Sounding Out Heritage

Southeast Asia

POLITICS, MEANING, AND MEMORY

David Chandler and Rita Smith Kipp

SERIES EDITORS

Sounding Out Heritage

Cultural Politics and the Social Practice of
Quan Họ Folk Song in Northern Vietnam

LAUREN MEEKER

University of Hawai'i Press
Honolulu

Printed in the United States of America

18 17 16 15 14 13   6 5 4 3 2 1

Library of Congress Cataloging-in-Publication Data

Meeker, Lauren, [date] author.
    Sounding out heritage : cultural politics and the social practice of quan ho folk song in northern Vietnam / Lauren Meeker.
        pages cm. — (Southeast Asia: politics, meaning, and memory)
    Includes bibliographical references and index.
    ISBN 978-0-8248-3568-2 (cloth : alk. paper)
    1. Folk music—Vietnam, Northern—History and criticism.
    2. Folk music—Political aspects—Vietnam, Northern.
    I. Title. II. Series: Southeast Asia—politics, meaning, memory.
    ML3758.V5M44   2013
    782.42162'95922—dc23
                                                                    2013008409

University of Hawai'i Press books are printed on acid-free paper and meet the guidelines for permanence and durability of the Council on Library Resources.

Designed by Publishers' Design and Production Services, Inc.

Printed by Sheridan Books, Inc.

CONTENTS

ACKNOWLEDGMENTS

This book is by no means wholly my own; many different voices speak through the words I have chosen to put down on the page. First, I am grateful for the financial support provided for this research by fellowships from the Fulbright-Hays Doctoral Dissertation Research Abroad Program, the Social Science Research Council's International Dissertation Field Research Fellowship Program with funds provided by the Andrew W. Mellon Foundation, and to LA&S Professional Development support from the State University of New York at New Paltz.

At Columbia University, my thanks go to Rosalind Morris, who has had a profound impact on this book and my scholarship in general. Her comments and encouragements pushed me to think in deep and innovative ways about my material. John Pemberton and Marilyn Ivy also had an important impact on my thinking and writing throughout my time at Columbia. Thanks also go to Patricia Pelley for her comments and, especially, to Laurel Kendall for her comments, conversations, and encouragement throughout the life of this project.

In Vietnam, my debts are incalculable. First, I would like to thank the Vietnam Institute for Culture and Arts Studies, its director Dr. Nguyễn Chí Bền and all the staff at the Institute for sponsoring my research and for all the assistance they have provided me over the years. I owe a particular debt of gratitude to Nguyễn Thị Kim Chi for being all things at all times for me. Her generosity and friendship helped make life in a foreign place that much better. Thanks also go to Đỗ Thị Thanh Thủy, Nguyễn Thị Thu Hương, and Bùi Hoại Sơn. My discussions with musicologists Tô Ngọc Thanh, Thao Giang, and Lê Danh Khiêm were also invaluable to my research. My thanks also go to the members of the UNESCO *quan họ* clubs in Hanoi and Bắc Ninh for their encouragement, teaching, camaraderie and for welcoming me into their clubs as a full member.

In Bắc Ninh, I would like to thank Trần Đình Luyện and the Bắc Ninh Department of Culture, Sport and Tourism for their cooperation and support for my research. My greatest gratitude in Bắc Ninh is reserved for the villagers who kindly and generously offered up their knowledge, talent, and friendship. In particular, Nguyễn Thị Bàn and Nguyễn Thị Sơn Hà and their family accepted me into their homes and hearts. They became family to me and taught me as much about life, love, and humanity as they did about Vietnamese culture. I also extend my deep thanks to Nguyễn Trung and the Bắc Ninh Radio and Television Station and to Xuân Mùi and the Bắc Ninh *Quan Họ* Folk Song Troupe.

I wish to thank all my friends and colleagues, in Vietnam and elsewhere, for their valuable insights on the ideas and words of this book in its various stages of development as well as the emotional support that sustained me through the process of research and writing. These include, but are not limited to Mai Tuyết Hoa, Vũ Song Hà, Nguyễn Trương Nam, Nguyễn Thị Thu Hương, Katie Dyt, Yukti and Ae Muktawijitra, Shahla Talebi, Lorraine Plourde, Brian Harmon, Jason Picard, Claudine Ang, Trung Nguyen, Jonathan Hubschman, and Ben Junge. Finally, none of this would have been possible without my parents, whose understanding and support have led me to where I am today.

All photos are my own.

Introduction

In 2009, UNESCO's committee on intangible cultural heritage inscribed *quan họ* Bắc Ninh folk songs on the Representative List of the Intangible Cultural Heritage of Humanity (Decision 4.COM 13.76). The committee's Decision describes how the "element" (*Quan Họ* Bắc Ninh Folk Songs) meets each of the selection criteria, including its role as a symbol of local and regional identity; that the inscription would promote greater awareness of musical traditions and cultural dialogue; that measures have been taken to safeguard the element; and that the local communities and authorities were involved in and gave their free consent to the process (UNESCO 2010:8). The road to inscription involved several years of preparations and mobilization of information by local and national officials, researchers, both domestic and foreign, and *quan họ* singers in Bắc Ninh and Bắc Giang provinces. These efforts were coordinated by the Vietnam Institute of Culture and Arts Studies (VICAS). The political implications of inscription are evident in the language of the Decision, in particular in the statement about *quan họ*'s potential value once inscribed on the list: "Inscription of the element on the Representative List would contribute to ensuring visibility and awareness of musical traditions on local, national and international levels, promoting social integration and enhancing inter-regional communication, cultural dialogue and respect for diversity" (ibid.). Thus, international recognition of *quan họ* comes with a heavy responsibility for this local folk form: *quan họ* must radiate out beyond its local origins to promote cultural dialogue regionally, nationally, and internationally.

The inscription language refers to the social importance of quan họ to local communities and its role in the work of international cultural exchange. However, what is not evident in the Decision and inscription materials is that the soundscape in which quan họ is found has a history and that designating quan họ as intangible cultural heritage is just the most recent episode in that history. The cultural politics of post-colonial nationalism, socialism, and reform have shaped and reshaped the soundscape of quan họ. For over half a century, quan họ folk song has had an extensive presence in the Vietnamese mass media and been the focus of interest and intervention of government officials and scholars in the region. As a result, quan họ is well known in Vietnam beyond its locality of origin, the villages of Bắc Ninh and Bắc Giang provinces. The form that scholarly and governmental interventions in the region have taken in this period has evolved over time. In the most general terms, it has shifted from a concern with post-colonial and socialist nation building to a concern with preserving the disappearing cultural heritage in the face of rapid development and modernization. Consequently, quan họ has become one of many focal points through which formations of state power and national and local identity are contested and enacted in contemporary Vietnam.

This book explores the cultural politics that have shaped the quan họ soundscape and the people who sing and listen to quan họ. It weaves together an examination of the construction and evolution of Vietnamese discourses on folk music, cultural nationalism, and cultural heritage since the August Revolution of 1945 with an ethnographic account of the changing social practice of quan họ folk song as it has moved from the village onto the stage. Through the lens of quan họ folk song and performance, I explore how discourses on culture have been an important source of political and cultural capital with which the Vietnamese government, intellectuals, and ordinary people represent Vietnam locally, nationally, and, increasingly, on the global stage.

In attending to the ethnographic details of quan họ practice, one becomes acutely aware of the pleasure that singers take in singing and listening to the songs and also how such pleasure is linked to the social and collective experience of singing. A theme that runs throughout this book is the connection between the sensory experiences (aural and visual) that occur within the quan họ soundscape and the emotional experience of performing and listening to the music. I examine in ethnographic detail how village practitioners of this socially embedded folk form negotiate the increasing attention to the form by those outside the village, their designation as "living treasures" who embody a traditional folk form, and their ordinary lives as people who love to sing quan họ. It also examines how professional singers of modernized quan họ are incorporated into this soundscape in an effort to highlight and popularize the culture of Bắc Ninh province in the national context.

Quan họ and its singers are embedded in the history and politics of the nation and this book examines a number of divergent readings of the past and present, from political ideology, local and national identity, the body, to the stage and television. The acceptance of quan họ on the Representative List of the Intangible Cultural Heritage of Humanity will certainly have a dramatic effect on many of the practices and discourses about the genre both in Bắc Ninh and elsewhere. This development necessitates continued work on the topics presented in this book.

FIRST ENCOUNTERS

Early one evening in the summer of 2001, I stepped up into the backseat of a black company-owned sport utility vehicle and sat down next to the CEO of a successful media company in Hanoi. We wound through the streets of Hanoi to pick up his friend before speeding off up the brand-new divided highway towards Bắc Ninh Town (now Bắc Ninh City). They were taking me to hear a kind of Vietnamese folk song as a thank-you gesture for helping the CEO practice reading English that afternoon. The CEO wanted to introduce me to his favorite kind of music and something that in his mind was truly Vietnamese. Upon entering the town, the CEO flipped open his phone and arranged to meet one of the singers along the way who would lead us to a local restaurant. Not long after, a young woman on her motorbike waved us down; this was his friend, the singer. We settled down on the floor of a small, private dock overhanging the restaurant's pond. Two other women arrived and the three women disappeared to change into brightly colored costumes. The six of us settled down around a large tray of food and the first singer began to tell a story of how, hundreds of years ago, two mandarins used to sing with each other and this eventually became known as quan họ. Then, they began to sing. I was captivated by the music.

What was this music? Aside from the legend told by the singer and the restaurant setting, I had no social context for this music. Was it used in a form of courtship or courtesanship? What was not being said here? Upon returning home that evening and in the following week before I flew back to the United States and to school, I began to seek out as much information as I could about this music. And, indeed, it seemed to be everywhere. I turned on the television and there it was. I asked my language teachers and they explained. I looked for books and compact discs and they were plentiful.

Once I began my field research into folk music and performance in northern Vietnam in 2003, my story of first contact had receded into the background as an aberration or as an inauthentic experience of quan họ. From that starting point, I was perpetually directed *back* by friends, teachers, and colleagues with whom I spoke on the subject: back in time, back to the village, back to a more authentic form than that which I had heard there next to the pond that night in Bắc Ninh Town. This going back would eventually take me to where, as an anthropologist engaged in ethnographic fieldwork, I was "supposed" to be. The locus of my research was meant to be the place where the "other" resided, which, my Vietnamese friends and colleagues told me was somewhere rural and the seat of an authentic form of the culture. Yet, while waiting for permission to conduct research in the villages, I wandered through different forms of "not-quite-authentic" folk song in Hanoi: UNESCO folk-song clubs, performances for tourists, televised folk song and performance. What was surprising to me at that time was that during these explorations, in seemingly contradictory fashion, many people emphasized these particular urban, staged, and recorded performances as representative, as real, as Vietnamese, even while they stressed that the villages were the places to find original quan họ. Eventually, by digging my way backwards towards what I was told was a more authentic style of singing, village singing, I came to realize that I was, in fact, re-enacting one of the dominant discourses on Vietnamese traditional culture. This discourse asserted that the authentic locus of Vietnamese traditional culture was in an idyllic, rural past, in a time and place where folk practices were as yet untainted by the upheavals of colonialism, war, revolution, and modernization and that it was essential to record and, if necessary, to restore these authentic forms of culture.

My early introduction to quan họ contained conflicting messages about authenticity that pointed to a much more complicated social construction of folk song than simply something that could be divided into what was "new" or "old" and "authentic" or "changed." My initial confusion about the message and social context of quan họ now—after several years of following many paths marked by different signposts to "the real"—points to the dynamic and open-ended ways that folk music is understood, performed, and represented in Vietnam today. New and old, past and present, village and city, rural and urban, these binary divisions that people often articulated on behalf of quan họ folk song blurred in the face of so much movement. How people variously situate and represent quan họ in Vietnam today, I will argue in this book, is a historically, politically, and socially situated practice. It is also a physical process located in, performed, and experienced through the body. The particular relationship between the past and the present in Vietnam is, in many ways, a constantly shifting ground for individuals and for society as a whole. It is the place where old forms of social relationships are contested and new ones are created. From this vantage point, speeding "back" up a new highway in a shiny black sport utility vehicle is in many ways an appropriate beginning for an examination of the complex ways that traditional culture is constructed, embodied, and performed in contemporary northern Vietnam.

This book is based on fieldwork conducted "back" in Bắc Ninh Province between October 2003 and May 2005, and for two months in the summers of 2008 and 2009. My methods included the anthropological approaches of participant observation combined with formal and informal interviews. I also recorded quan họ songs of village singers with whom I worked. I primarily worked with singers in the villages clustering within a few kilometers of Bắc Ninh City. Many of my village informants were elderly singers whom I followed around, interviewed, and with whom I attended events. I also interviewed several middle-aged female singers and observed their classes to teach quan họ to village children and youth. These women also attended village and regional events that I observed. I interviewed officials at the Bắc Ninh Department of Culture and Information (now renamed the Bắc Ninh Department of Culture, Sport and Tourism), in particular, researchers at its Center for Quan Họ Research. My research into village quan họ practice relies heavily on the memories of the elderly singers, their current activities, and on the rich body of work on quan họ published by Vietnamese scholars. My research on the new-style quan họ is based upon interviews with and participant observation of professional performers, attendance at performances by the Bắc Ninh *Quan Họ* Folk Song Troupe in Bắc Ninh City, and work with students and teachers at the Bắc Ninh Secondary School of Culture and Arts.

The remainder of this introduction provides some introductory background on quan họ folk song and the geographical, social, and political contexts in which it occurs. I also outline the theoretical frameworks that inform this book.

THE QUAN HỌ FOLK-SONG REGION

Quan họ is one of the famous folk song forms of our country and this shining cultural tradition is a source of pride for the people of Hà Bắc in particular and all the people [of the nation] in general. By way of its beautiful lyrics and music and through its history, *quan họ* folk song has reflected in part the activities, perceptions, thinking, sentiment, and aesthetic ideals of the people. (Đặng Văn Lung, Hồng Thao, and Trần Linh Quý 1978:9)[1]

Quan họ practice originated in a number of villages of what are today Bắc Ninh and Bắc Giang provinces. The bulk of the villages are in Bắc Ninh Province, whose capital, Bắc Ninh City, is located approximately thirty kilometers north of the national capital, Hanoi. The quan họ region, which covers about two hundred and fifty square kilometers, clusters around the "T" formed by the Cầu River in the North, which divides Bắc Ninh and Bắc Giang provinces and runs roughly west to east, and Highway 1, which runs north to south (see Đặng Văn Lung 1982:610).

Not all of the villages in this region have the custom of singing quan họ. It is commonly held that there are forty-nine "original" quan họ villages in Bắc Ninh and Bắc Giang provinces. The number of villages is said to correspond to the forty-nine male and forty-nine female attendants who accompanied the legendary founding ancestress of quan họ, the princess Vua Bà, daughter of one of the Hùng kings, on a trip to the region. It was she who taught the locals to sing quan họ and her attendants are said to have paired off to found the forty-nine quan họ villages.[2] Although residents of the area say that they are unsure of the identity of all forty-nine of these villages, scholars have identified forty-nine villages that they believe to be original quan họ villages (Trần Linh Quý 2006 [1974]; Lê Danh Khiêm 2000). Đặng Văn Lung, Hồng Thao, and Trần Linh Quý, three renowned scholars of quan họ, use two criteria to identify the forty-nine *quan họ* villages as they existed prior to the 1945 August Revolution. First, the village had made official partnerships or friendships (*kết bạn*) with groups in other villages and had sung with groups in other villages continuously for at least two to three generations; and, second, the village was recognized by other quan họ areas as a quan họ village (1978:20). Forty-four of the villages recognized by these and other authors (Lê Danh Khiêm 2000) lie in what is today Bắc Ninh Province and five are in Bắc Giang Province.[3] There are also a number of villages in both provinces that practice quan họ but are not considered to be "original" quan họ villages.

The quan họ region lies in the fertile flat plains of the Red River Delta. Historically, the majority of the quan họ villages have primarily relied upon wet-rice agriculture for subsistence, supplemented in some places by secondary occupations or handicraft production. Many of the significant quan họ singing events, as do many other communal village activities, follow the cycle of planting and harvesting. The region as a whole has a number of villages well known for cottage industries such as pottery, woodwork, bronze casting, papermaking, and so on (Ngô Đức Thịnh 2006:127). The region belongs to what was historically known as Kinh Bắc, the name assigned to the district (lộ) in 1241 under the Trần Dynasty (1225–1400) (Ngô Đức Thịnh 2006:126). Today, many cultural historians refer to Kinh Bắc as the "cradle" of Vietnamese civilization (Huu Ngoc 2001; Trần Quốc Vượng 2001) because it is considered to be one of the important locations of the origin (nơi phát tích) of the Kinh (or Việt) majority civilization (Nguyễn Văn Phú et al. 1962:11). Kinh Bắc is renowned as an intellectual center because of the large number of pagodas, temples, and other historical sites and because of its high number of degree holders under the imperial examination system.[4] Six hundred and forty-five of the two thousand nine hundred and ninety-one recipients of the tiên sĩ degree (those who had passed the regional exams and the national exam in Hanoi but had not passed the palace exam) between the years 1075 and 1919 were from Bắc Ninh Province. Over one-third of those passing the palace exam, the highest level, were from Bắc Ninh (Hoàng Kỳ 1982:641; Trần Đình Luyện 1997:101).

In some accounts, the high level of culture and scholarship in the region is directly linked to the difficulty or sophistication of quan họ lyrics. For instance, Lê Danh Khiêm, a quan họ researcher at the Bắc Ninh Culture Center, points out that many quan họ lyrics are based on poetry or derived from famous works of literature such as The Tale of Kiều (Truyện Kiều), Apricot Flowers Twice in Bloom (Nhị Độ Mai), and The Woman Graduate (Nữ Tú Tài) (pers. comm., 6/13/04).[5] Quan họ culture is thus said to be embedded in the historically and culturally rich Kinh Bắc region. The landscape of fertile green rice paddies, rivers, and occasional low hills rising out of the flat plain and its corresponding cultural traditions figure frequently in the lyrics of quan họ songs. The landscape is today often invoked in descriptions of quan họ that portray the songs and its colorfully costumed singers as part of a picturesque rural ideal. Contextualizing quan họ as such is an important element in the discourses that frame it as an age-old tradition rooted in the traditions and culture of the region. There is also a countervailing argument that emphasizes quan họ's origins as "folk" music or music of the people, an art form that derives from work songs and folk poetry (see Lê Hồng Dương 1972). This argument, which highlights the importance of laborers and the equality of men and women in quan họ practice, makes quan họ compatible with socialist and post-colonial reclamations of Vietnamese culture in the period following the 1945 Revolution.

RESEARCH AND POPULARIZATION OF QUAN HỌ

While very limited English language literature has been published on quan họ (Chan Ngoc Le 2002; Phạm Duy and Whiteside 1975; Dao Trong Tu 1984b; Nguyen and Hong Thao 1993), a rich body of Vietnamese language ethnological and ethnomusicological work on quan họ emerged after the 1945 August Revolution as part of the national project to collect and record traditions that were feared to be disappearing (Đặng Văn Lung, Hồng Thao, and Trần Linh Quý 1978; Lê Hồng Dương 1972; Hồng Thao 2002; Trần Linh Quý 2006 [1974]). Beginning in the 1950s, a number of scholars and musicians began to research and collect quan họ in depth, in part in response to the Vietnam Communist Party's efforts to create a new national culture for Vietnam after the Revolution, a project discussed in detail in chapter one of this book. Several researchers such as Trần Linh Quý and, in particular, Hồng Thao, a Bắc Ninh native, were well known to quan họ singers throughout the region for their work and dedication to the genre. Musicians such as Nguyễn Đình Phúc, Lưu Hữu Phước, and Lê Yên collected, transcribed and arranged quan họ songs. They subsequently published research articles in *The Music Review* (*Tập San Âm Nhạc*) and song collections, including one with two hundred fifty songs published by the Department of Arts (*Vụ Nghệ Thuật*) and three volumes of songbooks (totaling sixty transcribed songs) published by The Music Publishing House (*Nhà Xuất Bản Âm Nhạc*) (Nguyễn Văn Phú et al. 1962:4–5). The Hà Bắc Department of Culture (today the Bắc Ninh Department of Culture, Sport and Tourism) was also actively involved in quan họ research and collection (Nguyễn Văn Phú et al. 1962:11), and eventually organized a series of six conferences on the subject in 1965, 1967, 1969, 1971, 1974, and 1981 (Lê Hồng Dương 1982). The published proceedings from the 1971 conference, "Some Issues Concerning Quan Họ Folk Song" (Lê Hồng Dương 1972), provide an important collection of articles on quan họ. This body of work has continued to grow up until the present day (see Nguyễn Thị Minh Đoàn 2000; Lê Đanh Khiêm 2001; Trần Chính 2000). As a testament to this body of literature, in 2006, the Vietnam Institute of Culture and Information published a collection of articles on quan họ, with original publication dates from the 1950s up to the date of publication, that totaled more than one thousand pages (Nguyễn Chí Bền et al. 2006).

Vietnamese scholars' efforts to research, collect, and preserve quan họ village practices have paralleled efforts to develop and popularize the genre. These efforts were institutionalized in the late 1960s with the establishment of the professional Bắc Ninh *Quan Họ* Folk Song Troupe, discussed in chapter three. The troupe, comprised of professionally trained singers, developed a new modernized style that it popularized regionally and nationally through staged performance, and radio and television broadcasts. The "old" and "new" style quan họ are dramatically different in musical and performance style, lyrics, and performance venue. Nonetheless, both styles are proudly held up as local Bắc Ninh culture by singers, scholars, and local officials. The tension between these two styles of singing, old or village and new or modernized, is a crucial context for many of the arguments presented in this book.

The changes to quan họ practice are, in many ways, a localized manifestation of the dramatic political, social, and economic changes that Vietnam as a whole has undergone as a result of the 1945 August Revolution, the war of resistance against French colonialism, the American war and, more recently, as a result of the economic reforms (*Đổi Mới*) initiated in 1986 at the Sixth Party Congress. Today, scholars and officials worry about the loss of traditional knowledge in the face of modernization and, more recently, of globalization.

While the revolutionary and the post-reform discourses on national culture have significant differences, both rely upon references to an authentic version of folk culture. Even before the Revolution, many intellectuals argued over the need either to reject traditional culture or to reclaim it as part of anti-colonial mobilization, yet the Revolution definitively brought culture directly into the center of the political and ideological project of the new government (see Kim Ngoc Bao Ninh 2005; Pelley 2002). Feudalism and colonialism were seen to have had a negative effect on Vietnamese culture. Thus, in the decades after the Revolution and before reform, the Party and government of the new nation actively and aggressively worked to build a "new culture" that would reflect their goals for a progressive socialist modernity of the masses and people of Vietnam. In this period, historians, culture workers, and ethnologists reached into the past to find an essential Vietnamese history and culture "untouched" by the ravages of colonialism that they could call their own. Folk culture became an important part of this project because it was seen to belong to the peasants and their village culture and, as such, was said to be real or original. In the period following the August Revolution, memories of the past referenced an "essence" or "spirit" of the people and nation (*tinh dân tộc*) that had transcended the histories of colonialism and war. That which was seen to be outside history, to transcend it—folk culture—was at the very foundation of the vision for the socialist present.

Since the economic reforms were initiated in 1986, the revolutionary cultural discourse has been giving way to discussions about Vietnam's cultural heritage, a concept that increasingly plays a central role in shaping both scholarship and cultural policy. Literally, "changing for the new," *Đổi Mới* is often referred to as "renovation." These reforms began a process of political and economic liberalization to deregulate markets and institute limited political reforms. Reform has had a tremendous impact on many aspects of social and cultural life in Vietnam, including the diverse ways that Vietnamese relate to and remember their past. In post-reform Vietnam, references to an essential Vietnamese spirit still echo, in particular, in the discursive differentiation between the practice of quan họ in the village and the mass-mediated form by which it has become popular among a wider public. Increasingly, authentic quan họ is said to reside in elderly quan họ singers, whose memories provide the essential key to reconstructing past practices that had disappeared because of wartime necessity or socialist ideological pressure.

PLACING QUAN HỌ

In contemporary Vietnam, the discourse on authentic or "original" (*nguyên si*) quan họ is often articulated in terms of place and time. Where quan họ singers are from (Bắc Ninh or elsewhere), how they are trained (in the village or a conservatory), and how old they are (trained before or after 1945) are crucial elements in the discursive construction of quan họ singers as "authentic." This construction of authenticity relies upon memories: the memories of elderly singers used to reconstruct an "original" form of practice, and the collective cultural memories of an idealized past located in rural life.

In recent years, academic discourse in Vietnamese studies has focused sharply on memory, particularly on discursively constructed memories of the past in the reform period. As Hue Tam Ho Tai remarks, "Commemorative fever is threatening to blanket the Vietnamese landscape with monuments to the worship of the past" (2001:1). She argues that the upsurge in commemoration is a by-product of reform but is not simply a salvage operation. After reform, "the decline of High Socialist orthodoxy, relative prosperity, and prolonged peace have encouraged other actors besides the state to try to occupy the space of memory" (2001:3). The past is now remembered, re-articulated, and reconstructed by different actors and through a vast variety of cultural practices including religion (Taylor 2004), ritual (Malarney 2002; Luong Van Hy 1993), commemorative practices (Giebel 2001; Malarney 2001), academic discourse (Endres 2002), art (Taylor 1999, 2001), film (Dang Nhat Minh and Pham Thu Thuy 2003; Bradley 2001), and folk music and performance (Norton 2009). The state, performers, and ordinary people have deployed memory, in these contexts, as an important ingredient in the process of reconstruction of the past through the revival of cultural practices that had been lost or suppressed under colonialism, socialism, and more recently as a result of the younger generation's lack of interest. In this process, the memories of the elderly, in particular, have become a valuable repository of traditional culture.

Memory in Vietnam, however, cannot be confined to a relationship with the past. It is also a way of experiencing the present as a possible future. When people look back to the past, they are not simply remembering things past but are also engaging in a social act that reflects the cultural conditions of present society and aspirations for the future. Remembering the past as "tradition" is a contemporary social act. It is also an essential part of the process through which quan họ, or cultural practices more generally, become representative of "tradition" in the present. Drawing on Georg Simmel's "The Ruin" (1959 [1911]), Katherine Bergeron's work on Gregorian chant demonstrates this process for songs, which embody decay because they vanish "in the moment of becoming." As soon as they are sung, they exist only as memory or as the potential for a future performance. Bergeron argues that it was as an embodiment of decay that Gregorian chant established itself as a sign of "pastness *in* the present" (1998:19). Through the process of decay, epitomized by the ruin, "history shrivels up and becomes absorbed into the setting" and a new whole subsequently emerges (Benjamin 1977:179). The notion that songs vanish in the moment of performance is a powerful metaphor for loss of traditional culture in contemporary society more generally. In a rapidly developing Vietnam, the "new whole" that emerges is a representation of tradition, epitomized by village life and its customs that are feared to be rapidly disappearing.

The customs and practices of quan họ developed in the context of village life. Yet, this is a way of life that is rapidly changing as industrialization and development transform the face of the Vietnamese countryside. As is true elsewhere in Asia, Vietnam has seen a decline in rural populations and an accompanying growth in urban populations. In 1999, 76.5% of Vietnam's population lived in rural areas and about a quarter of GDP was comprised of agriculture (Phan Huy Lê 2006:37, notes 1, 2). By 2009, the rural population had dropped to 70.4% of the population, indicating a dramatic change in the country's demographics (General Statistics Office of Vietnam 2010:38). While the percentage of the population living in rural areas is decreasing, the village and its way of life nonetheless remains a significant trope in cultural discourse. Village studies in Vietnam (see, for example, Hickey 1967) have helped to establish the discursive focus on "the village" as the locus of tradition and as a place relatively untouched by history, as exemplified by the often repeated folk saying that "the laws of the king bow to the laws of the village" (*phép vua thua lệ làng*). A number of anthropological studies complicate the notion of the untouched village by demonstrating how, for instance, French colonial institutions and the socialist transformation dramatically altered the social and political organization of village life (Luong Van Hy 1992; Malarney 2002) As John Kleinen asserts, the dramatic historical, geographical, and sociocultural differences between Vietnamese means that "[w]riting about 'the' Vietnamese village is impossible, simply because such a village does not exist" (Kleinen 1999:2).

Nonetheless, while recent scholarship contests the notion of a quintessential Vietnamese village, a nostalgic and idealized vision of the countryside persists in Vietnam; people speak of it in these terms in ordinary life and it is pervasive in the mass media. This rural ideal is often pitted against a more modern, though potentially corrupt, urban culture. Drummond and Thomas attribute nostalgia in Vietnam, figured as "a profound and heavily romanticized vision of rural life and the 'village,'" in part to "a growing discontent with the alienation and anomie of urban and industrial life" (2003:8). These representations of the city as "the site of materialism, superficiality, spiritual alienation and corruption" are pitted against the countryside as "the repository of traditional values, national identity" and a place where relationships "are based upon emotion rather than money" (ibid.). Schlecker also argues that urban dwellers in North Vietnam relate the concept of "home place" (*quê*) to "a specific ideal of belonging and relatedness" (2005:510). However, he argues that "rather than a return to old ways, lavish contributions to home places are evidence of an ideal of belonging that developed alongside and in response to state-socialist programs of social integration" (ibid.).[6]

Locating the rise of this romanticized vision of the countryside solely among urban populations only partially explains the widespread and pervasive imaginary that is central to people's engagement with traditional culture, in particular with folk music. The vision of the "corrupt city" pitted against the "moral countryside" also circulates beyond the cities "to a large rural audience with newly acquired access to the media of popular culture" (Drummond and Thomas 2003:8; see also Harms 2011). Imagining the countryside in this manner is not limited to urban dwellers but also shapes the way villagers in rural areas think about and represent their own local cultures. Today, even Vietnamese village dwellers are able to conjure up a nostalgic image of an idyllic past, but one that is, ironically, already located in their own home place. Therefore, while urban dwellers imagine rural peasants to be living in a traditional past, they in fact share a similar narrative reconstruction of that past with those same rural inhabitants.

FROM TRADITIONAL CULTURE TO CULTURAL HERITAGE

The representational practices that link "authentic" quan họ folk song to a rural ideal rooted in the rich cultural history of Bắc Ninh Province are closely related to another broad concern of the book: how the state, academics, and performers have redefined and deployed the concept of "traditional culture" in response to different political and social pressures. The concept of traditional culture in Vietnam is closely tied to national and local identity. Since the 1945 August Revolution, local folk culture has been included as an integral part of national identity under the concept of "unity in diversity" and "one nation of many peoples" (see Pelley 2002). As discussed in chapter one, the concept of unity allows distinct local cultures, such as quan họ Bắc Ninh, to be incorporated into a broader national Vietnamese culture. Folk songs have played an important role in this process.

According to ethnomusicologist Phong T. Nguyen, folk songs are the "most collected and researched genre in Vietnam," something that he attributes in part to government encouragement and support (Nguyen 1998:479). Some scholars claim that folk songs are important because they are an authentic Vietnamese musical form that has been less affected by foreign influences than other musical genres (Nguyen 1998; Dao Trong Tu 1984c). However, other Vietnamese scholars have criticized how folk songs were collected and altered in the interest of politics in the revolutionary period. They argue in favor of returning to an "unaltered" version of those songs (Tô Ngọc Thanh 2001; Bùi Trọng Hiền n.d.). Tô Ngọc Thanh contends that since the early 1990s, Vietnamese research on folk music has made "important steps" in this direction with help from Western techniques, UNESCO support, and with the use of CDs and CD-ROMs for music collection and popularization (2001:29). Indeed, this reference to Western techniques and UNESCO is particularly salient. In recent years, an internationally informed concept of "intangible cultural heritage" that promotes international visibility for local cultures on the world stage of culture has become central to cultural policy and to the discourse on folk music in Vietnam, as evident in the language of the UNESCO inscription of quan họ, discussed above. The cultural heritage framework has been strongly articulated through UNESCO and its resolutions beginning in the 1970s and proliferating in the 1980s.[7] UNESCO's Convention for the Safeguarding of the Intangible Cultural Heritage entered into force on April 20, 2006.

In Vietnam, a re-orientation towards a globally defined notion of intangible cultural heritage is evident in the semantic shift away from "traditional culture" (*văn hóa cổ truyền*) to "cultural heritage" (*di sản văn hóa*) in scholarly discourse, in the increased number of international conferences on traditional culture organized in Vietnam, in legislation, and in a steady stream of submissions to UNESCO requesting inscription of Vietnamese folk forms on the Representative and Urgent Safeguarding Lists of the Intangible Cultural Heritage of Humanity.[8] In addition, beginning in the mid-1990s, Vietnamese scholars, in coordination with the Ministry of Culture and Information and local Departments of Culture and Information, began to work towards the creation of a legal and institutional framework for the preservation and restoration of intangible cultural heritage (Đỗ Thị Minh Thúy 2004a; Nguyễn Chí Bền 2003, 2004).

Nguyễn Chí Bền (Director of the Vietnam Institute of Culture and Arts Studies [VICAS]), claims that the *Đổi Mới* reforms allowed the thinking about culture to be "institutionalized in government documentation" (2004:6). It also resulted in a mobilization of efforts to designate, preserve, and archive cultural heritage. For instance, in 1995, the Vietnamese government approved a program called "General investigation and inventory of Vietnamese people's cultural intangible heritages," whose aim was "to collect all cultural intangible forms and assets, including traditional music and dance of all 54 Vietnamese ethnic groups," which was to be carried out by the Vietnam Institute of Culture and Arts Studies, the Research Institute of Folk Culture, and the Department of Culture and Information of the provinces of origin of the different folk forms studied (Tô Ngọc Thanh 1997:40). In 1997, the Ministry of Culture and Information assigned the Vietnam Institute of Culture and Arts Studies two responsibilities: "to advise and supervise the implementation of the projects to preserve and develop intangible cultural heritage initiated by Departments of Culture and Information in localities; to directly implement a number of projects to work towards building a database of Vietnamese intangible cultural heritage" (Nguyễn Chí Bền 2003:627). This assignment was followed in 1998 by Resolution Five put forth at the Eighth Party Congress (Số 03-NQ/TW), entitled "On building

and developing a progressive Vietnamese culture rich in national character," which is considered to be a major milestone in the work of development and preservation of culture in Vietnam (see Đỗ Thị Minh Thúy 2004a;
Nguyễn Chí Bền 2004). Among other things, it called for greater efforts to
preserve and develop cultural heritage and for the linking of cultural policy
and economic activity.

The resolution, considered by cultural workers and government officials
to be a turning point in the work of preserving, representing, and developing
cultural heritage in Vietnam, was a direct response to wider international
trends linking culture and economic development. Đỗ Thị Minh Thúy, for
example, claims that Resolution Five was a direct response to UNESCO's
program, "World Decade for Cultural Development, 1988–1997" (2004b:8–
9) which had four objectives: "acknowledging the cultural dimension of
development; affirming and enriching cultural identities; broadening participation in culture; promoting international cultural co-operation."[9] Đỗ
Thị Minh Thúy claims that Resolution Five incorporated both the key concepts of the UNESCO program and, more broadly, "the general progressive
trends of the world" (2004b:9–10).

Another major milestone in the development of the concept of intangible cultural heritage in Vietnam was the 2001 "Law on Cultural Heritage."
The law lays down guidelines for the preservation and development of tangible and intangible cultural heritage, which is defined as:

> products of the mind/spirit with historical, cultural and educational
> value that are contained in memory and writing, that are passed down
> by oral transmission, through occupations, performance, and all other
> means of containing and transmission including language, writing,
> works of literature, arts, science, orally transmitted speech, folk per-
> formance, ways of life and lifestyle, festivals, secrets about traditional
> handicraft production, knowledge about traditional medicine and
> pharmaceuticals, about culinary culture, traditional ethnic clothing,
> and all other folk knowledge. (*Luật Di Sản Văn Hóa* [Law on Cultural
> Heritage] 2001)

The Law on Cultural Heritage uses similar language to the UNESCO "Convention for the Safeguarding of the Intangible Cultural Heritage" established
in 2003.[10] Vietnam ratified the convention in 2005, signaling its participation in a global cultural sphere.

In direct response to the above policies, academic institutions and the
Ministry of Culture, Sport and Tourism have actively worked to submit

applications for different Vietnamese intangible cultural forms for inscription on the UNESCO lists. To date, *Nhã Nhạc*, Vietnamese Court Music (proclaimed in 2003, inscribed in 2008), the Space of Gong Culture (proclaimed in 2005, inscribed in 2008), *Quan họ* Bắc Ninh Folk Songs (2009), the Gióng Festival of Phù Đổng and Sóc Temples (2010), and Xoan Singing of Phú Thọ Province (2011) have been accepted to the Representative List. Ca Trù Folk Song was accepted to the Urgent Safeguarding List in 2009. In 2009, I was informed that the Ministry of Culture, Sport and Tourism had requested that the Institute of Culture and Arts Studies decide upon and prepare an application to UNESCO for a cultural form that would be appropriately representative of the city of Hanoi, which was getting ready to celebrate its one thousand–year anniversary.[11] Other involvement with UNESCO has included the creation of a list of "*quan họ* living treasures" in 2003 in a joint pilot project between the Department of Cultural Heritage, the Bắc Ninh Province Department of Culture and Information, and UNESCO's Hanoi office. Thus, researchers in Vietnam are developing projects and receiving significant funding from the government for projects that enhance the visibility of Vietnam's cultural heritage in an international context. The institutional infrastructure to implement policy and spread ideology among the people that was set up after the revolution as a part of its goals to re-shape the country's culture are still in place today and help to facilitate the refashioned goals of the state.

The UNESCO applications are important indicators of the growing internationalist outlook of cultural workers in Vietnam who recognize the value that Vietnamese culture has within a framework of world culture and the value—both monetary and symbolic—that international recognition has at home for their own work. Indeed, in a paper given at the conference "Going with the Past: Vietnamese Traditional Culture in Contemporary Society" held at Temple University in the fall of 2006, Nguyễn Chí Bền discussed the benefits of cultural heritage in Vietnam within a framework of "sustainability and development" and referred to the significant rise in government money allocated to the preservation of cultural heritage (both tangible and intangible) over the past ten years. Vietnamese cultural workers, the government, and scholars have enthusiastically embraced intangible cultural heritage as a new form of political and economic capital at home and abroad.

The recent shift from conceiving of culture within a frame of "traditional culture" to one of "cultural heritage" points to a change in orientation in the State's thinking about culture in Vietnam. As indicated above, UNESCO's activities have had a direct impact on Vietnam's cultural policies in the reform period. As Nguyễn Chí Bền (2004) asserts, since reform, Vietnam has developed a "culture market" and that government resolutions and legislation on the market economy have all had a strong impact on both the cultural life and the "culture market" in Vietnam. On the other hand, the effects of the market economy on culture are also frequently discussed in negative terms that bemoan the "commercialization" of traditional cultural forms. Read negatively, commercialization is equated with the degradation of "real" traditions; read positively, commoditization of culture establishes a place for Vietnam on the world stage both as an integral part of world heritage and as a new source of trade goods in an international market hungry for "cultural" goods.

As with money, which "does not truly measure unless its unit is a reality that really exists, to which any commodity whatever may be referred" (Foucault 1994:169), cultural heritage must both refer to a material reality and be involved in relations of exchange in order to be expressible "in the language of value" (Haug 1986:13) on the world stage. Heritage can be wielded as currency in the global exchange of culture because it can be abstracted into a general form, "culture," and at the same time referred back to a culturally specific material reality made up of objects and concrete practices of a particular place ("Vietnamese culture," for instance). In its general (culturally relativist) form, cultural heritage is the abstraction by which all cultures of the world come to be seen as equivalent. In its material form, *Vietnamese* culture asserts its legitimacy in terms of its local specificity. In the post-reform period, therefore, tradition is rewritten as heritage (*di sản*), which comes to stand in for the cultural reality precisely because it is construed as "inheritance" or that which had a material presence in the past. The Vietnamese word used to translate "heritage" is *di sản*, which means "inheritance" in the sense of material property passed on to the next generation. Ownership of heritage in the present is posited as direct material contact with the past and, therefore, is seen to link the modern present directly with the (absent or past) place of origin of Vietnamese culture. In this way, heritage is "a material memory" (Foucault 1994:181) that contains within itself a promise of return.

EMBODIED CULTURE, PERFORMED CULTURE

Precisely because folk culture is given objective (hence inheritable) status as heritage, it is the discursive ground on which a connection is made between past and future, urban and rural, and traditional and modern. Yet, while framing culture as "heritage" makes culture tangible such that it can be controlled, represented, and deployed in the interests of the state, it does not reveal the emotional experiences that bind singers to their music. Rather, the emotional and sensory experiences of singing become manifest in performance and are articulated in and experienced through the material practices of the body.

An overarching framework that informs this investigation is the assumption that the cultural reality is emergent in performance (Schechner 1985; Schieffelin 1985; Turner 1988). Victor Turner argues that ritual and performance are social dramas through which a society reflects on its own behavior (consciously or unconsciously) in a creative process that can induce change (1988:22, 26–27). Those participating in a cultural performance are not just participating in the production of an event, but also participating in the creation of the social reality in which they live (Schieffelin 1985). The choices that singers make about where and when to sing, how they speak about what they do with others, who participates in what events, and so on are both reflective and creative of the current practice of quan họ.

I am specifically concerned with the "material practices through which voices become audible" (Weidman 2006:12) and the bodily means that shape the encounter with quan họ. Singing quan họ is a form of social action situated in the body and a visible product of bodily action (Csordas 1990, 1994; Hughes-Freeland 2008). Attending to what Roland Barthes calls "the grain of the voice" or "the body in the voice as it sings" (1977:188) as it occurs in different registers of practice, technique, and discipline, reveals that the singing body is not merely an empty vessel through which the song is passed (Mauss 1979). The body in song or in motion actually generates cultural meaning. Quan họ practitioners engage with the music in concrete, audible, and visible ways. Examining how singers use and conceive of their bodies in song, the medium of performance (the village festival, the modern stage, television, etc.), and how these have changed over time reveals much about the social order in which performances occur. Material practices such as those articulated through bodies, stages, television sets, and amplifiers make up the soundscape of contemporary *quan họ* discussed in this book. These material practices not only make voices audible and culture visible but also generate new relationships among singers, songs, and society. Such processes, are just as important in shaping cultural identity (via folk song) as are political and historical definitions of folk music.

SINGING SENTIMENT

An important cultural meaning enacted and generated through singing quan họ is sentiment (*tình cảm*). Sentiment is the social glue that is said to bind quan họ singers to their music and to each other. Sentiment is variously expressed as ideology, enacted through song, generated through the exchange of songs, and conceived of in terms of the body. While it is true that how sentiment is perceived and enacted has evolved over time, it remains an important concept at the heart of quan họ practice. More generally, sentiment is highly valued in all social and familial relationships in Vietnam. Shaun Malarney, for example, in discussing funerary ritual in one village in northern Vietnam, maintains that sentiment is a "moral relationship" that is understood as a part of the "spirit of the village (*tinh lang*)" (2002:129).[12] The expression of this moral relationship, however, also involves the two sides of an exchange in a relationship of debt (Malarney 2002:130). Therefore, affective ties of sentiment are inseparable both from social and ritual exchange and from moral debt. Sentiment, construed as that which is intimate, warm, and communal, is increasingly traced back to an ideal of social relationships rooted in rural Vietnam. Thus, whereas sentiment is felt to be of central importance in one's relationships with others in contemporary society, discursively, it is closely connected with the space of modernity's other in contemporary Vietnam: the nostalgic and romanticized countryside that has been designated as the seat of cultural authenticity. This place of sentiment and nostalgic remembrance is firmly rooted in the present and distinctly shaped in dialogue with the institutional practices and cultural politics of the moment.

Sentiment is a form of cultural performance (Turner 1988) that demonstrates and creates one's embodiment of the social reality. That is, it demonstrates "social fidelity" (Weidman 2003) to an "authentic" quan họ. Performing quan họ does not connect the viewer, listener, or performer to the reality of an original folk song. Rather, it is the very process of transmission—whether through the body, the stage, on television—that generates the cultural reality. Because folk music in contemporary Vietnam is fetishized as having an objective reality (as heritage), it can be traced in its movement through different media and provide the anthropologist the means, both metaphorical and material, with which to analyze how contemporary cultural identity is shaped through song and how this identity has changed over time. The physicality of the medium of performance and its effect on the way people experience and construct relationships with folk music is developed in particular in chapters two, four, and five, which discuss, respectively, embodied practices of performance, staged and televised performance, and amplification at folk festivals. However, the notion of mediation and embodiment—whether it is through discourse, the body, television, or a stereo system—and how it is socially constituted run throughout the book.

The following chapters together present a picture of the soundscape of quan họ folk song and the various forces and people who have shaped and transformed it since the August Revolution. This soundscape has a history whose most recent phase is taking shape in the context of cultural heritage as a political, economic, and social force, locally and globally. The Vietnamese, along with other peoples and nations around the world, are in the process of shaping and re-shaping their cultural identity in response to these forces. Quan họ is an important folk form through which the Vietnamese are sounding out their heritage.

1

Music after the Revolution:
A "Unified Contradiction"

A cartoon by Būi Công Kỳ in a 1956 issue of the *Music Review* (*Tập San Âm Nhạc*) (vol. 4: 32) shows three musicians next to a pond with the sign *áo dân ca* (folk-song pond). Two of the men are fishing, one sitting and one standing with a guitar slung across his back, and the third man is standing looking on holding a violin. There is a briefcase on the ground on which is written *dân tộc tính* (national character). The seated musician is saying, "this professional hand will make a salad of raw fish!" (*gỏi cá*) (Fig. 1.1). The cartoon emphasizes the "realness" of folk song by explicitly commenting upon its rawness and reflects the idea that folk music is a repository for national character. However, the cartoon poses a critique of the process of composition by "fishing"; these three musicians are sitting idly in the cartoon neither engaged in productive work nor in active composition. It also critiques the act of putting one's name (as author) to something that belongs to all. Above the cartoon on the same page is a fictional exchange between two people (X and Y), entitled "National Character," that expresses similar sentiments as the cartoon. X is telling Y about his newest composition, which he describes as "rather good." The first phrase, X explains, is taken from a *Quan họ Bắc Ninh* song, the second from a *Hò* song from the central region, the third from *Chèo* to give the song humor, and the last phrase, which is full of sentiment (*tình cảm*), is taken word for word from a folk song from the southern region. At this point Y asks, "So which phrase is a phrase that you thought up?" X responds, "I didn't think up a single phrase, that way it is of pure national substance" (Khóa Sơn 1956:32).

The cartoon and the dialogue are exemplary for two reasons. On the one hand, they reveal the way in which folk songs were used as the raw material for a new national culture imbued with national character in the several decades following the August Revolution of 1945 and the establishment of the DRV (Democratic Republic of Vietnam) in the North. On the other hand, the cartoon and dialogue offer a critique of this practice that captures the conflict between authorship and politics central to debates about music at the time. The critical question was how to create a new musical canon for Vietnam that expressed something transcendent (that which had escaped the ravages of colonial oppression) and something progressive (the socialist revolutionary expression of a new society). The arts of the period emphasized and promoted the new culture and society of Vietnam that began with the Revolution and yet they also sought to find continuities with the past. Central to this project was the concept of "unity in diversity," which relied on defining a "national character" (tính dân tộc) that was shared by all.

In a 1957 article, Văn Đông questions whether the concepts of "national character" (dân tộc tính) and "local character" (địa phương tính) are

FIG. 1.1. "This professional hand will make a salad of raw fish!" ("Folk song pond," cartoon by Bùi Công Kỳ, in *Tập San Âm Nhạc* [*Music Review*] no. 4, p. 32, 1956.)

contradictory and remarked, "maybe, if they are, it is a unified contradiction (*mâu thuẫn thống nhất*)" (1957:3). He ends the article by remarking that "when speaking of national character, do not think that it is local character, but [when speaking of] national character one cannot not speak of local character" (1957:4). The notion of a unified contradiction aptly describes the difficulties of defining the nation as a singular entity that embodied many diverse localities and the work of building a musical tradition befitting that nation. While the emphasis on unity glosses over the incommensurability of the local and the national, this tension remains in discourse on music during this period.

This chapter considers some of the ways that folk music in Vietnam was re-valorized and "disciplined" as a part of the new northern nation's emphasis on unity and building a new socialist society. I use "disciplined" here in Katherine Bergeron's double sense to mean both the set of musical practices that train the body (the hands, the ear, the voice) and in the broader sense of discipline as musical canon, which relies upon those disciplinary practices to reproduce and legitimize itself (Bergeron 1996). Discipline implies intention on the part of those defining the canon and the complicity of those learning it. In revolutionary Vietnam, the work of building a new musical culture was not simply coercive. The practices and debates that musicians and composers engaged in were cultural performances (Turner 1988) through which Vietnamese composers and musicians negotiated and created a national musical identity within the context of socialism. Victor Turner argues that cultural performances can be "active agencies of change" through which cultures reflect upon themselves and through which they can sketch out new ways of living and being (1988:24). Through these cultural performances, folk music and culture came to be seen and utilized as something purely "Vietnamese" and as the building blocks of a new national culture. In this chapter, the set of disciplinary practices explored include the collection and revision (*chỉnh lý*) of folk music, the composition of a repertoire of new national music based on a standardized "Vietnamese" national style, and the dissemination and teaching of this new style through printed materials.

I have chosen to begin discussion with the period following the August Revolution in large part because of the symbolic and ideological resonance 1945 continues to have on the practice and scholarship of traditional music in Vietnam today. As David Marr says more generally of 1945, "for many it symbolized the end of foreign rule, although the issue would need to be contested in blood for another nine years" (1995:221). The moment Marr is marking is Hồ Chí Minh's reading of the Vietnamese Declaration of Independence on September 2, 1945 in Hanoi, which Marr says "contained a dramatic world view, a capsule history, some bold assertions, vivid phrases, and emotional imagery—all of which managed to capture the imagination of, first, the immediate audience of several hundred thousand, and then millions of Vietnamese who heard the speech repeated or read it in newspapers" (ibid.). Today, many musicologists and folk performers use 1945 as a temporal marker of authenticity. Those folk artists trained before 1945 are seen to belong to an authentic past and, thus, to perform a "purer" form of folk music. While 1945 is an important historical landmark, it is also an ideological tool, one that changes over time and that is used in the construction of national cultural identity. Practically speaking, the power of the DRV was not fully secure until after the French defeat at Điện Biên Phủ in 1954. However, the government and the Vietnamese Communist Party worked hard to normalize 1945 as a symbol of the division between an oppressive past and an enlightened socialist present. Many of the legal and discursive frameworks within which traditional culture and music were embedded in the years following the August Revolution are still evident, if in an evolved form, in the shape of the debates and perceptions of Vietnamese folk music today.

Debates about the value (or backwardness) of Vietnamese folk music and its place in Vietnam's modernization began long before 1945. By the early twentieth century, some Vietnamese intellectuals, as a part of a wider movement of intellectual dissent and anti-colonialism (Hue Tam Ho Tai 1992; Marr 1971, 1981), debated the impact of Western music on Vietnamese music and concerned themselves with how to balance "tradition" and "modernity" in musical production. According to Jason Gibbs, late 1920s Vietnam saw significant changes in musical life as a result of the introduction of Western classical musical training and the "Western popular song." This was followed by the development of a new form of Vietnamese popular song or "reformed music" (*nhạc cải cách*) in the late 1930s, a form of music that was criticized by some as being too Western and therefore lacking in Vietnamese character (Gibbs 1997:11–12; Thụy Loan 1993).

With the Revolution, however, came a new set of political and practical necessities that overlaid those earlier debates. Historians and intellectuals of the period worked hard to document and establish a new canon of history and to delineate a "new culture" reflective of a unified and distinctly "Vietnamese" nation and people (Kim Ngoc Bao Ninh 2005; Pelley 2002). This aggressive state project to eliminate the traces of a "feudal" past, create a new cultural nationalism, and to realize socialist society reached into all domains of Vietnamese society, including music.[1] However, this project relied upon contradictory premises: that the break between the feudal past and the socialist present was absolute and that the new socialist culture must be built upon a quintessential or untainted Vietnamese past. As expressed in a 1957 article entitled "Some Important Features of the Arts Movement in Vietnam since the August Revolution," despite important cultural continuities with the past,

> [s]ince the August revolution, the face of Vietnamese arts and literature has completely changed, Vietnamese arts and literature have stepped from one historical period into another. Today, we have a completely new system of arts and literature; even though it is still young (*non trẻ*), it is still very wholesome (*lành mạnh*) and very promising, a system of arts and literature which clearly has national, mass and realistic character. (Những nét lớn của Phong Trào Văn Nghệ Việt-Nam từ sao cách mạng tháng tám 1957:3)[2]

Musicians in the post-revolution period were actively involved in contributing to this new culture that was to be revolutionary in content and Vietnamese in character.

FOLK MUSIC AND ETHNOLOGY

Many artists and musicians sought to find evidence of the "quintessential" Vietnamese past in folk traditions. The collection and study of folk music is embedded in the cultural politics of the Revolution and the history of the development of Vietnamese ethnology, both of which helped to shape the "new culture" (*văn hóa mới*) of revolutionary Vietnam. Tô Ngọc Thanh emphasizes that in order to understand the ways music was collected and composed after the Revolution, one must understand the ideology that set two tasks for the revolutionary engaged in this work: first, to highlight (*khái sáng*) the Revolution and enlighten the people and second, "to correct the heritage" (*sửa chữa di sản*), that is to reform it on behalf of modernization and advancement (pers. comm., 4/15/04).[3] As ethnologist Le Van Hao argued in 1970 from within the framework of this ideology: "to carry out research into the traditional artistic treasury does not mean to collect everything without discrimination but, on the contrary, to make a judicious choice, criticize and discard what is bad and preserve what is good, and adapt it to the new circumstances to serve the new requirements" (1972:33–34).

Prior to 1945, it was the French who primarily conducted ethnological research in Vietnam. Researchers such as Gustave Dumoutier (1890), Gaston Knosp (1922), E. Le Bris (1922), and Georges de Gironcourt (1942) published ethnological works documenting the history, songs, instruments, and musical customs of Indochina in journals such as the *Bulletin des Amis du Vieux Hue* and the *Bulletin de l'École Française d'Extrême Orient*.[4] After the turn of the twentieth century, much of the serious ethnographic work on Vietnam was carried out by the *École Française d'Extrême Orient* (EFEO), which began publishing its *Bulletin* in 1900 and subsequently established its offices in Vietnam in 1901. Not all French colonial researchers were directly employed by the colonial administration; nevertheless, very few of them explicitly questioned the colonial project in their work (Kleinen 1997). Much of the research by French ethnologists was carried out within the context of the colonial state and was often explicitly geared towards colonial policy development (Kleinen 1997; Salemink 2003).

A number of Vietnamese were employed as researchers, assistants, and translators at the EFEO. While they were unable to advance too far within the colonial system, many of them later went on to prestigious careers in ethnology in Vietnam after independence in 1945 (Kleinen 1997). Among these was Nguyen Van Huyen who went on to become one of the most renowned ethnographers in Vietnam. Until recently, one of his books was used as the definitive textbook on Vietnamese ethnology and his book *Les Chants Alternés Des Garçons et Des Filles En Annam* (1934) remains an important work on folk song in Vietnam.[5]

Works produced by French ethnologists held a conflicted place in Vietnamese ethnology developed under the DRV. While some of the French ethnological work was utilized later by Vietnamese ethnologists, it was with qualification as to its colonialist orientation. In explaining the progression of Vietnamese ethnology, Mac Duong (1977) and Phan Huu Dat (1999 [1978]) make reference to pre-colonial sources as a sort of proto-ethnography and to colonial ethnographic works while carefully pointing out their shortcomings. Mac Duong discusses the positive contributions of French researchers to the ethnographic understanding of Vietnam but at the same time condemns their work as complicit in the enslavement of the Vietnamese people. He argues that French researchers "underestimated the role of the ethnic and cultural uniqueness of the peoples of Indochina and Southeast Asia as a whole" and that "[i]n the realm of the history and culture, they were inclined to exaggerate the role of external influences in the emergence of local cultures" (1977:77–79), an objection that expressed concern to clarify Chinese influences on Vietnamese history. Evans, however, remarks that Mac Duong's simultaneous critique and acceptance is reflective of the situation in Vietnamese anthropology in which "we find no outright rejection of all things 'bourgeois' and 'imperialist,' but a sincere and serious attempt to go beyond these earlier studies" (1985:122). An acceptance of earlier ethnographic materials facilitates the identification of a specifically "Vietnamese" culture.

Vietnamese ethnologists sought to show that the Revolution marked a point of cultural enlightenment for the Vietnamese people, before which there was ignorance of the richness of their own culture. For instance, Le Van Hao, a southern ethnologist who did extensive research in the North after the Revolution, claims that since the Revolution, "important discoveries" have been made in the field of music and poetry whereas "[i]nvaluable literary masterpieces were known to only very few people before the August Revolution" (1972:20).[6] Hao's claim, of course, has class overtones as well as historical and ethnological ones. The implication is that before the Revolution only a small group, the scholar-gentry class, would have had access to such "literary masterpieces."

Vietnamese writers tend to locate the origins of Vietnamese ethnology in the 1950s. The 1950s and 1960s saw the establishment of a number of institutions devoted to ethnology. In 1958, the Division of Ethnology was created within the Institute of History. In 1968, the Division became the Vietnamese Institute of Ethnology and a Department of Ethnology was established within the Historical Division of the University of Hanoi (Phan Huu Dat 1999 [1978]; Mac Duong 1977). Many Vietnamese ethnographers began as historians and, consequently, shared many of their same concerns (Evans 1985:120).[7]

In 1956, three departments dealing with traditional music and performance were established under the auspices of the Ministry of Culture: The Department for Traditional and Folk Music Studies (*Ban Nghiên Cứu Nhạc Cổ Truyền và Dân Gian*), The Department for Chèo Theater Studies (*Ban Nghiên Cứu Chèo*), and The Department for Tuồng Theater Studies (*Ban Nghiên Cứu Tuồng*). The common goal for these departments was to undertake a systematic collection of folk music, song, and theater in Vietnam (Tô Ngọc Thanh, pers. comm., 4/15/04). Phạm Văn Chùng outlined the goals for collection as follows: "We research and collect folk song not to satisfy individual pleasure, to research for research's sake, but our primary purpose in acquiring the national inheritance is as a reference [and] to build a new institution of music" (1956:1).[8] He argues for detailed research on the content and structure of folk song, which recognizes its proximity to the lives of the people (*nhân dân*) and on the particular local characteristics of different genres. Furthermore, "the work of preserving folk song is not only to transcribe, publish or preserve a few materials just so that a number of professionals can compose, but it must also take into account the people so that the true work of preservation is to 'return folk song to the people,' to make folk song live again in the mouth of the people" (*làm dân ca sống lại trên miệng nhân dân*) (Phạm Văn Chùng 1956:2). Folk song is seen to be a direct expression of the people. The call to place the voice "in the mouth of the people" at this particular historical moment effectively situates the voice in an "other" place, one that is past, natural, raw, or in a word, "folk." Yet, the folk lives on in the people (those who belong to the modern socialist nation and, in this case, listen to or compose national music). The voice of the people is thus framed as a true expression of national character and yet such a voice can only begin to speak in the new nation with the help of culture workers. Musicologists and composers believed it their responsibility to "return" the voice to the people.[9]

The folk was seen as something that persisted despite the oppression of Chinese and French colonialism, dynastic rule, and the ravages of several wars. Finally, under the new society, it would be shaped into a body of music appropriate to the new socialist nation. Pelley explains that Vietnamese Marxism was "heavily indebted to Romantic nationalists like Herder and Renan" although in the revolutionary period, the government rejected open support of such ideas (2002:43, 142–143). Nevertheless, the claim that the essential character of the Vietnamese was to be found in folk music resembles Herder's romantic nationalism, in which the key to a people's national soul was expressed through its folk poetry. Only by being true to the national soul, according to Herder, could a people develop and survive as a nation in the present (see Wilson 2006). The folk, that is, was already there and already "Vietnamese" in the modern socialist moment; it was up to the people, as listening subjects in the new nation, to recognize its inherently national character and utilize it in the construction of a new tradition of Vietnamese music.

The collection of folk culture was central to the process of paradigm development of the period, which sought to highlight and resurrect the true and essential Vietnamese spirit as that which persisted despite years of oppression and foreign domination. The harder the ethnologists looked, the more proof they found of the "variety and richness" of Vietnamese culture. The Revolution discursively marks the moment at which the abundance of culture that had heretofore been suppressed overflows into the modern socialist present and becomes accessible or available to all citizens of the modern nation.[10] Le Van Hao emphasizes the cultural solidarity among all Vietnamese that is reflected in the abundance of folk culture in his discussion of the advances made in the study of the arts and folklore: "Researches [*sic*] on Vietnamese folklore over the past 15 years have gathered a large amount of documents, analyses and syntheses which give irrefutable proof of the depth, variety and richness of Vietnamese traditional culture" (1972:32–33). His article is a catalogue of this research. Likewise, in his discussion of the collection and research of folk music in twentieth-century Vietnam, Tô Ngọc Thanh remarks that since 1945, studies of all different kinds of folk culture have "proliferated." He sets this up in contrast to the early 1940s, in which such studies were "very rare" (*hiếm hoi lắm*) (2001:29).

Nonetheless, Le Tuan Hung argues that while the government did recognize that much traditional music and theater was in danger of being forgotten in the years 1954–1975, it made little effort to counteract this loss because it did not prioritize "the preservation of purely cultural and artistic activities" (1997:41). Instead, he argues, cultural policy encouraged musical production that advanced revolutionary themes through revision of traditional styles or creation of modern revolutionary styles (ibid.). According to Tô Ngọc Thanh, many researchers lacked the necessary methodological training and understanding of ethnomusicology as a discipline to create systematic and comprehensive collections of folk music. Hence, collections were made without a thorough understanding of the cultural context in which they were found. For example, in early *Chèo* Theater collections, these researchers did not include biographies of performers, photographs, or "performance sheets," nor did they collect the "recitative" (*vỉa*) in *chèo* because it did not have musical "structure."[11] Furthermore, Vietnamese folk music was often evaluated according to Western musical principles and only those elements that could be seen in terms of such a system were deemed worthy of collection (Tô Ngọc Thanh, pers. comm., 4/15/04). Indeed, these collections were initially valued less for their role in preserving or recovering culture per se than for the progressive uses to which they would be put as the restored "voice of the people" and as the raw material with which to compose a new national music in the traditional style.

REVOLUTIONARY CULTURAL POLICY

The Vietnamese Party official most central to the creation of cultural policy in revolutionary Vietnam was Trường Chinh, who held numerous posts in the Party and government including that of Party Secretary General (Kim Ngoc Bao Ninh 2005:16). Revolutionary cultural policy centered on two of his writings: "The Theses on Vietnamese Culture" (1943) and "Marxism and Vietnamese Culture" (1948). These two documents remained central to cultural policy for the next thirty years (Kim Ngoc Bao Ninh 2005). David Marr writes that after the publication of "The Theses on Vietnamese Culture," which was meant for internal Indochinese Communist Party circulation, "all cultural output had to be judged by the degree to which it stimulated patriotism, mass consciousness, and scientific objectivity" (Marr 1995:187).[12]

In his "Marxism and Vietnamese Culture," Trường Chinh argues that that these three principles must be taken together as a whole.[13] The principle of nationalization (*dân tộc hóa*) requires artists to give their complete loyalty to the country by creating art as propaganda in order to fight the French and also to seek out the positive aspects of Vietnamese culture that were suppressed under colonialism. Scientific objectivity (*khoa học hóa*) requires artists to fight the backwardness (*lạc hậu*) in much of Vietnamese culture by opposing elements that are superstitious, mystical, and anti-progressive. The principle of mass consciousness (*đại chúng hóa*) requires that art serve the masses by being grounded in the real life and desires of the masses. Revolutionary culture should be socialist realist culture (*văn hóa hiện thực xã hội chủ nghĩa*) that was both "scientific" and "materialist" (Trường Chinh 1985 [1948]:60).

Trường Chinh's formulations on culture subsequently colored artistic and musical output in Vietnam. An excerpt from a letter from the Vietnamese Workers' Party Central Executive Committee sent to the Second National Arts Congress in 1957 reconfirmed artists' responsibilities to the new nation: The arts were to "serve the people and the revolution," in particular the workers, peasants, and soldiers (*công nông binh*), to "uphold the national character," to "absorb an international essence" particularly from the arts of other socialist countries, to create socialist realist works of art, and to address "positive topics and the new person" (Phấn Đấu Thắng Lợi: Cho Một Nền Văn Nghệ Dân Tộc Phong Phú [trích thư của Bản chấp hành Trung ương Đảng Lao động Việt-Nam gửi Đại hội Văn nghệ Toàn quốc lần thứ 2] (The Struggle for Victory: Towards a Diverse System of National Arts [letter from the Vietnamese Workers' Party Central Executive Committee to the Second National Arts Congress]) 1957:6–8).[14] Thus, "the common responsibility of intellectuals and arts workers in the North is to contribute to the implementation of the arts revolution in the new period, contribute to building up a new people for the new society with regards to thinking, intellect and sentiment" (ibid.:6).

For Vietnamese musicians, musical authenticity was intimately connected to the intentionality of art (that is, its ability to serve the masses) and the temporality of art (its connection to a pre-colonial "pure" past and its simultaneous grounding in the here and now of revolutionary time). An important concern for composers and musicians in this period was determining how music could serve the people or the *công nông binh* (workers, peasants, soldiers). Musicians debated the difficulty of conforming to the ideal of creating socialist realist works in artistic and aesthetic terms. They generally agreed that music must be connected to "reality" or "have realism" in some way but how this was to be achieved or what precisely that meant was open to debate. Some authors claimed that to achieve reality one had to inject words about laborers, revolutionaries, or peasants into one's compositions. Others claimed that to write revolutionary music one had to have experienced revolution firsthand (Nguyễn Văn Tý 1956). Still others claimed that it was necessary to look back to Vietnam's musical past. They claimed that for the new national music to be based in reality, it had to build upon a foundation of folk music seen as the real music of the people (Đoàn Chuẩn 1956). What tied all these opinions together, however, was the belief that musical composition had to be grounded in "reality" (*thực tế*) and had to appeal to the people in a meaningful way.

MUSICAL NATIONALISM

The Revolution, the War of Resistance against France (1945–1954), and the American War (ending in 1975) provided ideal venues for the beginnings of a musical nationalism in Vietnam. The phrase "the sound of the singing drowns out the sound of the bombs" (*tiếng hát át tiếng bom*) characterizes attitudes towards singing in this period, which was seen as an expression of optimism in the face of war. The wars necessitated an emphasis on national unity for practical and strategic reasons. This translated into an ideology of inclusiveness with regard to ethnic minorities within Vietnam and to the wide variety of local cultural practices. In order to defeat the French and later to drive out the Americans and re-unify the country, the revolutionaries had to rely on the help of ethnic minority groups (Marr 1981:183, 321; 1995:179–182) as well as on people who would otherwise be maligned by communist ideology, such as wealthy landlords (Luong Van Hy 1992; Malarney 2002). However, the ideal of unity was difficult to maintain conceptually in the face of the actual division of the country into North and South following the Geneva accords in 1954. Following the division of the country, writings on music emphasize a unity in spirit that finds its strength in a commonly shared "national character" or "national spirit."[15]

In writings in the years following the 1954 division of the country, some scholars and musicians claimed that North and South were unified in spirit despite the country's temporary physical division. The first issue of the *Music Review*, for instance, is concerned with the organization of the Arts Congress that was to take place that year.[16] In a letter from the Executive

Committee for the Congress that opens the Review, the overriding concern is how the arts can contribute to the re-unification of the country. The letter is directly addressed to "all our brothers and sisters in the arts of the whole country" (*cùng toàn thể anh chị em văn nghệ trong toàn quốc*) and concerns "the world of the arts in the whole of Vietnam from South to North" (*đoàn kết giới văn nghệ Việt-nam suốt từ Nam chí Bắc*) (Tiến tới Đại hội: Văn nghệ Toàn Quốc [Approaching the Congress: Arts of the Whole Country 1956]). In the same issue, composer Nguyễn Xuân Khoát writes in his "Letter Sent to Our Musician Friends of the South" that "We are just about to meet each other. We will reunite to become a force that will shoulder the common responsibility in the task of building a new institution of music that is worthy of the glorious age-old traditions of our nation" (1956:10). Such appeals to musicians and friends in the South indicate that musicians felt that a unified musical community hinged upon the transcendent nature of Vietnamese national character.

NATIONAL CHARACTER AND THE "IDEOLOGY OF SENTIMENT"

Hoàng Kiều, a noted music researcher and composer of *chèo* plays, opens his article "National Character in Music" with the statement: "The arts in general and music in particular must have national color [or character] (*mầu sắc dân tộc*) in order to have value" (1956:7). Defining national character and determining how to incorporate it into compositions was a central theme in many period writings. A common thread in many of these writings was that national character was closely associated with "sentiment" (*tình cảm*), which in turn was rooted in the folk traditions of the people. For example, Đoàn Chuẩn defines national character as the sentiment of the masses that originated in its folk music. This sentiment is what has enabled folk music to survive from "one century to the next" (1956:4). His article "Returning to National Music" (1956) narratively reenacts the way in which a composer (here the author) looks back for inspiration to traditional music (*nhạc cổ*). Ultimately, he "wakes up" to the value of traditional music and realizes that he "must return to the road of composition of national music by way of a love of traditional national music (*nhạc cổ dân tộc*), by searching for the essence of this music, by absorbing it gradually into the body. Then, from there, new compositions will have national character" (ibid.).

Hoàng Kiều defines national character as that which includes the "thinking, sentiment, language and customs" of a people (*dân tộc*) and also something that develops and changes with the times. To have national character, a composition must convey the thinking, sentiment, and life (*tư tưởng, tình cảm*, and *đời sống*) of the people today and at the same time enhance and educate the people (1956:9). This definition indicates that he sees national character as rooted in the embodied sentiment and actions that constitute social life. Nguyễn Xuân Khoát also emphasizes the role of emotion (*cảm xúc*) and sentiment (*tình cảm*) in musical nationalism. He documents how, through the process of composition, he comes to understand "the ideology of sentiment" (*tư tưởng tình cảm*) as an expression of national character. Initially, he went through a "period of borrowed emotion" in which he simply imitated his musical forefathers without full understanding but, finally, he comes to understand that the national character must have an emotional foundation in reality (*thực tế*) (1972:22–23).

These and other authors (see, for example, Tô Vũ 1972; Cừ Huy Cận 1972; Nguyễn Phúc 1972) are struggling to reconcile the ideological and political imperative to create a new musical canon based upon nationalism, mass consciousness, and scientific objectivity with the humanistic and social dimensions of musical production. To understand the connection that these authors make between national character, ideology, and sentiment, it is important to distinguish between "emotion" and "sentiment" in the Vietnamese context. Emotions are something felt and experienced whereas sentiment is fundamentally relational and is embedded in and constituted by social (or political) actions and exchange. To have sentiment implies engaging in correct social behavior that is a reflection of proper values and feelings towards others. It is through sentiment that one belongs to the collectivity (here figured as the socialist nation). Thus, one might feel certain emotions as a result of performing certain acts of sentiment. These authors are arguing that sentiment is, in fact, a form of thought or ideology (*tư tưởng tình cảm*) that can be expressed (*diễn đạt*) and achieved through proper action, in this case by incorporating folk music in new compositions. The result is a Vietnamese hybrid ideology that marries a Vietnamese focus on sentiment with the international socialist politics of the new nation. Locating the true realization of socialist ideals in the realm of sentiment ties ideology to the affective and social dimension of Vietnamese life.

These authors were working through these ideas in the middle of what is known as the Nhân Văn Giai Phẩm period (NVGP), a short-lived period of intellectual dissent in which a number of writers, artists, and musicians expressed their dissatisfaction with the limitations put on their creative and intellectual freedom of expression by the Party. The period was named after the two journals most closely associated with the movement: *Nhân Văn* (*Humanism*) and *Giai Phẩm* (*Works of Beauty*). A number of composers were closely associated with this movement, including Tử Phác, Đỗ

Nhuận (who eventually switched over to the official, opposing stance), and Văn Cao (the composer of the national anthem).[17] As Kim Ngoc Bao Ninh remarks, "Coming so soon after the establishment of the socialist state in North Vietnam and coinciding with a period of dramatic events in the communist world, the NVGP period came to exemplify the inherent conflict between the government's vision and the intellectuals' expectations of the new state and society" (2005:122). The more open atmosphere of these few years in the 1950s, before the government came down harshly on many of those involved in the Nhân Văn Giai Phẩm affair, ended by 1960.[18] In the American War period that followed, many of the debates that pitted ideas of artistic freedom against policy and ideological demands dissipated as intellectuals rallied in defense of the country.

Musicians during this period saw themselves and the process of composition in which they were engaged as a medium (literal and metaphorical) that would reconnect the Vietnamese spirit contained in the folk past with the modern socialist present. They embraced the fact that they were directly involved in the political process of education of the masses through the arts, even if they were troubled by how to reconcile this project with their own idea of the artist as an individual creative force.

"GOOD" AND "BAD" MUSIC AND THE POLITICS OF CORRECTION (CHINH LÝ)

A report on the preparations for the 1956 National Arts Congress (Đại Hội Văn Nghệ Toàn Quốc 1956) in the Music Review details how musicians were active participants in implementing cultural policy.[19] To begin with, they restructured the way that musical genres fit into society by classifying them in newly socialist terms. Before the conference, the subcommittee for the conference, directed by Nguyễn Xuân Khoát, collected and reviewed more than one hundred works from before the August Revolution that were to be used as "exemplary in the analysis and summary of the development of music" (Ngành Nhạc Chuẩn Bị Đại Hội [The Discipline of Music Prepares for the Congress] 1956:3). In its work, the subcommittee labeled works collected as "good" (tốt) or "bad" (xấu) on the basis of their "artistic value" and on their "ability to serve the masses" (ibid.:3–4). It designated different categories of composition (luồng sáng tác): secret and revolutionary compositions, compositions that utilize ethnic or national materials, compositions that revive historical topics, romantic composition, dance music, religious music, and compositions without lyrics (ibid.).[20] Each of these categories as set up for the 1956 conference can contain "good" and "bad" songs, or songs that do or do not express revolutionary and socialist values. The categories themselves also reflect the cultural ideology of the Party. The form of composition concerned with the revival of historical topics, for instance, clearly indicates the importance of reconstructing a Vietnamese national history and culture in the face of the perceived destruction of Vietnamese culture and history under colonial rule. In addition, classification (as a form of social scientific methodology) of songs as "good" or "bad" allowed Vietnamese musicians to work towards "scientific objectivity" in conformity with Trường Chinh's three principles for artistic production. The committee set up a system of musical value based on the ideology set out in socialist cultural policy.

Folk music collection and classification in Maoist China followed similar guidelines. Yang Mu argues that after the Red Army's "long march" (October 1934–October 1935) and under Mao's guidance, a large number of Chinese folk songs were re-written as "revolutionary songs" and re-distributed as traditional songs that expressed the revolutionary spirit of the people (Yang Mu 1994:308). His analysis of the *Anthology of Chinese Folk Songs* (the anthology was begun in the 1960s and resumed again after the Cultural Revolution in 1979), which is used by scholars in and outside of China for research, shows that inclusion of songs in the anthology was based on ideological concerns. "Revolutionary songs" were given priority for inclusion and some songs had sections deleted or altered to make them conform to the government ideology (ibid.:311). These criteria were put forth by Mao in the 1937 conference in Yenan. At the conference, Mao not only stressed the need for the arts to serve the masses and revolutionary purposes but also spoke of the necessity of musicians and artists to go among the people to find the "raw materials of literature and art" and "only then can they proceed to creative work" (Perris 1983:8). Mao recommended learning from folk and popular forms, which, as in the Vietnamese case, reflect the importance of the nationalistic element in revolutionary programs.

In Vietnam, while folk music and culture came to be seen as a repository for that which was essentially "Vietnamese" or for national character, it also carried with it the possibility of "backwardness," "primitivism," and "ignorance" at odds with a modern mass culture of the new socialist nation.[21] In addition to labeling songs as "good" or "bad," Vietnamese Party policy dictated that collected folk songs should be "corrected" (*chinh lý*) to make sure they conformed to revolutionary goals of nationalism, mass culture, and scientific objectivity. Correction of folk songs refers to changes made to lyrics and or musical structure in order to make the songs more modern and, therefore, more palatable to the modern socialist masses or to make them more revolutionary in content. For example, the song "Waiting" (*Đợi Chờ*) was published in the *Music Review* (Nhật Lai and Ta Phước 1956) as a "Tây Nguyên folk song." However, it was given new Vietnamese lyrics as follows:

> Go to combat for the sake of a peaceful home
> Be happy to go to combat and to forget me
> You must love the poor
> Love them far more than you love me
> But certainly allow your heart to love anyone
> I will always love and wait for you.[22]

Correction assumed that there was a fundamental authentic core or "essence" present in folk music and song that persisted and was to be left intact through time. Over this essential core, however, the lyrical content of a song had to be directly relevant to modern society, its history, and its politics. Music was seen as a tool that directly linked "correct" socialist content to something authentically Vietnamese.[23]

RENOVATION OF FOLK MUSIC

Phong T. Nguyen argues that there are three categories of change made to folk songs: *chỉnh lý* or "correction" of lyrics, *cải biến* or "revision of old melodies without the addition of new melodies," and *sáng tác* or "composition based on certain melodic motives of fragments of folksongs" (1991: 4). A form of new composition, falling into Phong T. Nguyen's third category (composition or *sáng tác*), that drew upon folk collections as its raw material was Vietnamese renovated national folk music (*nhạc dân tộc cải biến*) also known as modern national folk music (*nhạc dân tộc hiện đại*).[24] The inclusive nature of this music, which presented numerous folk music styles and genres, addressed the national agenda of the new state insofar as it contributed to the concept of Vietnam as one nation with many peoples (Arana 1999). This genre is also important to consider because of its relationship to Western musical structure and its reliance on Western notation.

Le Tuan Hung identifies seven principal technical features of revised or renovated music that marked a change from "traditional" music: 1) melody: traditional pitches were replaced with Western tempered pitches and microtonal ornaments were simplified or abandoned; 2) tempo was always increased to make the pieces sound " 'optimistic,' 'joyful' and 'heroic' to 'reflect the revolutionary mood of the society' "; 3) original structures were sometimes retained and sometimes arranged to fit the Western A-B-A song form in which B was an interlude developed from the original folk song;[25] 4) "texture";[26] 5) while many folk songs were traditionally unaccompanied or accompanied by percussion only, renovated music was always accompanied; 6) Western tonal harmony is usually preferred; and 7) many singers of renovated music "use the strong and projected vocal style of European classical music" (1997:44–47).[27] Vietnamese music not influenced by Western music, on the other hand, does not rely on fixed pitches and it typically had a single melodic line without harmonization and an orchestra would be composed of single instruments grouped together (Thụy Loan 1993: 58). Ornamentation or the addition of musical and verbal flourishes to a base melody was central to the full realization of a song or piece.[28]

Modern national folk music is most often an amalgamation of different melodies, motifs, and styles drawn from traditional music from around the country—of the Kinh majority and ethnic minorities—which are then arranged into new chamber music–style compositions meant for stage performance. The local nature of these elements is subsumed into a greater "Vietnamese" local. Modern national folk music is structurally Western but stylistically it is meant to represent something specifically "Vietnamese." It is often played on traditional instruments which have been modified or "improved" for use in modern national folk music performances as the instruments, in their original form, were unsuited to Western harmonic structures (see Arana 1999).

In modern national folk music, motifs and melodies from collected folk songs were repeatedly integrated into new, fast, and optimistic compositions until they were immediately recognizable as "Vietnamese" and "traditional" (truyền thống) by listeners who might otherwise not have been at all familiar with the music of localities other than their own. Arana explains that musical borrowing is not a new process in Vietnam and that in fact, there has traditionally been spontaneous borrowing between different folk music genres, which is one reason "why composers have no problem inserting popular but unrelated melodies into larger works, and why Vietnamese listeners have no problem accepting them" (1999:101).[29] Another reason Arana proposes for this ease of inclusion is that different melodies in Vietnamese musical practice were "typically associated with particular emotive content and meaning" evoked by the musical characteristics employed by different musical "modes" and immediately recognizable to listeners. These characteristics include pitches used, the relationship between pitches used, ornamentation, and melodic patterns and motifs (1999:102).[30] Arana writes, "the continual reiteration of familiar melodies in the nhạc dân tộc hiện đại repertoire serves to trigger a particular emotional response in the listener, and it is only through familiarity with a body of pre-existing melodies that this response can occur" (ibid.). Therefore, the modern national folk music genre was a new form that exhibited certain continuities with earlier Vietnamese musical practices, in particular that people identified with the music emotionally.

Modern national folk music assembled diverse musical fragments drawn from folk music found throughout the country into fluid and unified compositions. In these compositions, the locally specific sound fragments indexed the nationalist ideal of unity in diversity. The compositions provided a common musical language necessary for the creation of musical citizenship in the new nation. The nationalizing effect of this performance style is heightened by the costumes assumed by musicians who would don the appropriate "ethnic" clothing for its corresponding piece. These outfits, like the music they accompany are also "modified," which might mean they are made of brighter or livelier colors or have a hint of unspecified ethnicity by sewing bands of embroidery on a vest. Thus, "staging" Vietnamese renovated music is geared towards "making people believe" (Attali 1985:57) in the nation and in the music. This project relies on listeners to recognize certain (folk) sounds as "Vietnamese" and as belonging to the nation as a whole. However, it is not the stage per se that creates identification; rather, the social processes of staging, composing, performing, and listening (repeatedly) to this music generates an emotional identification with the nation.

WESTERN NOTATION

Even while it represented itself as essentially Vietnamese, modern national music was inextricably tied to the structures and methods of Western music. Western notation provides a useful metaphor for examining how the new musical reality of the nation was actively shaped and disciplined. Etienne Darbellay (1986), in his discussion of "tradition" and "notation" in the early Baroque period, explains that in general the evolution of notation involved the increasing precision and "inviolability" of the musical message. He claims that notation gave rise to a new concept of the composer as author, rather than as transmitter of a message. This composer-as-author communicates a "univocity" capable of being preserved in notation. As such, the composer establishes ownership of the message and ensures that it can be "understood and communicated by somebody else." Darbellay explains that "[s]ucceeding developments, precipitated by this process, show that hereafter the content of the message will reside more and more in its form" (1986:60–61). While the transcription of folk music differs from the composition of art music, as Darbellay describes it, the move from oral to written music is one of standardization. When written down, the music is "petrified" (Adorno 1990) on paper. What once were free-floating notes are rigidly fixed, tied to the musical staff. This is especially marked when the earlier form of pre-notated music is characterized by ornamentation and/or improvisation. The subtle variations in word choice or notes that occur from singer to singer and from generation to generation that characterized oral transmission become deviations from a standard that trouble the nationally recognized form upon which they are based.

Notation has, for instance, resulted in more precise or exact tempo in the performance of *chèo* folk theater. A ninety-one-year-old *chèo* singer in Khuốc village, Thái Bình province told me that a significant difference between today's singing, which has been "adapted" or changed, and his own old style is that, in the past, "the way of keeping the beat was not exact." Now, however, keeping time "has a method" and "is more exact." Furthermore, in the past, he said, singers were good at improvising on the spot in performance but did not have "do mi fa son [do re mi]; we just knew that this place fit with that breath (*hơi*)."[31] This singer's comment indicates that the very method of singing *chèo* has changed, become more precise, as a result of notation.

Don Michael Randel maintains that certain elements of notation (for instance, that it handles pitch better than timbre and duration) shape scholarly work on the Western canon (1996:12–13). As such, music that cannot easily be assimilated into the system of Western notation is often excluded from the canon. Because of its pentatonic and seven tone scales and lack of fixed pitches, traditional Vietnamese music is systemically at odds with the Western tonality contained within its notation. Thus the overwriting of Vietnamese music by the conceptual and organizational framework of Western notation requires a fundamentally different conceptualization of music and the canon.[32]

In Vietnam, there is no indigenous system of musical notation. Although a rough notation system derived from the Chinese system is used for instrumental music (Knosp 1922; Hoàng Yến 1919; Dumoutier 1890), songs are passed on orally from person to person. The concept of oral transmission, conceived as central to the practice of traditional music in Vietnam, is complicated by the introduction of notation. Many researchers and musicians with whom I spoke on the subject of the use of Western notation for the transcription of Vietnamese folk song spoke of it as a necessary yet inadequate tool for preservation. Without it (in the absence, that is, of an indigenous system of notation), too much would have been lost (see also Norton

2009:42–44).[33] However, Western notation fails to capture the nuances of tone, embellishment, timbre, and vocal technique that are often the very characteristics that distinguish one form of local song from another.[34] On the printed page such differences are nowhere evident. As Đặng Đình Hưng remarks in his article "Singing Folk Song" (*Hát Dân Ca*), "[o]ften times merely looking at the notation on the page creates a way of singing completely [the singer's] own to the point that these are no longer folk songs and upon hearing the songs, [people from] localities cannot recognize them as their own" (1956:30). Đặng Đình Hưng's comment reveals more than just the perceived inability of notation to capture the local or distinctive character of a song; one also gets the sense from the comment that interpretation of the song outside its original context and the highlighting of the individual singer that notation causes are inherently at odds with what he perceives to be the authentic rendering of a folk song. This is folk song in the mouth of a "singer" and not of "the people." Once set down in notation, a folk song, no matter what its original genre (*chèo, quan họ*, and so on), is open to interpretation from within any other genre. Failure to uphold the nuanced performance techniques that characterize each genre in one sense indicates the contradiction at the heart of the project of unity in diversity. The project is constituted by the very differences that its unity ultimately effaces.

The Vietnamese oral tradition of folk song is in important ways defined by its local styles. Different localities have distinctive folk performance styles. Variations in lyrics and music occur even from village to village in the same region. Through the transcription of oral forms of music into notes and measures, notation imposes discipline and orthodoxy on folk music; yet at the same time, as indicated by Đặng Đình Hưng, it also runs the risk of making folk music entirely unrecognizable (i.e., unreadable as "folk") when placed in the wrong "mouth." Western notation, figured as rational and scientific (see Dao Trong Tu 1984b), became the system through which folk music, or that which is "raw," was composed as national. Because it was new (and different from oral transmission), musicians and musicologists had to teach the people to read and perform music in such a way that it conformed to revolutionary ideals.

MUSICAL LITERACY IN THE NEW NATION

Several series of songbooks published by the Music Publishing House (*Nhà Xuất Bản Âm Nhạc*), under the Ministry of Culture, in the early 1960s demonstrate how notated folk songs (*dân ca*) were envisioned as a part of a larger Vietnamese musical tradition and could be used to help people achieve musical literacy in the new tradition.[35] These songbooks covered three areas: new music (*nhạc mới*), ethnic or national music (*nhạc dân tộc*), and foreign music (*nhạc nước ngoài*). The national music group includes books of folk songs by region (such as *Dân Ca Liên Khu V, Dân Ca Nghệ Tĩnh, Dân Ca Tây Nguyên*, etc.), by ethnic group (such as *Dân Ca Tày, Dân Ca Mèo*, etc.), and by genre (such as *Dân Ca Quan họ, Những Điệu Hát Tuồng Phổ Biến* [*Popular Tuồng Songs*], etc.). Also in this group was a series of twelve *Dân Ca* (Folk Song) books that included music from each of the above categories. The two songbooks in the *Dân Ca* series I obtained (numbers 7 and 12), instead of listing past and expected future publications in the songbook series on the back cover (as did the other series), have lessons in the fundamentals of Western musical notation (*ký âm thường thức*). Number seven, for instance, teaches about tempo: it lists different musical terms for tempo (*largo, lento, adagio*, etc.), how to pronounce the words in Vietnamese (*Lạc-gô, Len-tô, A-đa-gi-ô*, etc.), their meaning in Vietnamese, and their corresponding beats per minute. The lesson on the back cover of *Dân Ca 12* teaches how to use and notate scale.

Therefore, on the backs of the very collections of folk song from around the country, which are meant to demonstrate unity in diversity, the new Vietnamese listening subject finds a lesson in how to read and compose a national musical tradition. It is only on the general *Dân Ca* songbooks that the lessons in musical notation are given. The songbooks dedicated to regional or ethnic minority music, on the other hand, omit the lesson in music theory and notation, allowing them to maintain their local character within the wider national context. The *Dân Ca* books that include selections from all over the country, are presented as the proper forum in which the people should be learning to compose or read music. The 1957 issues of the *Music Review* also include supplementary inserts that contain a series of beginning lessons in music theory for readers to teach themselves how to read, write, and play music.

On the back of a *Dân Ca Tây Nguyên* (Tây Nguyên Folk Song) book, songs in the national music category are referred to as *loại nghiên cứu* (types [of song] for research).[36] The songbooks, thus, were seen as source materials with which new musical citizens could educate themselves. In this same context, the folk song "The Magpie Crosses the River" (*Con Sáo Sang Sông*), is introduced in the *Music Review* as follows:

> We publish the song "The Magpie Crosses the River" in three versions, Northern, Central and Southern for you to use as research materials. The three versions express, once again, that the land and culture

of Vietnam cannot be divided, that Vietnam is one unified country. (1956:33)

This passage expresses a desire for the disciplinary unification of Vietnamese music by way of standardized research materials that are made available and legible to all Vietnamese despite the temporary division of the country.[37] As oral tradition, Vietnamese folk songs found throughout the country, such as "The Magpie Crosses the River," varied significantly in performance from place to place and even from singer to singer. Văn Cao, for example, claims that he is aware of eleven regional variations of this song but that there are many more waiting to be discovered (1972:160).[38] Thus, the effort to create a body of standardized research materials is an effort to create a foundation of common musical literacy for a new national listening subject. The song "The Magpie Crosses the River" was published to demonstrate that, despite regional variation and the military and political division of the country, all three versions are tied together by an underlying essential spirit that makes the song "Vietnamese." That is, local diversity itself is here defined as Vietnamese.

CONCLUSION

After August 1945, folk music became a critical tool with which musicians, in concert with other culture workers in the new nation, forged a link between an essentialized Vietnamese past and the modern socialist present. In seeking how to delineate a new musical canon for the nation, they had to transcribe a concept of national character into a new and distinctly Vietnamese style and also find ways to discipline a whole nation full of newly created listening subjects in line with the revolutionary cultural policy. Fundamental to this project was the idea of unity in diversity and its attendant work of collection of folk music, which sought to incorporate the local into the very definition of the national in what one author called a "unified contradiction."

The concept of a unified contradiction can also be extended to the nature of the new national music that emerged out of the projects of decolonization and nation building following the Revolution. The project of creating a new national music was fundamentally intertwined with the Western and colonial structures of music and power against which the new nation and its music were defined. In the context of the "new culture," collection, correction, and composition of folk music can be seen as performative acts that engendered a particular form of Vietnamese national identity strongly

rooted in the state's ideology of unity in diversity. In their struggle to reconcile the ideological directives of the State with their own sense of musical
humanism based in the emotions, musicians and composers articulated an
"ideology of sentiment." This Vietnamese-socialist hybrid ideology linked
the idea of socialist political action to indigenous cultural ideas about sentiment as a form of proper action that sustains the social collectivity.

2

Embodied Practices and Relationships of Sentiment

We long for them as a fish longs for rain
We long for them as lunch makes the stomach hungry
We have longed for them for many months already
Today our friends intend to come back to "play" [to sing with us]
Coming to play they will see how our house is
Coming to play, I seek the friendship of someone to confide in.

When I was still young, I had such passion [for quan họ] that I'd go from here to there, the fifteen kilometers to Hoài Thị Village. . . . In the evening, after returning from harvesting and threshing rice paddy and after bathing, at 10 p.m., a group of us would walk over there, sing until four in the morning, then walk home again, eat again, go harvest the paddy again. We were that passionate, we were passionate about the music to that degree. (Female quan họ singer, Diềm Village)[1]

Depth of feeling, longing for absent friends, friendships that last a lifetime, passion for the music that compels one to sing through the night after a hard day's work in the fields: the lyrics of quan họ songs and the discourse of village singers in Bắc Ninh are permeated with feelings such as these. Yet, lyrics and words alone can only begin to convey the meaning of these feelings; they cannot fully embody "the felt sense, the 'guts'" (Lyon

1995:256) of what quan họ means to its practitioners because the passion for the music that the singer quoted above expresses is inseparable from the bodily practices of singing that are, in turn, inseparable from the social dimension of quan họ practice.

This chapter examines how social relationships and sentiment are situated in and generated by embodied practices of performance, following Csordas' claims that "culture is grounded in the human body" and that "the body has a history and is as much a cultural phenomenon as it is a biological entity" (1994:4). Following in the phenomenological tradition, Csordas expands upon Merleau-Ponty's discussion of Heidegger's concept of "being-in-the-world" and proposes the phrase as an alternative to anthropological works that result in representations of an other (1990, 1994). Unlike representation, which he argues understands culture in terms of "objectified abstraction," being-in-the-world "is fundamentally conditional, and hence we must speak of 'existence' and 'lived experience'" (1994:10). Margot Lyon argues further that studies of embodiment need to move beyond the phenomenological emphasis on "the sensory interface between body and the world that is experienced through it" to a view of emotion that attends to "the multiple facets of emotion . . . that are part of its foundational role in social relations" (1995:257). The immediacy of this approach to the study of culture allows for attention to a wider range of sensory and emotional experience that more accurately reflects how meaning emerges in social interaction. As Paul Stoller remarks in his discussion of his reawakening to the importance of the senses in the study of anthropology, "one cannot separate thought from feeling and action; they are inextricably linked" (1989:5).

At the same time, I do not reject the importance of representation in this examination of how quan họ is situated in the body. In fact, as quan họ moves onto the stage, representation itself becomes a way of "being-in-the-world." In his work on the role of the senses in visual ethnography, David MacDougall (2006) explores the moments when meaning emerges from experience. These are the moments when we become aware of meanings as something seemingly apart from experience and, thus, we become aware of "being itself" (both our own being and that of others). He links this process, which is one of generalization, to vision because "[s]eeing not only makes us alive to the appearance of things but to being itself" (ibid.:1). An important role of cultural performances is that they allow cultures to see themselves in action and, thus, "sketch out what they believe to be more apt or interesting 'designs for living'" (Turner 1988:24). Seeing ourselves in performance is part of the very process of understanding the social meaning generated by that performance. As more and more attention is focused on quan họ by those outside the region, its village singers are called upon to reflect upon and to represent themselves to the outside world in new ways.

In this chapter, "the social practice of quan họ" refers to the set of actions, singing techniques, gestures, songs, and events that together constitute village quan họ. The social practice of quan họ is often called *quan họ làng* (village quan họ) or *quan họ cổ* (traditional quan họ); however, neither of these terms fully captures the social dimension of quan họ practice. The social practice documented here refers to an ideal-typical form of quan họ based on a pre-1945 ideal of local practice in Bắc Ninh Province. I want to emphasize, however, that contemporary practice also includes all forms of current practice that singers themselves see as falling within this tradition. There are instances in which this form of practice could also be said to be performance, such as in singing events held in the public space of the temple or in the presence of researchers and television crews. It is important to note that today, villagers also put on staged performances of quan họ in their own villages. I am aware that by presenting the pre-1945 ideal, I run the risk of reifying a particular form of practice that exists today primarily in the memories of elder singers, and which is increasingly designated as a standard for cultural heritage, a critique that I have leveled against others elsewhere in this book. What I present here, thus, should be treated not as an exact picture of pre-1945 practice. Rather, because memories of past practices are fully embedded in the current cultural landscape, they are an essential key to understanding discourse about quan họ in contemporary Vietnam.

THE SOCIAL PRACTICE OF QUAN HỌ (*CHƠI QUAN HỌ*)

To understand the social practice of quan họ, it is necessary to understand the difference between the terms *chơi quan họ* and *hát quan họ*. *Hát quan họ* or, literally, "to sing *quan họ*," is the expression commonly used in the mass media, by non-singers, and in reference to staged performances of quan họ. By focusing on a single element—singing—out of an array of practices, the term *hát quan họ* plays down social practice and highlights theatricality. That is, the term references only the genre's most audible aspect. On the other hand, village singers most commonly use the expression *chơi quan họ*, literally "to play" or "to practice" quan họ.[2] The word *chơi*, in this case, refers to the set of social conventions, actions, gestures, relationships, songs, and style that singers employ in the social practice of quan họ in Bắc Ninh Province. Taken as a whole, the above conventions make up the "way of practicing or playing" quan họ, which singers call "*lối chơi*." Đặng Văn Lung, Hồng Thao, and Trần Linh Quý define *lối chơi* as

> the totality of the relationships between people in the activities of the art of *quan họ*. . . . The relationships manifest themselves in, on the one hand, the music and lyrics and, on the other hand, and not unimportantly, they also manifest themselves in the conventions of the way of practicing the activities (for example, way of singing, way of making friends with other groups (*kết bạn*), communication between groups), manifest themselves in body language, costumes, customs of eating and speaking, sitting, standing. (1978:19)

Participating in village quan họ is not just to sing but also to engage in an interconnected range of social practices and relationships.

Quan họ singers are organized into groups called *bọn quan họ*.[3] These groups exchanged songs (*hát đối đáp*) with other groups with whom they had partnerships. The groups provided training for young singers and were the organizational structures through which all singing events were arranged. Lê Danh Khiêm writes that:

> This organization is closely related to each specific village. A majority of the local "Bọn Quan họ" are established by the xóm [a subdivision of a village]. For example, in the past, Lim village had 4 xóm, each xóm had one men's bọn and one women's bọn. Diềm village had 10 bọn, Trà Xuyên had 6 bọn, Châm Khê had 4 bọn, Hòa Đình had 3 bọn, etc. (2001:189)[4]

A *bọn* was comprised of a group of either all women or all men from the same village and villages often had several *bọn* of different genders, as indicated in the quote above.[5] In the past, each *bọn* consisted of at least five singers.[6] Today, *bọn* usually consist of four to six singers.

These group relationships are still formed and maintained in contemporary quan họ village practice. However, younger singers trained after 1945 say that quan họ practice today is "more relaxed" and "informal," which includes the organization and exchanges between their *bọn*. Many villages today have one official village group (called the *đội quan họ*) that includes all village singers of both genders and children learning to sing. Diềm Village, for instance, established its village-wide *đội quan họ* in 1990. This official group is responsible for training new singers, representing the village at

events, such as festivals, taking place in partnered villages, and also providing stage entertainment at village festivals.

The singing members of a *bọn* are called, in the third person, *liền anh*
(a male singer) and *liền chị* (a female singer). The members of a *bọn* address
each other as, in order: second older sister (*chị hai*), third older sister (*chị
ba*), fourth older sister (*chị tư*), and so on or first older brother (*anh hai*),
second older brother (*anh ba*), third older brother (*anh tư*), and so on. The
omission of "first" sister or brother was a sign of egalitarianism in quan họ
practice. The order of the names is assigned according to the ages and abili-
ties of the singers, with the most accomplished being second older sister (*chị
hai*) or second older brother (*anh hai*). The oldest and most experienced of
the singers in a *bọn* would observe and pair off singers whose voices were
well matched in his or her group. These pairs always sang together in unison
(*hát đôi*) at singing events. In the past, the fifth (odd number) singer was
called *chị cả* (eldest sister) or *anh cả* (eldest brother). This person was the
eldest and one of the strongest of the singers in a group and was appointed
by the families of the group members. The *chị cả* or *anh cả* had an organizational and leadership role that included arranging meetings with other
groups and, especially, making sure that the singers followed proper procedure and behavior (Nguyễn Văn Phú et al. 1962:18). By 1962, however,
most *bọn* had dropped this custom (and the accompanying name) and the
young singers led themselves at singing events (ibid.).

At singing events and in song lyrics, quan họ singers always address each
other by the names above (second brother/sister, etc.) and never by their
given names. These terms of address deviate from the customary terms of
address in Vietnamese society, which are embedded in the social hierarchy.
The pronouns "I" and "you" in this latter system change according to the
relative age, gender, social position, and biological relationship of the speakers. Failure to use the proper pronoun with someone (especially someone
older or of higher social status) can be a sign of disrespect. In quan họ, on
the other hand, singers always refer to themselves in the diminutive *em*
(younger brother or sister) and address other singers with *chị* (older sister) or
anh (older brother) regardless of their actual ages. As one singer explained,

> If a group of women are only about twenty to thirty years old, for exam-
> ple, but the men are above forty to fifty, even so, they must call [the
> women] second older sister, third older sister, fourth older sister, fifth
> older sister. The women also must call the men second older brother,
> third older brother, fourth older brother, fifth older brother. That is,
> neither side is higher than the other. (Male singer, Y-Na Village)

Singers say that this custom maintains a sense of respect and equality among all singers. As put by another singer, "the sentiment of quan họ is very warm, we cherish each other like blood brothers and sisters even though we are not" (female singer, Thanh Sơn Village).

Before the establishment of the village-wide quan họ groups (đội quan họ), anyone who wanted to participate in quan họ activities had to belong to a bọn quan họ and each bọn would form a bond of friendship (kết bạn) with a bọn of opposite gender from a different village (Lê Danh Khiêm 2001:190). Groups from the same village never form official partnerships with each other, though they do sing with each other and with non-partnered groups from other villages on less formal occasions called "makeshift singing" (hát pha tạm) or "singing for fun" (hát vui) (Nguyễn Văn Phú et al. 1962:19). There are two kinds of "friendship relationships" between the bọn quan họ. The first, kết bạn, is formed between two groups from different villages who decide they want to sing together. The second, kết chạ or kết nghĩa, is a relationship between two villages in which the villages consider each other to be blood relatives and always participate in festivities, funerals, weddings, etc., of the other village, including quan họ activities (Lê Danh Khiêm 2000:84). Such partnerships were formed for various reasons, including defense against enemies, mutual aid (for example, help with building communal houses), as an expression of indebtedness for help given, to resolve quarrels over water use, etc. (Lê Hồng Dương 1982:535). If two villages have a kết nghĩa relationship, it is likely that they also have partnered bọn quan họ; however, this is not a requirement (Nguyễn Văn Phú et al. 1962:21). Only those bọn that have formed the friendship relationships with each other will organize a formal canh hát together, in which the two groups gather at a host's house and sing late into the night (see below). These three terms—kết nghĩa, kết bạn, and kết chạ—were often used interchangeably by people with whom I spoke in the villages and elsewhere.

There was a specific series of interactions that bọn would go through if they wanted to form a partnership (kết bạn) with another bọn (always of opposite gender). In some cases, a group (usually a men's group) would go to a village to seek out a woman's group with whom they were interested in forming a partnership (Nguyễn Văn Phú et al. 1962:21). Another common way groups found partner groups was at village festivals. Đặng Văn Lung, Hồng Thao, and Trần Linh Quý describe this procedure for the Lim Festival in Tiên Du District, as it occurred in the past, as follows:

> Arriving at Lim hill, a men's group as yet without friends would go to the festival to look for a woman's group that also was without friends

and would invite those women to share betel. If the women's side accepted the betel, it meant that they agreed to sing with them. There were also occasions on which the women took the initiative to invite the men. While they sang with each other at the festival, if the two sides felt they suited each other with regards to the way they treated each other and the way their singing voices harmonized with each other, then they would arrange to meet each other [on a future date] in the women's village to allow the men's side to bring offerings and request to form a partnership (*kết nghĩa*). (1978:38)

In the event that the groups agree to form a partnership, the visitors would offer incense and betel to the families of the hosts. The hosts would then bring them before the village notables and take them to pray at the communal house, and finally lead them back to the house to eat, drink, and sing (Đặng Văn Lung, Hồng Thao, and Trần Linh Quý 1978:38). According to one singer in Diềm Village, partnered groups would sing together at least once per month, sometimes more if there were special events like weddings or festivals to attend.

HOW TO PRACTICE QUAN HỌ (*LỐI CHƠI*)

The practice of quan họ (*chơi quan họ*) has strict rules of practice or a "method" called by the singers the *lối chơi quan họ* (way of playing or practicing quan họ). In order to understand the *lối chơi quan họ*, one must understand the concept of *giọng* or "voice" in quan họ.[7] This term overlaps with but is not equivalent to the English concepts of song (*bài hát*) and tune or melody (*giai điệu*), terms that are not generally used by quan họ singers in reference to what they do. In its broadest meaning, the term *giọng* is used to designate the three main categories of song that must be sung in order in a gathering of singers (*canh hát*): method voice (*giọng lề lối*), variety voice (*giọng vặt*), and farewell voice (*giọng giã bạn*). In addition, *giọng* is also used to indicate the individual melodies that occur within these three melody types. In the method category (*lề lối*) alone, elderly singers identify thirty-six melody variants (*giọng*), although many of these had been forgotten as far back as the early 1960s (Nguyễn Văn Phú et al. 1962:44). Elderly singers in Diềm Village, for instance, recite a poem that lists songs of the method voice category that the quan họ ancestress, the princess Vua Bà, was said to have taught the Diềm villagers. When one singer recited this poem to me, she listed about sixteen songs then broke off to say there were "many more." Nguyễn Đình Phúc quotes one singer who tells him, "If you allow us to sing for three days and nights continuously, we still would not exhaust all the works we know!" (Nguyễn Đình Phúc 2006:893). This statement is similar to claims that many singers made to me during my research.

Each individual melody (*giọng* of the latter type, above) has a number of different lyrical variations that are referred to by singers as *câu* or "phrases." *Câu* most often refers to the first phrase of the lyrics of a song. For example, the song at the beginning of this chapter is the *La Rằng* melody and falls into the broader "method voice" category (*giọng lề lối*). This specific song is referred to by singers as the *câu* "We long for them as a fish longs for rain" (*Mong người như cá mong mưa*), based upon the first line of the poem. There are many different "phrases" in the *La Rằng* melody. Thus, in each of the three tune categories (*giọng*), there are numerous melody variations (such as *La Rằng*), also called *giọng*, each of which has several different lyrical variations, called "phrases" (*câu*).

These distinctions are essential to understanding how an exchange of songs occurs at a *canh hát*. At a full *canh hát*, the three tune categories, method voice (*giọng lề lối*), variety voice (*giọng vặt*), and farewell voice (*giọng giã bạn*), must be sung through in that order. The method voice is the only category in which singers must follow a particular melody order (*giọng* of the second meaning, above). For instance, in Diễm Village, the melody order for the first segment of the method voice in the *canh hát* is as follows: *giọng La Rằng, giọng Kim Lan, giọng Gió Mát, giọng Bỉ*, and *giọng Cây Gạo*. Because the *canh hát* is structured as an exchange, singers say that "the five [songs] become ten" in this segment. For example, the first pair of singers might sing the "phrase" (*câu*) "I long for you as a fish longs for rain" (*Mong người như cá mong mưa*), which is an opening song (*bài ra*) for *giọng La Rằng*. Then, a pair of singers from the partner group might respond with the *câu* "If only I were at home" (*Nhẽ ra em cũng ở nhà*), which is also *giọng La Rằng*, but is sung as a "response song" (*bài đối*). Different pairs of singers would then repeat this exchange for each of the subsequent four melodies in the *lề lối* category. There are many different "phrases" that belong to each of the melody variants that could be sung in this situation; singers will select a "phrase" based upon personal repertoire. Village custom selects and sets the order of the five melody variants sung first in the method voice category. Singers must cover all five melodies in the method voice category before moving on to other melodies within this tune category or to the other two categories.

In a *canh hát*, the other two tune categories, variety voice (*giọng vặt*) and farewell voice (*giọng giã bạn*), follow the method voice (*giọng lề lối*) in this order. Songs in these two categories do not have a specified song order and singers can choose to sing whatever they like. However, they must adhere to the rule of exchange in which an opening song is responded to with a matching song. In a true *canh hát*, the absolute necessity to begin with the method voice category of songs highlights the centrality of conventions of social practice to this kind of music. Village singers say that a true *canh hát* is one that includes all three categories in order.

The songs in the first segment of a *canh hát*, the method voice (*giọng lề lối*), are considered to be the oldest and most difficult songs to sing. *Lề lối* means "the way of doing" things or "method" and is the same word used in "the way of practicing *quan họ*" (*lối chơi*). Barley Norton describes the concept of *lề lối* as it is understood by musicians of *châu văn*, the liturgical music that accompanies spirit mediumship rituals in the Vietnamese Mother Goddess Religion, as "the fundamental melodic identity of the song" (2009:143). He explains that

> [d]espite the differences in the vocal contour each time a song is performed, every realization has the same direction or movement—a "way"—in common. Musicians consider every realization of a song to be the "same" because each performance conforms to the same "way." (2009:134)

In *châu văn*, "way" refers to the skeletal melody of a piece that is then shaped in performance by a singer or musician. The variations in individual performance result in part from the melodic changes that occur with changes in lyrics from song to song because the tones in the music tend to follow the tonal inflections of the Vietnamese language (Norton 2009:143–144). Thus, the correct rendering of the "way" requires long years of practice and a feel for how each potential musical and lyrical situation conforms to the "way."

In quan họ, the concept of "way" is similar to this when used in reference to the *giọng lề lối* category of song in that each melody (such as *La Rằng, Bỉ, Cây Gạo*, etc.) conforms to a particular melodic "way" that is realized in a variety of "phrases" (*câu*). Generally, however, in quan họ, the basic melody is referred to as *giọng*, which, when realized in performance, rests upon the coordinated voices of two singers. While one finds variations in style and word choice in different pairs of singers, each pair together is highly coordinated when rendering any particular song. Thus, the "way" depends upon a long-term singing relationship in which the two singers, over time, become "as one." While *lề lối* in quan họ does refer to a category of melodies, it also refers to the set of social conventions and relationships of exchange fundamental to village practice more generally. Most importantly, quan họ is only fully realized as a social practice through the exchange of songs.

QUAN HỌ LYRICS AND TIES OF EMOTION

Đặng Văn Lung writes that "the topic of *quan họ* lyrics is emotional ties (*tình—nghĩa*). That is, the emotional ties between people (*tình nghĩa giữa những con người*)" (1982:611). Many quan họ lyrics express sentiments of attachment, love, and longing that results from being apart, as demonstrated in the lyrics quoted in the epigraph of this chapter, "We long for them as a fish longs for rain." Other lyrics expressing these sentiments include:

Far away, I am all alone
Who can truly understand my feelings?
. . .
If we love each other, we hope to make a life together
black shiny teeth and blue/green hair [from youth to old age].
(From *Bỉ đầu* melody, method voice, as taught by Bà Phụ, Diềm Village)

You left so the spider could spin its web.
The long night feels so cold and empty.
Do you miss me, the pure and beautiful girl, at all?
(From *The Spider Spins its Web*, farewell voice, taught by Nguyễn Thị
    Bàn, Diềm Village)

While lyrics speak of love and, occasionally, marriage to a beloved, village singers stress that the songs do not refer specifically to love between man and woman but rather to sentiments of attachment and friendship. Thus, these singers do not interpret the lyrics literally but rather interpret them within the social context of friendships derived from long-term singing relationships. Lyrics must be *exchanged* (*đối đáp*) in a social act for meaningful sentimental relations to form. Without the full array of social practices in which the song occurs, those lyrics would only *refer* to sentiment, not actually generate it.[8]

The importance of lyrics to the social practice of quan họ became clear in a discussion with an elderly singer from Bồ Sơn Village who emphasized the importance of *đúng văn* (correct lyrics). She said that today, many lyrics are wrong. They have been changed here and there, sometimes because people do not understand the lyrics and sing them incorrectly or sometimes because they are trying to make them more "modern." Furthermore, when someone else in the room mentioned to this same singer that lyrics today are often oriented more towards romance and love songs (that is, the literal interpretation of many lyrics), she immediately agreed. This singer then emphasized that many of the lyrics now are nonsensical *"không có nghĩa"* and therefore lose their interesting character. She laughed hard as she recited the new lyrics, emphasizing how silly or nonsensical they were to her. I asked where the changes in lyrics come from and she said that nowadays "they teach carelessly, wrong" (*dạy linh tinh, sai*) like quan họ on television. She said it is important to have "correct lyrics to make it interesting" but "the new teachers use incorrect lyrics." In fact, a number of the examples this singer claimed were the result of incorrect teaching, were actually local lyrical variants. What is important, however, is that she perceived these differences within the context of the changes wrought by modernization. "Correctness" does not refer precisely to the individual words of the lyrics because different singers and localities often substitute one word with equivalent meaning for another based on personal or local language usage.[9] Rather, she was referring to changes and intentional or unintentional mistakes, which result from a lack of understanding of the meaning of the poetry in the context of social relationships of quan họ singers. Thus, this singer was expressing the importance of the meaning of the lyrics as they were integrated into social life and the social practice of quan họ.

PLAYING AN INSTRUMENT IN THE THROAT

The social practice of quan họ, or to *chơi quan họ*, is inseparable from the embodied practice of singing and it is in the very act of singing that sociality is generated. In his essay, "Musica Practica," Roland Barthes distinguishes between "the music one plays" and "the music one listens to." These two musics, he claims, are "two totally different arts, each with its own history, its own sociology, its own aesthetics, its own erotic" (1977:149). The music one plays, Barthes argues, is a "muscular music." It is a "manual" and "kneadingly physical" music in which the body is the "inscriber and not just transmitter, simple receiver" (ibid.). Such a description aptly describes the social practice of quan họ in which the breath and sentiment are said to arise from the belly (see below), and sound is generated in the throat and the mouth.

Village quan họ singers sing in their speaking voices, which places sound in the throat and reveals what Barthes calls the "body in the voice as it sings" (1977:188). One singer explained to me that, to sing quan họ well, one's singing voice must "be in the throat." Clarifying this, she said "it is like playing an instrument in the throat" (*Nó như đánh đàn trong cổ họng*). What she was referring to specifically in this instance were the "supporting words" (*từ phụ* or *từ đệm*, also sometimes called *âm đệm*, "supporting sounds"), the "i's," "hứ's," "a's," "ô's," and "*tình tang*'s" of quan họ that are devoid of meaning yet give quan họ its distinctive sound. According to Lê Danh Khiêm, these sounds extend the poetry beyond its base of 6/8 meter (*thơ lục bát*) and, consequently, transform it into quan họ (pers. comm., 7/29/04). The base poems of many quan họ song lyrics are in 6/8 meter, which is one of two main meters found in Vietnamese folk poetry. It is said to be easy to remember because of its similarity to the cadence of Vietnamese speech (Huynh Sang Thong 1996). The supporting words or sounds expand the base poem of the song into a much longer composition. For example, the base phrases:

Nhẽ ra em cũng ở nhà   If only I were at home
Trong lòng bối rối như là người mong My heart is embarrassed like
             one who waits with longing

become:

Nhẽ ra hi i hi hi như ư ư hư a a đã **em cũng** hi hi i i i i ha hối ha ả à mấy a là a rằng hư là này rằng hự, hư ư lá la hối hư ư hư hư hừ, thì hư hư hà bên em ở ở nhà hì hì hì. hì í a ha a ha hối ha a ha hối ha a ha
Thì anh i hi i hi i hi hí hai a mấy i hai ơi mấy **trong** la a ha **lòng** hư ứ hự hối hự là, là a a em **bối rối** i hi i i i i **như** a à mấy a **như** a là mấy à i i hôi ha là **mong** ư hứ hư hôi hư hư hứ hư là.[10]

The songs in the method voice category (*giọng lề lối*), to which the above song belongs, are more drawn out than those in the other categories, making them much more difficult to remember and to sing. The supporting sounds not only extend the length of the song but also lend an internal vocalized rhythm to this otherwise unaccompanied music.[11] Lê Danh Khiêm, for instance, claims that these sounds imitate the sound of an accompanying instrument. He maintains that the supporting sounds stand in for accompanying instruments (*thay cho nhạc cụ*), which *quan họ cổ* does not use (pers. comm., 7/29/04). Several singers also pointed out to me that the supporting sounds are a kind of musical accompaniment to the song. *Quan họ cổ* is sung without musical accompaniment so these sounds provide a rhythmic movement to the singing that drives it along.

In the 1970s, quan họ scholar Trần Linh Quý developed four criteria or techniques with which to evaluate *quan họ cổ* (traditional or "ancient" quan họ) singing: *nẩy* (bouncing), *vang* (ringing), *rền* (resonant), *nền* (moderate or restrained) (Chan Ngoc Le 2002:73). Because the terms were devised by scholars to describe village singing technique, many elderly singers have difficulty explaining them. Younger singers on the other hand are generally more familiar and comfortable explaining and using the terms. The four techniques highlight the physicality of the sound of singing and its intimate relationship with the throat and mouth through their dependence on the supporting sounds. This is particularly true of *nẩy* (bouncing), which is a jumping or stopping of the voice mid-note, which lends to the note an almost percussive sound. Musicologist Hồng Thao claims that three criteria must be met in order to achieve *nẩy*, or "bouncing grains," in one's singing: "singing in real [speaking] voice," "singing in the middle register of the singer's pitch range," and "singing at a moderate pace to make the grains longer in duration. At a fast pace, the grains are too short to be effective" (Chan Ngoc Le 2002:75). *Nẩy* is very difficult to learn and scholars and village singers alike say that most professional singers cannot sing it, claiming that one must have begun to study quan họ at a young age to learn it.

The way in which breath is conceived of and used is also fundamental to the generation of sound in *quan họ cổ*. The social practice of quan họ is characterized by pairs singing (*hát đôi*). Each singer is paired with another singer from his or her group (*bọn*), thus of the same gender, who has a complementary voice. The two singers must *hát đều*, that is, sing evenly and symmetrically and the tone and quality of their voices must match. Furthermore, singers say that the two voices must complement and carry each other along so that they become "as one voice" and produce a single unified sound.[12] Noted quan họ researcher Hồng Thao, quotes a singer from Lim Village on how to sing quan họ well:

> [F]irst, the voices of the two people must blend with each other, the singing voice must be clear (*trong*), must be even (*đều*), one hears the singing of two people but it must really be like that of one person; second, one must know how to sing with bouncing grains (*nẩy hạt*), it sounds like there are drawn out vibrations as if there were tiny grains inside; third, one must know how to join the notes (*hát luyến*); fourth, one must know how to drop off the voice (*hát rớt*). (Tô Ngọc Thanh and Hồng Thao 1986:124)

The stronger of a pair of singers will lead, *hát dẫn*, and the other will sing "below" (*dưới*), called *hát luồn*. As explained by a singer in her forties from Diềm Village, the lead singer must be accomplished in two of the four characteristics, *nẩy* and *vang* (bouncing and ringing), while the "following" singer must have *nền* and *rền* (restrained and resonant). If both singers sing all four characteristics strongly, then the two voices will not "be as one;" they must "fit" with each other to make one voice.

Singers explain that the sound a pair of singers produces is not merely unified but also breathless—in the sense of freedom from breath, not out of breath. When one singer takes a breath, the sound is hidden by the voice of the partner singer. The result is an unbroken, continuous sound. What is hidden, then, is technique, as technique is understood in musical training influenced by the West. Indeed, the use of the breath was the first thing that I, as a Western-trained singer, had to "unlearn" in order to learn how to sing quan họ. In Western musical technique, the placement of the breath is seen as fundamental to the production of sound. One sings from the diaphragm and allows the breath to support and to carry the voice. The breath embodies mastery of sound itself and the ability to project it to others. That sound must be conveyed with emotion, but never so much emotion that it interferes with one's technical execution of the song and, thus, with the "communicative" nature of the song (Barthes 1977). Technique and emotion complement each other and support each other but remain distinct. The skilled performer certainly feels emotion in stage performances, which is perhaps necessary to trigger an emotional response from the audience. However, the emotion triggered on stage also references something outside the performance itself.

For village quan họ singers, on the other hand, breath is hidden under one's partner singer's voice and sound is said to be generated in the throat. While technical mastery of the song is important to these singers and those who hear them, its meaning lies in its connection to sentiment (*tình cảm*). Sentiment is at the heart of the social practice of quan họ. It is situated in the body and produced through the exchange of songs, gestures, and conventional language.

Singing Sentiment

In quan họ, not only does one sing in one's speaking voice and "play an instrument in the throat," one also sings "from the belly up and out" (*bụng ra lên*), as one village singer explained to me. The difference between singing "from the belly up and out" and supporting the breath in the diaphragm extends beyond mere placement of the singing voice in the body. It also indicates a fundamental emotive difference between this kind of singing and the kind of singing influenced by Western technique, a difference suggested by the word *bụng* itself. In Vietnamese, *bụng* ("stomach" or "gut") is the metaphorical seat of one's deep thoughts and emotions and is more akin to the English word "heart."[13] Therefore, the seat of the quan họ song, or the place from which it emanates, the belly, is also the seat of one's emotions. The quan họ song emerges from this bodily space of affective feeling or sentiment. To say then, that one sings "from the belly up and out" is not a technical reference to the place in which sound is generated or from which the breath emanates. It is, rather, a metaphorical statement about the meaningful relationships generated through the act of singing. The sentiment in the song springs from the belly but only becomes manifest through social exchange. Sentiment is understood as a form of social relationship; yet it also embodies deep emotions.

Lề Lối (way of doing) or *lối chơi* (way of practicing) quan họ is often articulated by village singers in terms of sentiment (*tình cảm*). One singer, in response to a request to speak about the practice of quan họ in the past responded, "it was materially poor but rich in sentiment" (female singer, Thanh Sơn Village).[14] When asked directly to explain the "sentiment" of quan họ, some older village singers, instead of remarking on the feelings shared by singers, immediately began to describe the *lối chơi* or the "way of practicing" quan họ, emphasizing that it involves an exchange of songs in which the two groups of singers sit opposite one another and so on.[15] The "way of doing" or "practicing" quan họ, that is, the gestures, the procedures, the singing technique, and so on, was inseparable in the minds of these singers from the affective feelings it generated. One elderly male singer remarked that when two pairs of singers exchange songs,

> The two sides understand each other very much; they understand each other by means of the spoken phrase, the sung phrase. Not in the sense that we tell each other that we respect each other; we understand each other *inside* the song. (Thị Cầu Village)[16]

While singers often told me that they greatly "cherish" (*quý*) and "respect" (*kính trọng*) each other, they do not express this outright to each other. These feelings are embedded in the act of singing, the lyrics of the songs, and in the body language of the singers.

As in northern Vietnamese society more broadly, sentiment in quan họ is associated closely with correct social behavior and practice that is situated in the body. In her discussion of the socialization of children in Vietnam, Helle Rydstrøm explains that in northern Vietnam, sentiment (*tình cảm*) is closely associated with social education (particularly of girls) and is understood as a form of a "social competence" rather than as a psychological state (2003:52–53). Sentiment is very much context dependent such that it cannot be understood apart from its practice (ibid.:54). In addition, the practice of sentiment in northern Vietnam is closely integrated with ideas of the body and person in which "a person is referred to as *being* in her or his body, and people speak of the body as simultaneously integrating a complex of ideas about physiology, sociability, individuality, fate, and emotions" (ibid.:5).

Likewise, in the social practice of quan họ, adherence to the conventions of the genre demonstrates one's social competence and, thus, one's embodiment of sentiment. Thus, sentiment in quan họ is its practice and is the feelings that that practice generates. The very act of exchanging songs establishes and confirms a social relationship based upon sentiment among singers. Lê Danh Khiêm remarks that the essence of exchange relations (*thực chất giao lưu*) in quan họ is found in the friendships formed between groups of singers (2001:190). One singer explained this exchange explicitly in terms of sentiment: "to speak of sentiment in quan họ is like this . . . when we meet each other at festivals the underlying principle is that we met, exchanged and sought each other out [that is, found singing partners]" (male singer, Thị Cầu Village). This singer then went on to explain the process of exchanging betel and inviting other groups to form partnerships to which his singing partner, also present, responded, "this sentiment is a highly valued sentiment." The first singer then remarked that while many children find it easy to study singing (*học hát quan họ*), it is much more difficult for them to learn how to practice (*chơi*) quan họ because of its strict rules.

The practice of quan họ involves great intimacy that is generated and maintained through outward actions. However, these actions are constrained by strict social conventions that dictate bodily comportment. The unity of sound and evenness of tone achieved by pairs singing discussed above is enhanced by the body language of the singers. Singers remain still while singing, sitting on mats with their bodies and faces angled in toward their partners.[17] Singers look each other in the eye as they sing, a sign of intimacy in Vietnam, which heightens the sense of closeness of the relationship.[18] There are also rules for the way one sits, with one knee bent up and the other leg tucked under or both legs tucked to the side with the feet facing backwards; that is, one does not stretch out the legs. Singers will frequently rest an arm on a bent knee, then rest the hand on the cheek almost hiding the mouth behind the hand (Figs. 2.1, 2.2). The visual result is almost as if the two singers are whispering between themselves. However, aurally, their voices project strongly. The visual effect suggests that the sound is generated

FIG. 2.1. The body language of village quan họ 1.

as a result of the intimacy between the two singers rather than as a result of two people engaging in the act of singing. At the same time, each pair is in communication with a pair from the partner group of opposite gender who must reciprocate in song. Thus, shared sentiment is inseparable from the body and the conventions of exchange in quan họ practice. This communication occurs, as discussed above, "inside the song."

The way that quan họ singers define sentiment draws upon broader societal understandings but is also firmly situated in its own set of social practices. One important way in which sentiment is expressed is through the obligation to maintain exchange relations. Shaun Malarney claims that, in Vietnam, relationships based upon sentiment, the most prized of the non-kin relationships, are primarily expressed through exchange relations (2002:130). In northern Vietnam, for instance, "Vietnamese describe the system of exchange that takes place at weddings and funerals as 'exchanging debts through eating and drinking' (*an uong tra no mieng nhau*)" (ibid.:133). When a family holds a funeral, the gifts brought by other families will be recorded, so that they can be adequately reciprocated in the future with a return gift of equal or slightly larger size. An excessively large gift is seen as

FIG. 2.2. The body language of village quan họ 2.

an attempt to "buy sentiment" (ibid.:132), which would disrupt the system of debt upon which sentiment rests. Likewise, in Vietnam, food or drink offered to a guest in the home cannot be absolutely refused. Even if one has just eaten, one must take a few bites to show one's acceptance of the hospitality offered. If guests arrive, one should always have something to offer, however simple—fruit, candy, cookies, and at the very least, tea. A fine balance must be maintained between formal acceptance of what is offered and how much is actually consumed. Hosts will exhort their guests to "be at home" (*như ở nhà*) and "don't act like a guest" (*đừng làm khách*) but the guests must nevertheless know and observe the boundaries of this expressed hospitality. This exchange follows the logic of the gift as formulated by Mauss (1990) in which gifts appear voluntary but are in fact obligatory and their acceptance indicates one's acceptance of a social relationship.

The conventions of polite exchange used in quan họ are specialized expressions of this generalized pattern of exchange in Vietnamese society. In quan họ, the offer and acceptance that characterize exchange constrain bodily practices. Sentiment is generated through formulaic polite language and gesture, through forms of address that are respectful and expressive of equality, and through strict adherence to the proper song order. Language and behavior are always considerate (*ý tứ*), respectful (*kính cẩn*), and sensitive (*tế nhị*). Singers say that in quan họ one should "eat half a mouthful, speak half a word" (*ăn nửa miếng, nói nửa lời*). In other words, restraint must be exercised in behavior and speech. There are, for example, rules for how one eats. One should not clatter one's chopsticks against the bowl as one eats and never take too much. Unlike in everyday social life in which one is exhorted "not to act like a guest," in the social practice of quan họ, one should always "act like one is a guest" (*làm khách*).

When speaking, the voice should always be very quiet and gentle, almost a whisper (*nói sẽ sang* or *khẽ khàng*). If one were sitting right next to the speaker, one could hear what was said but those sitting a little farther away would have to strain to hear. Singers always preface a song, eating, offering betel, and so on with invitations in language that is very formal, polite, and self-deprecating. Before eating, for instance, the oldest member of the host group (in the example below a woman's group), invites the other group to eat as follows:

> Each year we have but one day together. Today is the great festival of my (*em*) village. Second, third, fourth and fifth brother have set aside a little time. First we together (*chị em chúng em*) have the important work of praying for and wishing good health to the parents of our group. It is already rather late so we are about to serve a tray of food so that we can wait on our guests. We are rather clumsy at eating, speaking and cooking; here are some salty things, and some bland things.[19]

The forms of "my" (*em*) and "we together" (*chị em chúng em*) used in the above statement offer respect to the partner singers by using the diminutive "younger sister/brother" form. It is also important to note the emphasis on the collective nature of the invitation when the speaker says "we together." It is essential that each of the members of the host group invite the members of the other group to eat in turn.

Singers do not just invite the other singers to eat, but also must invite the other group to sing: "It is already very late, so we (*chúng em*) would like to please invite second brother and third brother from outside (*ngoài nhà*—that is, the guests or those from the other village) to sing a response song so that we can learn from it, so that we can follow along after second and third brother" at which point the men's group will reply: "So now we (*chúng em*) are also only second to *quan họ* over there; we are full [of food] already so now we would like to invite second sister and third sister to sing first and we will follow after."[20] Before singing a song, the singers will always formally and politely "request to sing this song" or "request to respond with this song."

Elder singers describe that in their youth, if the second pair was unable to reciprocate with a matching song, the pair would "lose" (*bị thua*) that round. However, this was not a failure of communication but rather built into the social conventions of the singing event. Some singers explained that they used tea cups to "keep score." That is, if one side "*bị thua*," they lost a cup to the other side. One sure way to lose a round this way was if the other side sang a "*bài độc*" (literally, "toxic song" or "malicious song"), which was a new song one of their members had written that had no response song. If the other team had a new song of its own to respond with, they would not "lose" the round; if not, they would lose a point. Many of the singers in the past were not literate but a group would have one person who was literate and who composed new songs. All of the singers I spoke with during fieldwork were hesitant to emphasize this former competitive aspect of quan họ practice, the reasons for which I can only speculate. It may be that as singers age and pass away, emotional ties have become more important than competition or it may be that as the genre becomes more public with the intervention of the state, singers are less inclined to emphasize competition. Nonetheless, one singer in her eighties did proudly point out to me that she had never "lost" (*bị thua*) in all her years of practice.

CONCLUSION

Attending to the body in the song and the body as it sings with others, reveals the intensity and passion that singers have for quan họ more clearly than an investigation of technique, lyrics, or actions alone could do. These emotions bind singers to the music and drive them to walk fifteen kilometers after a long day in the fields to sing with friends, as the singer in the epigraph described. Village singers frequently emphasized that they "did not know how to get tired" when singing quan họ, a statement that has physical truth (I witnessed elderly singers maintain their energy into the wee hours of the morning) and metaphorical weight, indicating that social knowledge of quan họ is situated in and generated through the body.

The bodily practices of village quan họ occur in an intimate space of long-term friendships as indicated by the shared meals, songs about love and friendship, equality of status between singers, and the traditional quan họ venue, the *canh hát*. At the same time, emotions and behavior are constrained by conventions of practice such as polite and modest body language, respectful and quiet speech, proper song order, and the rules of exchange must be adhered to. The correct performance of these conventions signals correct social knowledge and morality within the quan họ context; through correct performance, singers demonstrate that they possess proper sentiment. In the social practice of quan họ, it is through the *act* of exchanging songs and gestures, and through the "way of practicing" (*lối chơi*) that sentiment rises up and out of the belly. By adhering to and enacting the rules of conduct of quan họ village practice, singers both create and demonstrate their proper sentiment.

3

"How Much for a Song?"

Local Stories, National Representations

"If you want to understand quan họ folk song, you have to go to Bắc Ninh Province." Friends, academics, and musicians have told me this since the early stages of my research into folk music and performance in Vietnam. It was here, they claimed, that the true and "ancient" (*cổ*) form of quan họ folk song was to be found. Ultimately, the precise quan họ locality I was to reside in was decided by my sponsoring institute in consultation with local authorities in the Bắc Ninh Department of Culture and Information to ensure my placement in an appropriately representative musical house, in a "real" quan họ village. These claims indicate that locality plays a critical and central role in the notion of authenticity in relation to folk music and in how value is assigned to national culture. Arriving in that place to which one "must go," I found that local narrations of quan họ history and culture at times coincided with the portrayal generated in the "center" (*trung tâm*), that is, by those academics and culture workers affiliated with the provincial or national governments, universities, and institutes who are in a position to publicize, publish, and legislate about Vietnamese culture.[1] However, when the central narrative was reiterated by village singers, other stories—about commercialization, loss, and generational conflict—also emerged, indicating a sense of unease with the externally generated narratives.

This chapter will trace how quan họ folk song has been "heard" and defined across the changing political and socioeconomic situation in northern Vietnam since the August Revolution of 1945. In doing so, it will examine how particular voices (both narrative and singing) come to be constructed as representative of tradition in particular times and places. In recent decades, the dynamics created by the relationship between local and national musical identity have increasingly institutionalized binaries between "old" and "new," "rural" and "urban," and "authentic" and "commercialized," in which "real" folk music is seen to reside in a rapidly receding rural past. As such, the voice of folk music is increasingly seen to reside in the bodies of the elderly and in specific rural localities. In this chapter, I focus on the particular paradoxes that occur when the center places a monetary value and a culturally determined "heritage" value on socially embedded practices. Yet, in order to receive that assignment of value, these practices must be uprooted from the very social context upon which that value depends. The ethnographic detail I present here points to more generalized questions about the relationship between culture as heritage and culture as social practice.

In the study of culture, Homi Bhabba argues for attention to the boundaries that mark cultural, ethnic, racial, and other differences, for it is there that the process of cultural articulation takes shape in today's world (1994). Likewise, attention to the interplay between the national and the local in Vietnam, as revealed through the stories emerging at the boundaries of the national discourse, demonstrates how that which falls outside the unifying discourse of the center is often vital to the constitution of that very discourse. Those stories that fall beyond the centrally defined purview of local culture and that are "inaudible" to the national discourse (they go unheeded and unrecorded or are only told among locals) raise questions about the authority of voice. Who has the right, or more particularly, the power, to speak for whom? Gayatri Spivak, in her discussion of the subject status of Indian women, for instance, argues that these women, as subalterns, cannot "speak." The choices for exercising "free will" are themselves circumscribed by subordinating power relations (Spivak 1988:303). Gail Hershatter reformulates Spivak's query in reference to Chinese history. Hershatter ultimately rejects the contention that the subaltern cannot speak. She argues instead that the subaltern is "nested" within an array of other relations of subalternity. Instead of the voiceless subaltern, Hershatter finds "many subalterns making cacophonic noise, some hogging the mike, many speaking intermittently and not exactly as they please, and all aware to some degree of the political uses of their own representation *in that historical moment*" (Hershatter 1993:125; emphasis in original). The stories that I present in this chapter also reveal singers' complicated relationship to power and representational authority in which, at times, they can be heard speaking in the language of the state (or the center) and, at other times, appear to speak outside that language.

While inaudible stories appear to perform a commentary on and a critique of what is told, the question must be asked: if such commentary remains "local," then can these voices speak in a world that is increasingly concerned with defining and marketing culture as something shared and public in the form of heritage? More plainly, is there a place for the inaudible or invisible social forms in a world that demands visible and universally accessible culture? A national discourse that constitutes itself through the incorporation of local stories requires a selective and focused form of listening. National discourse "hears" the stories that contribute to it and dismisses those that would critique it. Yet, those latter stories serve to highlight the boundaries of that very discourse in which they find no place. Those same inaudible stories are often precisely those that epitomize the socially embedded place of quan họ in the life of the village.

BRIDGING THE GAP: THE DEVELOPMENT OF THE QUAN HỌ MOVEMENT

Provincial and national level discourses since the 1950s tend to place quan họ in a historicized narrative of interruption. Indeed, there was reportedly a significant interruption of quan họ practice in the period from 1945 until 1965 during the War of Resistance against France and the beginning of the American War, up until the first Conference on Quan Họ was organized by the Bắc Ninh Cultural Service in 1965. Trần Chính writes that in Diềm Village during this period, quan họ practice in its traditional form came to a "standstill." However, some singers did choose "some elegant and compelling songs, gave them new lyrics according to the requirements of political responsibility and taught them to the youth in the civil defense corps, to the youth union, and to children to perform at public events in the village and in arts performances in the district and province." Several of the songs Trần Chính lists, "Please Don't Go" (Người ơi người ở đừng về), "Song of the Magpie" (Lí con sao), and "Pretty Bamboo" (Cây trúc xinh), are some of the most popular and nationally recognized quan họ songs today.

However, he continues, quan họ activities were "scattered" and "sporadic" because they "absolutely did not have the means to carry out activities which were characterized by lề lối or hát canh as before" (Trần Chính 2000:64).[2] In other words, while certain songs were performed for entertainment in politically acceptable venues, the social practice of quan họ was virtually absent from the village during that time. Lê Danh Khiêm also argues that from the late 1940s until the early 1960s it was "as if people did not sing *quan họ*" or, if they did, they were labeled "backward" (*lạc hậu*) (pers. comm., 6/13/04). In a 1956 article in the *Music Review* (*Tập San Âm Nhạc*), the authors remark that during the ten years of the War of Resistance, quan họ practice was interrupted; no festivals were held, and people regarded it as backward. After the end of the War of Resistance, in 1954, they claim, quan họ was restored (*khôi phục*) but only by elderly singers; very few youth sang these songs anymore (Lưu Khâm, Nguyễn Viêm, and Nguyễn Đình Tấn 1956:17–21).

Part of the concern to not appear "backward" was connected to the Democratic Republic of Vietnam's (DRV) ritual reform and anti-superstition campaign. Soon after the August Revolution, the newly formed DRV set about reforming ritual as a part of its goal to transform the sociocultural practices and ideology of the people. This initiative aimed to bring cultural practices in line with party goals of building a new revolutionary society based on a "confident, modern rationality" and social equality (Malarney 1996:542). According to Shaun Malarney, the DRV's goals were to secularize ritual by eliminating superstition and denying contact between the world of the living and the supernatural, to eliminate waste by targeting elaborate and expensive ritual wedding and funeral feasts, and to eliminate signs of social hierarchy that it characterized as "feudal" (2002). While I have not encountered direct evidence that quan họ was specifically targeted by this campaign, my conversations with researcher Lê Danh Khiêm and others reveal that quan họ was swept up into the general campaign, and that consequently, certain practices were dropped. Village festivals, an important venue for quan họ practice, were discontinued throughout the region during this period.

Quan họ seems to have occupied a conflicted place in the history of this campaign. Some of its practices, such as singing quan họ at village temples to worship local deities during festivals and singing to pray for rain in times of drought, could indeed be labeled "superstitious" and incompatible with the "modern rationality" of revolutionary society. Devotional songs such as these use the same tunes as those sung in secular venues but with different lyrics tailored to the occasion. Again, while I am unsure if these practices were specifically targeted or if they died off because of the general atmosphere of the period, they are only today being revived in village practice at the urging of scholars. There is, however, evidence of direct criticism of certain song content in this period. Lê Hồng Dương, for example, quoting the song "Wise Bird" (Chim khôn), claims that some quan họ lyrics were negatively influenced by feudalism:

Chim khôn đỗ nóc nhà quan	The wise bird lands on the mandarin's roof
Trai khôn năm thê bảy thiếp	The wise man has five wives and seven concubines
Gái ngoan chỉ có một chồng.	The well-behaved woman has only one husband.

However, this negative influence was, for Lê Hồng Dương, outweighed by the positive effects of the overall character of quan họ lyrics and activities, which were an important "weapon" in the struggle of the masses against feudalism:

Having love between man and woman as its primary subject, the practice of *quan họ* had become a means by which every song that rang out made people love their homeland all the more through their dedication to their labor, love people all the more by bringing them closer together in the struggle against their environment and the ruling classes. Women in *quan họ* practice not only had equality with men but also took the initiative and were determined of purpose, contrary to women in society at that time. (Lê Hồng Dương 1972:10–12)

Quan họ practice was, in opposition to prevailing social norms of pre-revolutionary times, strongly egalitarian. In addition, aside from the devotional songs discussed above, its song content was secular, allowing it to be incorporated comfortably in a revival of Vietnamese national folk culture under the socialist state, as Lê Hồng Dương's quote indicates. As such, it could be said to be "of the people (*nhân dân*) of Hà Bắc specifically, and of the nation (*dân tộc*) in general" (Đặng Văn Lung, Hồng Thao, and Trần Linh Quý 1978:9).

In writing about quan họ during the revolutionary period, Đặng Văn Lung, Hồng Thao, and Trần Linh Quý do not portray the interruption of quan họ as absolute. They claim that before 1954, during the Resistance War, "following the party directives to build a national music that is [based in] reality and has the people's character, many musicians sought out *quan họ* singers who had been evacuated to the Bắc Thai free zone to ask them about *quan họ* Bắc Ninh. As a result, they were able to collect and correct (*chỉnh lý*) a number of *quan họ* tunes" (ibid.). At this time, The Voice of Vietnam Radio also introduced *quan họ* to people across the country and abroad. Then, from 1957 to 1961, the movement to research *quan họ* began (ibid.).[3] Thus, despite claims that village practice was interrupted, there was a continued academic and political interest in quan họ as folk culture building throughout the revolutionary period.

Beginning in 1965, the Cultural Service of Hà Bắc organized six successive conferences on quan họ, at which it was determined that quan họ could be restored and the movement (*phong trào*) to restore and develop quan họ began.[4] The movement sought simultaneously to encourage youth in local villages to sing *quan họ cổ* ("ancient" or village quan họ) and also to develop and popularize new-style quan họ. In a paper at the 1969 Quan Họ Conference in Hà Bắc, Lê Hồng Dương divides quan họ into two developmental periods: first, "the period from whence [quan họ] began to the end of the French colonial period," or the period prior to the August Revolution in 1945 (legends place the origins of quan họ back several hundred years); and second, the period from the August Revolution until the time of the conference on quan họ in 1969. He remarks that there is almost no documentation on quan họ from the first period but that elder village singers insist that during that time, quan họ was already "thriving" (*thịnh vượng*) and the practices and melodies were "stable" (*ổn định*). He concludes that this was "the period in which *quan họ* Bắc Ninh was born, became fully formed, stable, and developed" (Lê Hồng Dương 1972:13). The idea that quan họ songs and practices were "stabilized" during this earlier period is still echoed in scholarship today. This idea introduces a concept of temporality into the portrayal of quan họ that, in a reversal of village practitioners' claims that quan họ is a genre for youth, valorizes and authenticates only the oldest singers, or those that trained prior to the 1945 Revolution. It also allows for the establishment of a collectible, "stable" body of materials from those elderly singers and, hence, begins to codify "authentic" quan họ. Lê Hồng Dương divides the second period into three subperiods: from the August Revolution to the establishment of peace in 1954, in which there was very little quan họ activity; from 1954 until 1965, during which many small arts troupes (*đội văn nghệ*) were established around the country; and finally the period from 1965 until the time of his writing, in which the research and development of quan họ were strengthened and contributed to the war effort (ibid.:14–16).

Lê Hồng Dương's paper indicates that by the mid- to late 1960s, a new orientation to quan họ as folk culture was emerging, one that sought a restoration of the "stable" and fully developed form of quan họ that was severed from the present in 1945. By the time of the American War, which lasted through 1975, quan họ had to be rescued from the ravages and interruption of several decades of war. Therefore, by the American War period, the discourse on quan họ had shifted toward "rescue" and "restoration," concepts that were in tune with the wider framework of military and ideological mobilization of the nation at the time. It is important to note that while academic interest in quan họ restoration appears to build steadily through-out the post-1945 period, the emerging discourse rests heavily on the notion (real or constructed) that the practice of quan họ was interrupted in the villages. Village singers with whom I spoke, for the most part, did not empha-size or "remember" this period as one of interruption to the same degree as the above-mentioned writers. On an individual level, quan họ continued to exist in the bodies and memories of each singer even while they may have had to alter their singing practices due to external circumstances. For instance, some claim that they continued to gather informally with friends to sing even when circumstances did not allow them to organize a full *canh hát* (gathering of singers).[5]

THE EMERGENCE OF PROFESSIONAL QUAN HỌ

The Hà Bắc *Quan Họ* Folk Song Troupe (Đoàn Dân Ca Quan Họ Hà Bắc)—now renamed the Bắc Ninh *Quan Họ* Folk Song Troupe (Đoàn Dân Ca Quan Họ Bắc Ninh)—was established in 1969 as part of the "quan họ movement" in an effort to stimulate the preservation and the popularization of quan họ throughout the country and even internationally. The troupe is impor-tant in that it was largely responsible for the development and initial popu-larization of new-style quan họ, which is generally characterized by faster tempo than village quan họ, simplified lyrics, and the addition of musical accompaniment. New-style quan họ includes songs that can be enjoyed as discrete units and that are seen as appropriate for stage performance. New quan họ includes old tunes with new or modified lyrics, new lyrics set to "old" tunes, and entirely new songs in the "quan họ style." This style is what is encountered on the stage, radio, and television and is the most commonly recognized and well-known form of *quan họ* in Vietnam today. This is even true to a certain extent within Bắc Ninh Province itself. Many Vietnamese outside Bắc Ninh know only this style of quan họ and would have little or no familiarity with village quan họ practices.

In his article "Glory and Hardships: Remembering the Early Days of the *Quan Họ* Troupe," Xuân Mùi, one of the troupe's first performers and now its assistant director, reiterates the above argument of interruption for the later American War period. He remarks that during the war, people mainly sang songs that were expressions of revolutionary heroism and not the kinds of songs one finds in quan họ, and because the younger genera-tion increasingly associated quan họ with the elderly, "it was as if the time of *quan họ* was really at an end." It was in this context, he claims, that the newly established quan họ troupe "became an important 'bridge' between the *quan họ* elders and the youth in the region." He writes, "[w]e were the students of the elder village singers, but at the same time we were the teachers of the region's youth" (Xuân Mùi 1998:150, 152).

A mythology of interruption, then, becomes the means by which an officially sanctioned, provincially and nationally recognized form of quan họ literally inserts itself into the field of quan họ practice. War severs one generation from the next, resulting in a failure to pass on quan họ. The emphasis on the failure of the transmission of knowledge from one generation to the next, then, allows for the troupe to incorporate itself within the genealogy of an "authentic" and "original" quan họ and allows the state to legitimize this intervention. Such a perspective also gives the troupe a healing role. It sutures the gap in quan họ practice opened up by the violence of war and by Party ideology, across which quan họ had become inaudible, and allows for its continuance. A second issue that this discourse underscores is that war marks the dissipation of interest in quan họ by the younger generation. After the war, quan họ became an "old people's" custom. Indeed, Xuân Mùi relates that in the troupe's early years, when its members were studying quan họ in the villages, village youth would ask them why they were studying something old fashioned and for old people (ibid.:151). The troupe saw itself as a bridge between the generations, one that would reconnect the old, authentic sensibilities with new, modern sensibilities.

However, while the troupe's singers were all recruited from within Bắc Ninh Province, the first members of the troupe had to learn how to be "locals" from elderly Bắc Ninh villagers. The first singers in the Bắc Ninh professional troupe trained directly with village singers in Bắc Ninh under the tutelage of Nguyễn Đức Sôi, an elderly village singer. From 1969 to 1970, groups of three to five singers and musicians would go to different quan họ villages to study with and collect songs directly from different village singers, returning repeatedly to the villages until they got the songs right. Then they, in turn, taught these songs to the rest of the troupe. The early work of the troupe also included learning about the cultural practices of quan họ (Đức Siêu 1998). This early training of the first troupe members also suggests that the interruption to quan họ was less absolute for the locals than it was discursive for academicians and professional singers.

THE BẮC NINH PROVINCE SECONDARY SCHOOL OF CULTURE AND ARTS

Today, performers for the professional Bắc Ninh *Quan Họ* Folk Song Troupe are primarily recruited from among the best students majoring in quan họ performance in the Faculty of Music at the Bắc Ninh Province Secondary School of Culture and Arts (Bắc Ninh SSCA), established in 1998 in the provincial capital of Bắc Ninh City. The particular construction of local identity expressed by students studying quan họ at the school illustrates how local identity is set up in opposition to national identity yet is simultaneously enabled by it. Like students at the National Conservatory of Music in Hanoi, students in Bắc Ninh study a variety of subjects, including Western musical theory and history as well as a number of different Vietnamese traditional music genres. However, students in quan họ performance studies in Bắc Ninh focus primarily on quan họ.[6]

I interviewed students from the National Conservatory, who came from all over the country. When I asked why they decided to study traditional music, many mentioned that one or both of their parents were musicians or worked with music. On the other hand, music students at the Bắc Ninh SSCA, all from Bắc Ninh Province, tended to speak of their reasons for studying in regional terms, often expressed in relationship to the body. One student told me that she thought that "the blood of quan họ had already absorbed into her body," and another felt that he had been "imbued" with quan họ since he was a child and that this profession had "absorbed into him." Yet another student told how one of her teachers, in response to questions of why people from Bắc Ninh can sing quan họ best, often stated that maybe it is "something in the water." She stressed that her teacher said this in jest. Nevertheless, this and the other responses are a strong expression of the importance of locality and one's very physical and embodied ties to it, even in the face of or perhaps because of, the nationalization of quan họ.

When asked about their first introduction to quan họ, many of these students in Bắc Ninh claimed to have first heard it on radio or television. Most students' first encounters with quan họ were with its modernized and nationally recognized form, which is aired on both the national and Bắc Ninh television stations. Yet, despite the fact that their initial attraction to quan họ came by way of a form that was also broadcast and recognized nationally, these students directly linked the pervasiveness of quan họ in Bắc Ninh Province to its locality. They said that quan họ "is everywhere" in Bắc Ninh, and that if one grows up there, one cannot avoid it. Indeed, the local Bắc Ninh television station frequently airs programs about quan họ, thereby giving quan họ a more pervasive media presence in Bắc Ninh. Singers also frequently performed quan họ at local events and at weddings, continuing a village practice in which singers from partnered villages would send representatives to sing at weddings, funerals, and festivals. As their introduction to quan họ via its nationalized form indicates, these students' claims to locality are dependent on and derive meaning in reference to a wider geographical context.

Students and teachers at the school proudly noted that as a part of their curriculum, students were able to spend several weeks in Diềm Village, known locally as the village where quan họ originated. Here, they studied *quan họ cổ* from *nghệ nhân*, who are amateur artisans or musicians, usually villagers, who have reached a high level of expertise in a particular craft or musical form and who are also actively involved in passing on this skill (Fig. 3.1).[7] This designation also indicates that *nghệ nhân* have been officially recognized for their expertise and, as such, are important to the work of designating culture as heritage.[8] The four *nghệ nhân* who taught the Diềm class were all elderly women over the age of seventy. This class was perceived as a model of "oral transmission" (*truyền khẩu*) because it was taught by *nghệ nhân*, who themselves learned orally. In actuality, the students' learning was transcription based. In the Diềm class, the *nghệ nhân* would first recite the lyrics of the song for students to write down and then sing the song line by line.[9] *Nghệ nhân* in Diềm said that in the past, no one wrote anything

FIG. 3.1. Students from the Bắc Ninh Secondary School for Culture and Art learning *quan họ cổ* from *nghệ nhân* in Diềm Village, 2004.

down; they just had to remember, unlike students today. They also claimed that they learned the songs much faster than students today, in part because from a young age, they had continually followed older singers around and, therefore, had been constantly surrounded by the songs. A singer's understanding of technique, lyrics, and custom, was developed to the depth that it was through full immersion in quan họ culture.

The students in the Diềm class, therefore, literally transcribe the gap between an older, orally trained generation of singers and a new, musically trained generation. This transcription is crucial to upholding the perception of village quan họ as "original" quan họ, which is largely defined by its oral transmission. Transcription can also be seen as the continuation of the legacy of the Bắc Ninh *Quan Họ* Folk Song Troupe's role in bridging the gap between old and new quan họ and allowing for the legitimization of a nationally recognized form of quan họ. Furthermore, locating the act of transcribing quan họ in its "origin" village (Diềm) highlights the process by which immaterial practices (or "intangible cultural heritage") are objectified. This is essential to the representation of folk culture as authentic local culture. Transcription is the material means by which the authentic "voice" of quan họ is transposed into the modern national present. The question, to which I will return below, is what happens to the voices of those whose "voice" is transposed?

With the exception of the Diềm class, the students at the Bắc Ninh SSCA primarily learned new-style quan họ. Most of these students thought of the old forms as something they were required to know to have a complete understanding of the music, but not the form that they preferred musically or that they would be singing during their careers. The school, therefore, has become intimately connected to the ways in which quan họ has been modernized and popularized in the mass media and on stage. At the same time, the school maintains a self-perception based on its locality. Bắc Ninh with its quan họ villages, is ultimately essential to the school's inclusion in a nationally defined and recognized genre of Vietnamese traditional music.

THE BẮC NINH *QUAN HỌ* COMPETITION

The regional quan họ competition, held annually in Lunar January since 1991 at the Culture Center in Bắc Ninh City, has become an important event for villagers, aspiring professional singers, provincial officials from the Department of Culture, Sport and Tourism, and national officials from the Ministry of Culture, Sport and Tourism. It is here at the Bắc Ninh *Quan Họ* competition that old and new practices and practitioners converge. At the same time, the competition discursively highlights and institutionalizes the split between "new" quan họ and "old" (village) quan họ. The spatial segregation of new and old quan họ at the event visibly and aurally divides the two forms of practice, thereby further institutionalizing the gap between them. Each year, the competition is split into two venues. The stage competition for solo singers (đơn ca) of new quan họ is held inside the auditorium of the Culture Center. The exchange singing for pairs (đối đáp), modeled after village practice, is set up outside, in the courtyard next to the banyan tree (cây đa), a symbol of village community.

In 2004, the indoor stage competition began with speeches by local dignitaries, followed by a performance by the professional Bắc Ninh *Quan Họ* Folk Song Troupe, giving this setting an official and formal atmosphere. Competitors in the stage competition were judged not only on singing ability but also on performance and costumes. On the second day of the competition, indoor stage contestants could choose to sing quan họ or another type of song, or do something else, such as a dance number or flower arranging (Fig. 3.2). This part of the competition did not solely identify ideal or typical quan họ performers, but also well-rounded representatives of local Bắc Ninh culture. Contestants were judged on their performance of local culture and practices, such as carving betel (têm trầu) into the phoenix shape, associated regionally with quan họ. But the familiarity of these performances to a national audience was also important. The stage set, lighting, musical accompaniment, performance styles, and so on were arranged in a way that replicated other cultural performances and television stage sets for traditional performances. These performances helped insert "new quan họ" contestants into a unified national culture based on a foundation of local culture.

The outdoor pairs-singing competition, on the other hand, was set up in a more "traditional" style. In 2004 and 2005, quan họ groups from participating villages sat at folding tables set up in a square "u" configuration around three sides of the stage, which was a low, raised platform covered in red carpeting. A low, carved wooden table set with flowers, a teapot, and cups sat in the center of the stage. The judges' tables lined the open end of the "u," under the banyan tree, upon which was hung the large, round quan họ hat (nón quai thao). Two pairs of competing singers from different villages would sit across the wooden table from each other (Fig. 3.3). Each pair of contestants alternately sang two songs, one opening song (bài ra) and one response song (bài đối). These songs were chosen from a pool of 150 songs that the organizing committee determined to be foundational to the "traditional" repertoire. If a pair of singers did not show up, the opponents

FIG. 3.2. Quan Họ Regional Beauty Contest. Indoor stage at the Annual *Quan Họ* Competition held at the Culture Center, Bắc Ninh Town, 2005.

were automatically considered to be "fluent in the song" (*thuộc bài*), meaning they could execute it well and from memory. Pairs-singing contestants were judged on their singing: whether they were "balanced" (*đều*), if they had memorized the song completely, and if they successfully used the four quan họ criteria of *vang* (ringing), *nảy* (bouncing), *rền* (resonant), and *nền* (restraint). The correct balance of these criteria by the two singers lends quan họ its distinctive sound.

The spatial organization of the outdoor competition emphasizes the social exchange seen to characterize village quan họ practice. The competition space is set up in an enclosed square shape, contestants face each other across a table set up with tea, and the "audience" is relegated to an outside, unstructured space (there are no chairs set up for non-participants), as if they are looking in on something. This setup directly references village quan họ practice, which did not, strictly speaking, have an audience outside the other singers or assistants present. However, at the contest, the space implicitly addresses an audience in that there are large speakers set up to broadcast the sound beyond the immediate competitive space, and banners announcing

FIG. 3.3. Pairs singing at the Annual *Quan Họ* Competition held at the Culture Center, Bắc Ninh Town, 2005.

the contest and the New Year are hung from the banyan tree overlooking that space. Furthermore, because the outdoor competition focuses on and judges only singing, it isolates and valorizes only the most audible aspect of an array of social practices that make up the totality of quan họ practice. A pot of tea and the positioning of singers facing inward is a direct reference to the social context of quan họ; yet its transfer to this public venue, in which village singers are judged by music teachers from the conservatories and scholars of music and folk culture, indicates that village quan họ can be audible as heritage only when removed from its social context.

In the competition, competitors were divided into two age groups: youth (from sixteen to twenty-nine years old) and middle-aged (from thirty to sixty years old). The creation of competitive categories based on age helps to institutionalize categorizations of singers that associate new quan họ with youth and beauty and old-style quan họ with age and tradition. Indeed, the indoor stage competition was dominated by youth. Here were people seeking future careers and opportunities in traditional music performance. At the pairs competition outdoors, on the other hand, a majority of contestants were older. Even among the younger pairs singers, it was clear that singing was a hobby and something done for enjoyment, rather than for employment. There was a monetary incentive to compete, as the prizes are cash awards.[10] However, from my interviews and discussions with participants, I do not think this was a primary motivation for participation in the competition.

Today, interest in quan họ has sprung up in a number of villages in Bắc Ninh that are not "traditional quan họ villages." Quan họ arts troupes have been established in these places, and they now come to participate in the yearly quan họ competition held in Bắc Ninh City. For example, a woman from a village in Tiên Du District learned quan họ outside her village a number of years ago and then returned to teach people in her village. Her team of singers is drawn to the competition because it gives them a chance to meet and compete with other singers from different villages. This indicates that despite the competition's inability to accommodate or perpetuate all traditional practices of village quan họ, people are adapting older forms of social practice found in quan họ to new conditions of practice enabled by the competition. These forms, unlike new quan họ, are not professionally or commercially motivated but socially motivated.

The quan họ competition, the professional troupe, and the training of students at the Bắc Ninh school contribute significantly to the institutionalization of quan họ as Bắc Ninh culture within a national framework. They operate within venues and organizations officially recognized by village, provincial, and national governmental bodies dedicated to culture. These kinds of institutional practices serve to validate and popularize local practice more widely on the national level, but they also reinforce a sense of pride and investment in quan họ locally. However, the shifting political and socioeconomic situation since reform has led to a growing emphasis on locating "authentic" quan họ in the villages of Bắc Ninh. I now turn to the stories that emerge from one of these places of "origin."

DIỀM VILLAGE: THE ORIGINAL QUAN HỌ VILLAGE

The story goes something like this: thirty kilometers north of the national capital of Hanoi, in the heart of Kinh Bắc, the "cradle" of Vietnamese civilization and ancient culture of the Red River Delta, lies Bắc Ninh City, the provincial capital of the quan họ region. Here is the scenic land of mountains and rivers and Bắc Ninh girls in their billowing dresses, renowned for their beauty. Turning off onto a dirt road, at the edge of town, one bounces along another five kilometers, past brilliant green rice paddies tended by farmers in conical hats, dark ponds, occasional small clusters of cows grazing precariously on the banks of the paddy fields, children bicycling back and forth to school (trucks piled high with rice stalks or building materials chugging along with their exposed transmissions and choking clouds of dust and black exhaust, a silver SUV with the colorful Vietnam Television logo painted on its side) . . . and finally, past a few small local graveyards with their round mounds.[11] One has arrived at Diềm Village, the original quan họ village, according to one legend. It was here that the princess Vua Bà, daughter of one of the legendary Hùng kings, taught the local people to plant mulberry to feed silkworms and to sing quan họ. The legend, as told by one singer, is as follows:

> The sixth Hùng king chose a husband for his daughter, the princess, by arranging a wrestling match in which the winner would be allowed to marry her. However, the princess did not like the man chosen and her father allowed a second contest, a match of capture the ball (*cướp cầu*), to take place.[12] However, the same young man won and the princess had no choice but to agree to marry him. Before her wedding, she requested that the king allow her to take a sightseeing trip. The king agreed and chose forty-nine men and forty-nine women as retainers to accompany the princess. However, they were swept away by a great storm on the road. Afterwards, she founded a settlement in what is today Diềm Village and taught the people how to plant mulberry to raise silkworms and how to sing quan họ. She then married off the forty-nine men to the forty-nine women, and each pair founded one of the forty-nine *quan họ* villages.[13]

There are other stories as well. When I asked the singer who related the above version of the legend of Vua Bà about the meaning of the word quan họ, she told me a story about two mandarins, one from Võ Giàng (an old name for the district in which Diềm Village is located) and one from Tiên Du (also in Bắc Ninh), who were the best of friends. After the two men had retired, they often visited each other's homes, bringing along their grandchildren, and sang with each other. The two men always called each other *anh*, that is, they dispensed with the age distinction in their use of pronouns. This indicated that they considered each other equals, and expressed how much they respected each other. This also highlights the principle of equality that is very important in quan họ practice. Eventually the locales of their two houses became quan họ villages. In this story, the *quan* of *quan họ* refers to the mandarins; and *họ* (family name or line of descent), to the two founding families. The singer then related an alternative story in which the king was traveling along a road when he heard a young woman in a nearby field, singing about cutting the grasses. Entranced, he stopped his horse (*họ ngựa*) to see who it was. That is, the king and his attendants (*quan*) stopped (*họ*) the horses.[14] This singer, however, emphasized that the main (*chính*) origin story is the story she told earlier about Vua Bà.

There is no consensus among locals or academics about which of the two latter stories relays the "true" meaning of the words quan họ. In fact, the lack of consensus has itself been incorporated into the discourse of the quan họ story. The telling of such legends is invariably followed by statements asserting that there are "many stories" and that people cannot agree on which one is correct. This claim suggests the presence of a pluralistic counterdiscourse to the homogenizing national discourse, while simultaneously repeating the national discourse's claim to "unity in diversity."[15] It is, however, generally agreed that these stories constitute an integral part of the history of both quan họ and Diêm Village. They are, furthermore, often the first stories told in response to inquiries about quan họ in Diêm Village. The history of the village and its self-representation are intertwined with legend to the point that historical "fact" and legend are indistinguishable. Indeed, Trần Chính, in his book on quan họ in Diêm Village, argues for the historical and legendary validity of Viêm Xá (Diêm) as the origin village of quan họ in large part because those legends that attribute the origins of quan họ to Vua Bà, and that designate Diêm as the origin village, are the most numerous of the local legends about quan họ (2000:30–31).[16] Trần Đình Luyện, a historian and former director of the Bắc Ninh Department of Culture and Information, remarks that historical documents housed in the Vua Bà Temple and the village communal house, such as ancestor tablets (*bài vị*), royal proclamations (*sắc phong*), horizontal lacquered boards (*hoành phi*), and parallel phrases (*câu đối*), show that Vua Bà was the daughter of the Hùng king. These documents suggest that she was a historical figure. However, he maintains, the essence of the story told about her is legend, and "the integration of history and legend has become a reflection of the history of a founding village, Viêm Xá, and of a unique folk cultural activity of the Kinh Bắc—Bắc Ninh region. That is, *quan họ* folk song" (Trần Đình Luyện 2000a:58).

Patricia Pelley has argued that a central theme in post-colonial historiography in Vietnam—"the tradition of resistance to foreign aggression," which was taken on as a "principle of the past"—led to a tendency in which the "history of unity often collapsed what was genuinely historical into one-dimensional distillations of the past. The history of resistance converted myth into history and transformed history into myth, and necessarily suppressed the counter-histories that confounded it" (Pelley 1995:234). The motivations behind this kind of historiography do play a part in the conflation of history and legend in the origin story of quan họ. The "quan họ movement" arose in the wake of the war of resistance against France and continued though the American War period. As discussed above, quan họ had to be rescued from the interruption in practice resulting from multiple wars and the perceived loss of interest by the subsequent generations. Indeed, incorporating the fact that no one can agree on the validity of one story over another into the very discourse on the history and culture of quan họ in effect "unifies" all voices on the subject. The congenial inclusion of all stories means that no one story can stake a claim as *the* story. However, while this certainly plays a role in Diềm Village discourses on its own history, there are other stories that do not make it into the official collection of stories.

Diềm Village singers themselves are quick to point out the central place that their village holds in quan họ culture and proudly claim that their quan họ is the "oldest" (*cổ nhất*) in the region. The tensions arising from the increased attention quan họ is receiving at the provincial, national, and, most recently, international levels, however, complicates village singers' consciousness of their own history and place of origin in the quan họ story. Local discourses are influenced by the national and academic representations of the village that increasingly enter the language of the village singers themselves. This is particularly true in situations in which they see themselves as "official" representatives of their culture, such as on first meetings with foreign researchers or with television crews. At my first meetings with many village singers throughout the region, for instance, it was often assumed that I wanted to know about old-style quan họ, and I was often asked right away, "What songs do you need [to record]?" This question reveals the long-standing efforts of folklorists and ethnomusicologists to collect stories and music from these village singers. Yet it also reveals the ways in which particular interactions between village "resources," to borrow George Yúdice's term (2005), and the external writers of cultural history, ethnography, policy, and so forth become scripted and predetermined.[17] These scripted interactions ensure that informants give scholars the stories and songs the scholars want and expect while minimizing intrusion into their own lives. Even while village singers, both young and old, are adept at representing quan họ in officially sanctioned ways, some of the stories they tell point to a deep-seated discomfort with the cooptation of quan họ culture by the center. Such stories raise questions about who controls the cultural heritage of the locality—those who are perceived to embody it, or those who are invested with the power to represent it to the wider world, to publish it, to preserve it, to develop it, and so forth. These are also the stories that do not get told in the official versions of the history and culture of quan họ, either by the central authorities or by the villagers themselves.

One such story, told to me by an elderly singer in Diềm, particularly highlights the uneasy relationship that the village singers have with the central government. In 1990, she said, the government (*nhà nước*) uncovered a small iron box containing a long strip of yellow silk, two centimeters wide by forty centimeters long. Painted on the silk were characters, each of which indicated one of the oldest quan họ songs. She told me that the songs were painted on the silk several centuries before by Vua Bà, the founding ancestress of quan họ folk song, and that by some miracle it had survived intact and undiscovered in this box through time and several wars. When it was discovered, she continued, Diềm Village was recognized as the cradle (*nôi*) of quan họ. When I asked her what happened to this strip of silk and whether it was still in the village, she said, "No, it was taken away by the center (*trung tâm*); what a pity." To this singer, this story proved the claim that quan họ did indeed originate in Diềm Village, but it also raised questions about the relationship of the village to the center. She claimed that it was upon the discovery of this strip of silk in 1990 that the government recognized Diềm Village as the place of origin of quan họ. From then on, she remarked, the government participated in the annual village festival commemorating Vua Bà, whereas before that, only the village participated. I later asked a quan họ researcher at the Center for the Study of *Quan Họ* Culture of the Bắc Ninh Department of Culture and Information about Vua Bà's strip of silk with the quan họ songs on it. He had never heard of it and suggested that perhaps she had mistaken it for the *sắc phong* (royal proclamation) banner in the Vua Bà Temple. But when I later checked back with the singer, she was adamant that she knew the difference.

What is interesting about this singer's story is that the date she gives for the discovery, 1990, is the same date that the regional quan họ competition was established. The competition was first held in 1991. While this singer mistakenly claimed that it started in 1990, what I want to emphasize is not the correct dates but the coincidence of dates in her memory. Whether it resulted from the mysterious whisking away of Vua Bà's silk or from the newly established regional quan họ competitions, to her this date represented the beginning of a more visible and active participation of outside officials and academics in the quan họ activities and practices in the village. As she explained, before this date, only the village participated in the village festivals, but afterward, people from the center also came. It was at precisely the moment that quan họ attained national heritage status, then, that control over its representation and narration were perceived to be mysteriously whisked away to the center. It should also be noted that it was only several years later, in 1994, that the Vua Bà Temple was accepted into the national registry of historical relics and Vua Bà was officially recognized as the founding ancestor of quan họ (Fig. 3.4).

Since the early 1990s, quan họ has become increasingly important to provincial and national projects to preserve and revive traditional culture, and it now falls under the internationally defined concept of "intangible cultural heritage" as mediated by international organizations, such as UNESCO, and embraced by Vietnamese academics, institutions, and the Ministry of Culture, Sport and Tourism. In 2003, the Department of Cultural Heritage, the Bắc Ninh Department of Culture and Information, and UNESCO's Hanoi office concluded a joint project to identify "*quan họ* living treasures" in Bắc Ninh villages. In 2008, the Vietnam Institute of Culture and Arts Studies submitted a candidature file for quan họ to UNESCO's Representative List of the Intangible Cultural Heritage of Humanity, which was accepted in September 2009. In this context, control over the appearance, sound, and practice of quan họ takes on importance beyond its local place

FIG. 3.4. Front gate of the Vua Bà Temple, Diềm Village, Bắc Ninh.

of origin even while that locality becomes ever more important as a marker of traditional culture.

It is also important that Vua Bà's strip of silk records the oldest of the quan họ songs. These are the songs people fear are disappearing as the young generations lose interest in learning them; they are the songs that are most intimately linked and indispensable to the social practice of quan họ in the village. Therefore, the supposed removal of the silk strip and its songs is particularly evocative of the state's particular interest in *quan họ cổ* and of the state's increasing presence in the "practice" of quan họ. But this is an interest that, in the mind of the above-mentioned singer at least, coincided with the increased orchestration of village practice by the center.

ORCHESTRATING THE *CANH HÁT*

The subtle ways in which an official, administrative presence makes itself felt yet is not fully integrated into quan họ practice was made particularly clear at the 2005 Diềm Village festival. On the evening of the fifth day of the first lunar month, the night before the main festival day, a *canh hát* was to take place. As discussed in chapter two, the *canh hát* is a gathering of and exchange of songs between two groups of quan họ singers, one male and one female, from different villages, which takes place in someone's house. In the past, the *canh hát* was one of the main venues in which quan họ singing took place. A true *canh hát* must follow a strict singing order of three voices or categories of songs: method voice (*giọng lề lối*), variety voice (*giọng vặt*), and farewell voice (*giọng giã bạn*) (Fig. 3.5).

In 2005, the *canh hát* participants ranged in age from very old to younger singers in their mid-thirties from Diềm and Hoài Thị villages. The two villages have a partnership, or official friendship (*kết nghĩa*), and the singers from Hoài Thị were visiting Diềm as official representatives of their village at the Diềm Festival. This particular *canh hát* was an interesting mix of continuing practice and preservation. The oldest singers were not "preserving" or "reviving" a practice, but rather were engaging in practices they had engaged in since they were young, even though in the course of the event they often spoke of specific elements in reference to how things were done differently in the past. On the other hand, the younger participants and some Vietnamese authorities and researchers, myself included, who were also present, felt that they were participating in an exciting recreation of an "authentic" event.

Also interesting was the odd juxtaposition of the relaxed and embodied practice of the oldest participants with the occasional orchestrated

FIG. 3.5. A *canh hát* at the 2004 Diềm Village Festival.

interjection of event "structure" by the local official in charge of coordinating the event. For instance, after the singers had finished eating and shortly after they had begun to sing, a member of the Diềm Village Arts Team (Đội Văn Nghệ) who was coordinating the quan họ events for the festival came by the house to request that some of the singers go to the Vua Bà Temple to sing.[18] He said that the oldest singers could stay at the house but that some of the younger singers should go to "share quan họ." At this point, many of the Hoại Thị singers, except a couple of the very oldest, went to the temple. They felt obligated to do so in their official capacity as representatives of the partner village. Most of the older singers from Diềm, however, stayed put. The younger Diềm singers did not arrive at the house until later, as they were already participating in public events. The Hoài Thị singers from the temple along with a couple of younger Diềm singers from the Arts Team returned to the house after several hours at around 11:00 p.m.

One of the official interjections into the *canh hát*, which contrasted markedly with the embodied practice of the older singers, was the official request that some singers go to the temple. The oldest singers seemed to be participating in the event in a different social capacity than the younger singers. This difference was highlighted by the polite exemption from singing at the temple that the official granted them. The younger generation was considered to be responsible not just for carrying on and preserving the traditions of quan họ, as learned from older generations, but for transferring them from the private internal space of the home into a public performative space. This underscores a new sense that quan họ should no longer be kept solely in the house where only the singers can hear it but should be a focal point for local culture and pride on a village, even a region-wide level. Delegating to the younger generation the responsibility to "share quan họ" indicates that the younger generation maintains a different relationship with the state than do the older generations. The younger generation is seen to provide access to a local cultural resource, quan họ. However, somewhat ironically, "true" knowledge of quan họ is invested in only the oldest singers. The older singers are seen to embody the heritage but not the power to speak it. That is, they can teach it but cannot represent it, even while they are seen to be representative *of* it.

The older singers also appeared to inhabit a different temporal structure than that of the "official" festival organization. This became markedly clear at the "end" of the *canh hát*, at midnight. The event's organizer came by the house once again and made a short speech about the importance and sentimental value of the evening's event for the preservation of quan họ. He then announced that since it was late, the event was officially over, but that those who cared to stay and carry on this happy gathering might do so. Then rice porridge was served to everyone, after which the official repeated that now people could leave if they wanted to. However, he was the only one who left at this point. This official marking of the end of the event played no actual role in the structure of this *canh hát* except that it prompted the singers to remark that since they met this way "only once a year," they should stay. This discussion of whether to stay or go, although uttered in the presence of the official, was addressed to the other singers, indicating that this particular event existed both within and outside of its official or administrative framing. While this was a discussion among the singers, it had the feel of an unofficial response to this official framing of the event. The effect was that the singers themselves seemed to reclaim ownership of the event come midnight.

Furthermore, this conversation was primarily carried out in the customary polite and formal language with which quan họ singers address one another at a *canh hát* (although it was also interspersed with some less formal commentary). As they argued for staying in "quan họ language," the older singers seemed again to exist outside of, or to be exempt from, the official's construction of this event, an event that they nevertheless were at the heart of. They could speak against the grain of the official's speech, but only by speaking another "language," one that they alone possessed fully. Indeed, the older singers' arguments to stay were structured as a polite, formal, and ritualized conversation—a form that contrasted with the formal pronouncement and one-way speech of the official. This interaction was not confrontational per se, but rather seemed to exist in parallel to the organizational structure represented by the official.

This conversation was even more striking against the backdrop of claims by older singers that if one truly loves to sing quan họ (*mê quan họ*), then one "does not know how to feel tired" when singing, even if one sings through the night, for several days straight, stopping only to tend the fields during the daytime. The implicit statement, then, is that staying past the official midnight end of the event is an indication of real quan họ practice and ownership of that practice. It also references a different kind of "end" to quan họ practice. Singers frequently remark that the practice and tempo of *quan họ cổ* is not compatible with the fast pace of modern life. Therefore, that the practice of "real" quan họ at the 2005 *canh hát* could begin only after the event's end and the day's end indicates that *quan họ cổ* is out of time, in both senses of the phrase. The name of the event itself, *canh hát*, further emphasizes this sense of being "out of time." The phrase *canh hát* refers to a time in which singing, *hát*, occurs. *Canh*, by itself, is an archaic term meaning "an interval of time equaling one-fifth of the night."[19] Today, in an age when clocks and watches keep time for us, this form of time measurement has become obsolete and the term has taken on a more literary cast. That is to say, quan họ is not only disappearing as social practice, but as heritage, it is relegated to a rural folk past. Furthermore, official pronouncement of the event's "end" highlights how official involvement in quan họ practice is seen as an act of "restoration." Without an "end," the interruption in practice that enables the rescue of quan họ from the ravages of time, war, and the apathy of youth is no longer necessary.

Today, despite government, academic, and local participation in efforts to preserve and restore quan họ in the villages, there are few people left in the villages who practice quan họ as it was practiced in the past. As a result, academic interest in quan họ often focuses on the aging population of singers trained before 1945 as representative of quan họ and its imminent disappearance. There are very few singers left who learned and were practicing quan họ prior to 1945, and of those who are still alive, many have forgotten much of what they knew. The younger generations who are currently practicing quan họ in the villages, therefore, are seen as too far removed from "original" or "traditional" quan họ, and they are often excluded from studies of *quan họ cổ*. In television broadcasts of quan họ, for example, younger singers are frequently relied upon for visual and aural reconstructions of traditional-style quan họ gatherings, yet when it comes to collection of music and folk practices, they are often given less attention than older singers and are perceived to be less knowledgeable about quan họ practice than their elders. The older singers, in particular, often remark that quan họ is a genre for youth. Older singers will frequently claim that they are too old (vocally and in physical appearance) to sing quan họ anymore, but that they have an obligation to carry on for teaching and for preservation purposes. At times this view contrasts with that held by many young non-singers, who frequently remark that quan họ is a kind of singing for old people. This is not to say, however, that village practice of quan họ no longer exists as distinct from modernized, popular quan họ. Village practice itself has evolved, in its own way, with the times.

Younger village singers, however, are very much aware of these tensions. As one singer in her forties told me, today quan họ is organized more widely than it was previously. That is, it has moved beyond the confines of the home, the temple, and the village into a widely circulating, mass-mediated form. She also remarked that there are more people and villages participating in quan họ activities now than there were in the past. In the past, she said, they would sing only at the festivals, at events of their village or the villages that they had singing relationships with, or sometimes with their friends at home. Now, however, there are organized events such as the quan họ competition, and there are other competitions for all age groups. She told me, "In the past, quan họ was not organized into a movement (*chưa có tổ chức phong trào*) like it is today." This comment indicates the extent to which mass-mediated, modernized quan họ circulates back into the villages. Today those who want to participate in official quan họ activities join the Village Arts Team, which is modeled after the professional Bắc Ninh *Quan Họ* Folk Song Troupe and often performs modernized quan họ on the village stage. The village team was established in 1990 with the help of the newly established Center for the Study of Quan Họ Culture in Bắc Ninh City. At that time about sixty singers, both men and women, participated (Trần Chính 2000:36). Today, singers in the troupe range in age from very young children of both sexes to those in their mid-fifties, although among the youngest members there are very few boys. They learn to sing in classes held by older singers (usually middle-aged women) in the teachers' homes in the evenings.

COMMERCIALIZATION: HOW MUCH FOR A SONG?

Singers in the villages of Bắc Ninh stress that quan họ practice is characterized by the deep respect that singers have for each other, manifested in
the lifelong bonds of friendship between singers. These relationships are
simultaneously in tension with and fundamental to the new relations of
exchange between quan họ practitioners and the state, academia, and the
media. In my discussions with people outside the villages of Bắc Ninh, I
frequently heard concerns about the commercialization of quan họ, which
indicated a discomfort with the place of a socially embedded practice in a
growing market economy. However, among village practitioners, I found
less unease about commercialization than an unspoken distrust, or perhaps
skepticism, among older singers of the co-opting of quan họ as "heritage."
This co-optation, more than the modernization or popularization of quan
họ in the mass media, appears to wrest control over the practice of quan họ
from these villagers.

Fears of commercialization in Vietnam cannot be understood outside
the context of the drastic economic changes that the country has undergone since the reforms of the Renovation period (Đổi Mới) began in 1986.
The dramatic changes to the economic system initiated with Đổi Mới have
opened the door to new kinds of economic relationships centered on folk
music. Such relationships today increasingly fall under an internationally
defined "heritage" culture, particularly with Vietnam's increasing involvement with international organizations such as UNESCO. The current opportunities for the resurrection of folk practices and for innovation opened up
by reform take shape in concert with other political, economic, and institutional pressures.

The evolving relationship between the people and the state is evident in
the new kinds of exchange relations that are forming around quan họ practice and popularization. While I was on a brief visit back to Diềm Village
in March 2006, an elderly singer told me of several recent invitations to go
to Hanoi to sing only one song, for which she was paid what she considered
to be a lot of money. She expressed surprise that "they" would be willing
to pay so much for a single song. Her emphasis on the excessive and seemingly irrational cash value that "the center" gave her for one song implicitly
portrayed her own knowledge of the true value of quan họ as something
that does not in fact have a monetary value but rather a social one. She, like
other nghệ nhân, stressed the importance of sentiment (tình cảm) to the
relationships generated through singing quan họ. These singers frequently

emphasize that they greatly value (*quý lắm*) each other and that these sentiment-based relationships are very important to the practice of quan họ.

In village quan họ practice, the sentiment and strong lifelong bonds between groups of singers act out an idealized equality of exchange in which a matching song is always reciprocated and all singers treat each other as equals, regardless of age and gender. Ritualized reciprocity, stemming from the familial institution of social debt but adjusted to accommodate the ideal of equality, is embedded in old-style quan họ practice on several levels. In a *canh hát*, for instance, songs and food are offered to and accepted by partner singers within strictly defined rules of invitation and acceptance. In addition, partnered groups of singers from different villages are expected to participate in village festivals, weddings, and funerals in their partner's village.

New economic relations of exchange unsettle these traditional relations of reciprocity. The kind of exchange that characterizes the performance of a quan họ song for an audience who then pays the singer (too much) constitutes a rupture of the social relations quan họ singers are felt to embody and a form of forgetting. Quan họ thus practiced is no longer a long-term, deeply felt relationship of exchange based on "relatedness" but rather a short-term financial transaction; the cash payment pre-empts any relationship of social indebtedness. To the *nghệ nhân*, these two different forms of exchange are incompatible. The overestimation of the value of the song by those who hired the elderly singer reveals the misrecognition of one kind of value (the song that is familial and socially embedded) for another (the song and body of its singer as "heritage").

The cash value given to the single song indicates a shift in the representative value of the older singers to the center, as well as their commodification. Whereas a few years ago a conference or performance organizer in Hanoi might have hired professional singers to sing "old-style" quan họ, the "authentic" elderly singers *themselves* are now paid and brought into the city. As the representative (and hence, monetary) value of "authentic" quan họ and its practitioners grows in the heritage culture of Vietnam, quan họ is increasingly seen to be located in the village and in old age. Transporting these elderly singers to urban academic or performance spaces highlights a paradox arising out of the new heritage culture: quan họ songs become mobile and discrete objects (that is, removed from their traditional context of social practice) with cash value precisely because they are socially embedded and musically embodied practices. Therefore, as age in quan họ practice is institutionalized as "authentic," aged singers are relegated to history as representative living "relics." Consequently, they do not have the authority to speak outside the language of their own representative social practice.

The commodification of the *nghệ nhân* and their designation as "heritage" undermines the locally generated social relations and sentimental relations that define the social practice of quan họ.

CONCLUSION

The stories presented in this chapter demonstrate, in part, how the power and unity of the national narrative lies in its ability to "authorize" local voices to tell the stories that become the foundation of a national culture composed of local cultural diversity. The local stories that national narratives render inaudible, however, constitute the silent background of such discursive unity. Several of the quan họ narratives presented here indicate an inherent incompatibility between the *representative* value of quan họ as heritage and the *social* value of quan họ as the embodiment of a socially embedded form of musical practice. Once culture, as heritage, has a market value, authenticity is seen to lie less in *doing* culture than in visibly *representing* culture as heritage.

The framework of "inaudible stories" introduced in this chapter has wider implications for the study of culture in a world increasingly concerned with defining and preserving local cultural heritage. It is unclear whether such inaudible stories have a viable place in a global marketplace for culture that demands universal visibility for all culture. Representation, in this case, depends less upon a community of different cultural actors doing things than upon an investment-based notion of community where all actors contribute to fixing culture into what John Comaroff and Jean Comaroff (2009) would call a "brand." Who speaks for the quan họ "brand" as it continues to take shape in the coming years holds important implications for the communities and villages of Bắc Ninh. Such questions also have broad implications for studies of cultural identity and community. Is heritage culture an instance of more powerful forces trying to impose culture upon less powerful "others," or is it an emergent form of "imagined community which is truly global in its inception"? (Anderson 1991). The stories related here together speak to the complicated ways that quan họ singers and representatives of the center have negotiated the changing terrain of folk cultural representation in contemporary northern Vietnam. The authority to speak about quan họ takes on added importance in the context of internationally oriented claims to cultural heritage. Through its overt recognition and institutionalization of local folk practices, the unifying force of "cultural heritage" claims precedence and maintains control (even if not absolute) over the representation of Vietnamese culture without ever explicitly denying the semblance of locals' control over their own practices. Increasingly, however, those singers of the oldest generation who are said to embody the tradition most strongly are relegated to the realm of a rapidly receding rural past and, consequently, are divested of the power to speak about their own traditions in the modern context of cultural heritage. While these singers are often willing partners in the outside representations of their cultural practices, close attention to those inaudible stories (of yellow silk) and expressions that are "out of time" indicate that something meaningful always remains beyond the reach and control of any authoritative statement of authenticity and tradition.

4

Staging Quan Họ, Televising New Social Relationships

Before, it was said that one went to listen (*nghe*), not that one went to watch (*xem*). As I was growing up, I heard the elders say 'today I listened to quan họ at so and so's house' but nobody ever said I am going to watch quan họ. Now since the popular [professional] troupe began putting out music, we go watch quan họ. . . . When we sang, then the neighbors would come listen. No audience at all was invited but if people heard us singing, they would come by to listen to us singing. (Female singer, Bồ Sơn Village)

The quote above is an explanation given to me by a quan họ singer in response to a question I had posed: "Do you like to watch quan họ on television?" Her careful clarification of the semantics of "to listen to" versus "to watch" quan họ, points to a fundamental tension in quan họ practice in contemporary Vietnam. This singer's comment suggests that listening is a cultural practice embedded in the rhythms and social interactions of village life. Village singers do not perform for a theatrical audience. They do not require that anyone watch what they do, only that they listen to each other. Her claim that professional quan họ led to watching quan họ indicates that part of the difference between watching and listening to quan họ hinges on performing on stage for an audience that is not participating. Indeed, the assistant director of the professional Bắc Ninh *Quan Họ* Folk Song Troupe expressly articulated this difference as follows:

Watching artists perform [quan họ] is like watching TV. That is, at the same time, one can enjoy both with the eyes and with the ears. But if you are with the village singers (*nghệ nhân*), they don't express (*thể hiện*), they don't perform. . . . If you want to attract an audience, you must add movement. (Xuân Mùi, pers. comm., 6/17/04)

Theatrical audiences depend upon watching as much as listening and also depend upon the display of a visual aesthetic not present in the social practice of quan họ in the villages.

This chapter explores how the performance stage and television (as a form of stage) mediate between different social contexts of performance. Roland Barthes argues that the theater is characterized by the gaze, or the precise calculation of "the place of things *as they are observed*" and it is the geometry of the intersection of the gaze and the stage that is the foundation of representation (Barthes 1997:69; emphasis in original). With the staging and televising of folk music in Vietnam, the question of "the place of things" becomes central—not so much where things are placed on stage but, rather, where the stage itself is located in the social imagination. Staged quan họ exists in reference to, and indeed cannot exist without, another very different form of quan họ, the social practice of quan họ in which village singers create and express long-term meaningful relationships through the act of singing and in the context of village life. Staged performances of "new" or "modernized" quan họ refer to, but do not replicate, quan họ as practiced in the villages. Staged quan họ is also mobile. Performances in the province and elsewhere bring quan họ to a wider, non–Bắc Ninh audience, creating a second point of reference for the stage: Bắc Ninh provincial culture. Thus, while the quotes from the village singer and the troupe director, above, refer to the same genre of music, quan họ, they index very different social contexts of performance.

Vietnamese singers in the villages and professional stage singers frequently categorize quan họ in terms of a binary opposition between "old" and "new" quan họ. To be sure, these categories of quan họ practice are based upon readily identifiable differences in style, performance venue, lyrics, and so on and are clearly useful for the musicological description and classification of quan họ. Yet, in contemporary discourses about quan họ as traditional culture, quan họ practices falling into these two temporal poles of "old" and "new" are in constant dialogue with each other. Erik Harms argues that the discourse on urbanization in contemporary Ho Chi Minh City draws upon binaries between urban and rural, modern and traditional and he demonstrates how these binaries are tied up in the political, economic, and social transformation of contemporary Vietnam. He argues that these binaries are productive, they "do something" (2011:226), and by attending to them, we learn something about Vietnamese identity. In this context, this chapter explores how staged quan họ helps shape the Vietnamese contemporary cultural imagination and ideas about traditional culture in Bắc Ninh Province.

QUAN HỌ PERFORMANCES ON STAGE

The old-style quan họ sung in the villages of Bắc Ninh is said, to younger ears, to be difficult, somewhat strange, and monotonous. In contrast, new-style quan họ is faster, lyrically less complicated and accompanied by instrumental music. Furthermore, in the villages, singers wear old-style clothing, which is said to appear drab and old fashioned to younger eyes. Also, as one elderly singer told me, only rich families had colorful clothes to sing in. "Old-style" village women's clothing usually consists of a brown or black shirt worn over a white halter and tied at the waist with a single sash of a neutral color such as white or cream. The modern women's quan họ costume has been modified to make it more colorful and theatrical. Women's outfits now have sashes of bright neon yellow, green, red, and pink and two sashes are worn at once. The dress is made of bright colored cloth overlaid with a sheer dark layer. Such changes were made to add entertainment value and to liven up the quan họ singer for stage performance. In the past singers wore their nice clothing, out of respect and a sense of occasion, but it was not intended to attract an audience. Men's clothing is modeled after the mandarin-scholar's clothing, consisting of a long patterned blue or black tunic of silk gauze over an inner tunic or, if the wearer is rich, of satin. This is worn with white silk or satin pants and a turban. Today, men's turbans are bought (pre-wrapped) and worn over short hair whereas in the past they were wrapped around men's queues (Trần Linh Qúy and Hồng Thao 1997:47).

Staged performances of quan họ are always modernized quan họ and generally present a sequence of songs and dances. Many performances open with the songs "Guests Arrive to Sing at [our] House" (Khách Đến Chơi Nhà), also sometimes referred to as "Offering a Drink [tea] and Offering Betel" (Mời Nước, Mời Trầu). In opening with these songs, the performers reference the social practice of exchange central to quan họ. Some songs are sung by groups of all male or all female singers, some by solo singers, and some are duets sung by a man and woman. If a quan họ cổ, traditional-style, song is sung, it will be sung by a pair of singers of the same gender, to mimic the pairs singing (hát đôi) of village practice; however, it is rare that more than one traditional-style song is sung in any given performance and a response song is never exchanged on stage as in village practice. The traditional songs are seen as less exciting and not as suitable for stage performance as their modified versions.

As Xuân Mùi stated above, movement is added to quan họ on stage to make it a performance and more attractive to audiences. All songs are accompanied by stylized gestures and some songs are accompanied by dances, primarily performed by women. These dances make use of open, expansive yet slow and gentle gestures of the arms in a style that is vaguely reminiscent of dance in *chèo* theater.[1] Performers will walk and turn around on stage, but never jump or leap, leaving the viewer with the sense that the performers are mimicking movements naturally occurring in everyday life. Singers' movements are open and expressive in contrast to the controlled stillness of villagers singing quan họ. Performers face the audience when singing and project their voices. Female singers often use fans or the large round quan họ hat (*nón quai thao*) as props and men often carry a black umbrella. This performance style, developed by the Bắc Ninh *Quan Họ* Folk Song Troupe, has been adopted in all theatrical and televised performances of Vietnamese folk song.

Today, television is the most common medium through which people encounter new quan họ, especially outside Bắc Ninh Province.[2] Quan họ on television and quan họ on the stage have the dual purposes of providing entertainment and dissemination of culture and both are identical stylistically. On television, however, songs are not introduced by an announcer, as they are on stage, but rather the name of the song and singer are simply shown on-screen. Quan họ songs are often included as numbers in shows presenting regional folk songs from around the country performed by professional singers. These broadcasts may be taped on a studio stage set or taped outside in scenic views of Bắc Ninh landscapes and traditional architecture. The primary mediating process for new quan họ is the "stage" (whether it is encountered in a theater, outdoors, or on television).

ENACTING QUAN HỌ SCENES (*DỰNG CẢNH*) FOR AN AUDIENCE

On stage, singers often enact the lyrical content of the song (*dựng cảnh*) in a stylized way such that their body movements become a form of illustration and explanation of the songs. An eighty-two-year-old singer in Diềm Village, in response to a question about whether or not she likes quan họ on television, said it is interesting because you can see what the song is about whereas, in the past, they could only imagine it. She elaborated:

The singing voice on television is that which moved out from here, from the origin villages of the quan họ homeland. But when we sang in the past, we only knew how to sit and sing. We didn't have all this beautiful scenery like this [that we see on television]. Today, the government has collected the [songs of] *nghệ nhân* from these quan họ villages and put them on television and embellished (*tô vẽ*) them to make them more beautiful. . . . In the past, we just had to sit and say "spinning thread and threading the needle" but we didn't see thread or a needle anywhere. Now, the government says "spinning thread and threading the needle" and you have threading the needle. . . . Today, the government, society is advanced so if you sing about something, then you have [i.e., see] that thing. (Female singer, Diêm Village)

"Spinning thread and threading the needle" is a line from a quan họ song that is frequently performed on stage and aired on television; singers will pantomime the act of threading a needle as they sing (Fig. 4.1). Thus, as this singer indicates, quan họ on television is often a literal visual rendering of what is heard, or, the imagination made visible. When acted out visibly in this manner, quan họ becomes accessible to all. While this singer and her fellow village singers "knew how to sit and sing," most people (in the village and elsewhere) did not know how to sing. However, when the songs are acted out on the stage, anyone in society can "have the song by seeing it." What is also interesting about this singer's response is that she directly equates quan họ on television with the government and state (*nhà nước*). For her, the movement of quan họ out of the village, the involvement of the state in quan họ, and television are all linked together. She *sang* quan họ in the past, but what she *saw* on television was a reflection of the new society. The enacting of quan họ, that is, comes by way of the state and comes on television. Thus, television draws quan họ out of its village context to present it to the nation as a whole.

In contrast to the above singer's statement that quan họ on television is "very interesting," most other elderly village singers with whom I spoke said that they did not like it, or at least emphasized that they felt it was nothing like what they knew and loved as quan họ. Even the singer quoted above maintained a very clear distinction between what she sang and what she saw on television. Singers consistently stated that television quan họ "does not fit" (*không hợp*) with them, or that they cannot watch it. One singer even said that quan họ on television is "ridiculous" (*nhố nhăng*). These singers, as the living embodiment of *quan họ cổ*, distinguished clearly between what they know as quan họ and the new, faster, modernized form on television.

FIG. 4.1. "Threading the Needle." Students from the Bắc Ninh Province Secondary School of Culture and Arts being taped for television.

The comments of these singers illustrate the perceived gap between village quan họ and new quan họ and also between the old and the young singers. The elderly singers do not hear (or see) their quan họ on television but, rather, something else that does not "fit" with their ears. This music does not fit because it is not a part of the social gatherings through which long-term friendships were formed and deep sentiment generated.

What separates the new (stage/television) and old (village) forms of quan họ is the medium of transmission. In village quan họ, this is the body of the singers; in new quan họ, it is the stage (or the television screen). Each medium generates a different sense experience and refers to a different social order. Inherent in the movement of quan họ from the bodies of village singers to the stage and screen is an awareness of the incompatibility of the social registers in which each form occurs. This difference is in part manifested in the changes to the music caused by the addition of musical accompaniment.

According to one older singer from Châm Khê Village, village singers do not like the sound of quan họ on television because it has lost "the sounds of the music" (tiếng nhạc). He explained that, in quan họ cổ, each verse [of the song] has some sections of music [that act] as *lưu không* (interlude).[3] For example, "*tình tính tang la tang tính tình*" or "*ừ ư*." . . . These are music words (*từ cái nhạc*) of quan họ. But now these are cut out to put in the sounds of modern music, which interferes with those words.

In other words, these "meaningless" words that in *quan họ cổ* imitated the sound of musical instruments, have been replaced with instrumental accompaniment in new quan họ. In *quan họ cổ*, words without meaning (pure signs) represent the sounds of instruments. In modernized quan họ, the representations—the "music words"—are substituted with the "real" thing, the instrument itself.

When musical accompaniment is added to the song, the "sound" of the music no longer comes from within the bodies of the singers and the song itself but arrives from outside the song, from elsewhere. In the past, Vietnamese folksingers sat and sang and did not have to imagine what the lyrics of a song "looked" like since they were singing about actions and sentiments that were an intimate part of their lives in the village. Staging, on the other hand, allows those who have never been a part of the intimate world of village quan họ to "remember" themselves in a time and place in which they would have been engaged in "threading the needle." It is no longer through the singing body that is embedded in village life that folk songs are made meaningful but, rather, through the song that has become a representation of itself, in which the "music words" have been replaced with the "real thing." Representation, according to Foucault, "possess[es] the obscure power of making a past impression present once more" (1994:69). It is the imagination, in the form of impressions that resemble each other just enough to be compared, which enables that representation. Thus, "[t]here must be, in the things represented, the insistent murmur of resemblance; there must be, in the representation, the perpetual possibility of imaginative recall" (ibid.). The quan họ stage portrays quan họ as a form of collective memory or imagination of a past that is available to all: singers and non-singers, old and young.

LOVE ON THE STAGE

The most striking example of how the performance of quan họ can be seen to stage new forms of sociality that are available to singers and non-singers is in the particular way it enacts romantic love through a literal rendering of quan họ lyrics. When represented on the stage, the sentiment that was so central to the social practice of quan họ becomes something else. It becomes "love" or, more precisely, romantic love. The kind of love signified by the performance of quan họ on stage does not arise from the act of singing itself, as did the friendships of village singers. Rather, the song portrays love visually. On stage, lyrics expressing love, longing, and friendship are often acted out as visual fantasies of romantic love between male and female singers. On the quan họ stage, performers often enact open flirtations that are provocative by traditional standards. Men and women sing duets, touch each other on the arm or hand while singing, look directly at one another, and hide their faces together behind the large round quan họ hat (*nón quai thao*) (Fig. 4.2). One village singer called this latter gesture "exchanging feelings with the hat" (*giáo duyên bằng nón*) and stressed that this was not appropriate in village practice. Such openly flirtatious behavior between men and women belonging to partnered groups (*kết bạn*) was prohibited by custom in the social practice of quan họ. The relationship between singers, rather, was as one singer explained, "*vôi*," which is the lime powder that is used in betel chewing and also to make traditional house paint. She was using the word to mean very clear or pure to define the relationship between quan họ partners.

FIG. 4.2. Quan họ on stage. Performance by the Bắc Ninh *Quan họ* Folk Song Troupe, 2004.

An indication of the transformation of sentiment into romantic love is that the terms of address have changed: women on stage become *em* (the diminutive younger sister, or female lover) to the men's *anh* (older brother or male lover) signaling a romantic and unequal relationship. Romantically involved and married couples in Vietnam refer to each other with these terms, with women using the diminutive *em* and men the higher status *anh*. In the social practice of quan họ, however, singers always refer to themselves as *em* (younger sister or brother) and address the other singers as older brother or older sister, *regardless* of the other singer's age and gender, as a sign of respect and equality. The changed terms of address in the modern songs signal romance between male and female singers rather than social relationships among equals. Always calling the women singers by the diminutive *em* introduces an age and gender hierarchy into the singing relationship.

Another interesting indication of the changing relationship of love to quan họ is the widespread misconception concerning marriage between quan họ singers. Throughout my fieldwork, Vietnamese friends and acquaintances (non-singers) who were aware I was studying quan họ frequently emphasized that one of the more interesting aspects of quan họ was that singers were forbidden to marry each other. The commonly held conception is that while they sing about love, singers can never marry each other. In fact, the marriage proscription is only partially true; it pertains only to those singers from villages with the *kết nghĩa* relationship of friendship, since the members of the two villages are considered to be siblings, that is, blood relations. Those groups (*bọn*) who form friendships with groups from villages that do not have this formal relationship with their home village are permitted to marry each other, with some limitations (Đặng Văn Lung, Hồng Thao, and Trần Linh Quý 1978:33). Nguyễn Van Phù, Lưu Hữu Phước, Nguyễn Viêm, and Tư Ngọc suggest that while the feudal proscription against marriage between men and women from villages with the *kết nghĩa* relationship and friendships between unmarried women and men was not ironclad in practice, it is reasonable to assume that if singers freely formed relationships with each other in violation of custom and propriety it might endanger the organization of such singing events over time (1962:23). That is, if the young quan họ singers were openly and frequently to violate social norms limiting open flirtation and interactions with the opposite sex at their gatherings, presumably, their elders would have put a stop to such gatherings.[4]

The idea of an unattainable romantic love has precedent in Vietnamese culture; indeed, the heroine of Nguyễn Du's *Tale of Kiều*, the country's most famous epic poem from which many quan họ lyrics are drawn, sacrifices her own love and happiness for her family honor. After long years of struggle, when finally given the chance to reunite with her lover, she chooses a platonic spiritual union with him. This story, which is based upon a Chinese one, resonates with William Jankowiak's work on how Chinese popular literature has demonstrated the long presence of romantic love in China, particularly as it "reveals the personal anguish of people torn between filial duty and romantic desire" (1995:168). Because "the struggle between individual desire and social obligation" was so strong, it posed a threat to the interests and power of the family, which "often went to extraordinary lengths to ensure that its offspring would not haphazardly or impulsively fall in love" (ibid.:168–169). As such, some of the tales of love became morality tales "designed to teach the younger generation that love was not an end in itself but a by-product of marriage, the formation of the family, and the continuance of society" (ibid). In pre-revolutionary Vietnam, as well, one sees similar pressures between individual desire and family obligation.

And yet, romantic love is attainable in contemporary Vietnamese society as a result of significant changes to marriage practices and conceptions about love since the August Revolution, when love marriages were promoted by the state for the first time. Harriet Phinney traces how discussions in the 1920s about individual romantic love that were influenced by French literature and ideas under colonialism were supplanted during the revolutionary period by calls for common responsibility and love of nation. Revolutionary youth were exhorted to shift their loyalties from themselves as individuals and from their patriarchal families to the work of the Revolution and the nation (2008:336). Then, in 1959, the DRV passed the Law on Family and Marriage, which resulted in significant changes to marriage practices intended to help promote equality between men and women and improve the rights of children within the family (Malarney 2002:149–150). Throughout this period, the government worked to create what Phinney calls a "socialist love as part of its efforts to create a modern social subject" (2008:330). The law did, ultimately, succeed in removing much (but not all) authority in marriage from the family and "[f]or the first time in Vietnamese history, love became a *legal* basis for marriage" (ibid.:344; emphasis in original). Despite the rhetoric, however, couples in this period were still not entirely free to choose their marriage partners, as the state, in many cases, replaced the family as the authority figure (ibid.).

In the reform period, the state promoted yet a new vision of the "happy, healthy and wealthy family" that would "ensure the nation's success in the global market economy" (ibid.; see also Werner and Bélanger 2002), and which has introduced new tensions for youth. Tine Gammeltoft argues that the meaning of female sexuality in Vietnam today is contested by urban youths (especially women) many of whom make choices about sexuality based upon "personal inclination and moral conviction" (2002:116). Nevertheless, such choices may still be interpreted by families and society as immoral (ibid.:118). These young women are caught between complicated and often clashing notions of morality and virtue that often hinge on differing engagements with a concept of "traditional values." Kristin Pelzer notes that the word "tradition" is frequently used in "the ongoing dialogue, or skirmishes, between the sexes in contemporary Vietnam" and that, in this context, a "certain nostalgia for traditional Vietnamese values" has emerged in the period following reform (1993:317, 326).

In this context, romantic love on the quan họ stage is a public narrative that reflects the conflicted and changing history of romantic love in Vietnam. On stage, the political and social pressures influencing how love is perceived in the new society are tinged with nostalgia, longing, and searching for something just out of reach. One can marry the person one loves in the new society but there are still nostalgic resonances of past social restrictions. The common, if not entirely correct, perception that quan họ singers cannot ever marry each other indicates that love on the stage is seen to be a poignantly unattainable love. Yet, what is now unattainable is a representation of a rule that was not ironclad to begin with. It seems, then, that the unattainable romance of quan họ singers, as represented on stage, also enacts the discursive gulf between an idealized folk past and the modern present. In the remoteness resulting from the mediation between one form of quan họ and another via the stage, something else altogether is created. The stage creates a different relationship to desire and its fulfillment from that which occurs in the social practice of quan họ. In the social practice of quan họ, the fulfillment of desire comes through the act of singing itself and it is that act that generates affective ties. On stage, however, no affective social ties are formed between singers and the audience; the performance of quan họ can only represent those ties. In performance, the fulfillment of desire does not happen. However, something meaningful is created for performers and audiences of new quan họ. This new social meaning is closely connected to a sense of being a cultural, and in particular a Bắc Ninh cultural, "insider."

WE ARE ALL LOCALS ON TELEVISION

Vietnamese ethnomusicologist Tô Ngọc Thanh once told me that "we are all locals" on television. With the mass mediation of folk music on television, he was saying, everyone within Vietnam became an "insider" or had access to what were before isolated local musical forms unfamiliar to those outside the areas in which they were practiced. Certainly television has been used to great effect in the nationalization of Vietnamese folk music and performance. Audiences in northern Vietnam, for instance, have on-air access to the southern *cải lương* or reformed opera while audiences in the south have on-air access to the northern *chèo* popular theater. Around the country, people can listen to folk music forms that, in the past, would not have been performed outside their place of origin. Folk song broadcasts on the national television stations are structured as variety shows in which songs from around the country are played back-to-back and often distinguished from each other visually only by the subtitle indicating its province of origin and, at times, the singer's regional costume. The songs are identifiable as local yet because of the uniform style of their presentation, they become parts that make up the national whole and, thus, are mutually substitutable in the national context. These shows are structured so that anyone around the nation can identify with any form of local folk music from afar in the shared national context.

Tô Ngọc Thanh also argues that folk music must occur in its social context, as a social activity, in order to be "real" (*thật*). It cannot, he says, just be a "presentation" of that form. Thus, he directly links authenticity to the community of origin of a particular genre and to its continued existence as a living tradition. These two statements about folk music indicate that while he understands folk music on television to be in direct relationship with some form of substantive "authentic" folk music, at the same time, he perceives a gap or break between the two that happens via television. The question is, how is that which is presumed to be the unique experience of individual communities, local folk culture, represented by a medium that claims to have the singular ability to give viewers command over precisely that which they already have?

FILMING QUAN HỌ FOR LOCAL TELEVISION OR TELEVISING THE UNATTAINABLE

The Bắc Ninh Radio and Television Station is a small provincial station, with limited resources, located in Bắc Ninh City, the provincial capital of the quan họ region. The station produces three kinds of programming related to quan họ folk song: documentaries about quan họ, musical television dramas that tell a story about quan họ (*phim truyền hình ca nhạc*), and a program to teach quan họ to viewers. In addition, the station will occasionally air recordings of particular quan họ songs if it receives enough requests from viewers. Quan họ (and folk song more generally) also appears on television as one of many different forms of folk music in folk music-video shows. Typically, musical films of quan họ take place in an outdoor setting that appears untouched by modern life. This might be a natural setting such as a field or by a river (Fig. 4.3) or in some form of traditional (cổ) building such as an old house built in Vietnamese traditional architectural style or a temple.[5] Songs and stories take place, that is, in places with no evidence of "modern" life in order to give them a timeless feel.

A closer look at the folk music productions of this provincial broadcast station indicates that local directors and producers believe their authority to portray quan họ on television is based on their deep and accurate knowledge of quan họ. They contrast their own deep knowledge with what they see as the cursory knowledge of filmmakers from the national television stations. At the same time, portrayals of quan họ produced for Bắc Ninh television appear to emphasize a dreamlike and unattainable character, which I argue serves to highlight the mediated nature of the relationship between local quan họ (village) culture and the national (non–Bắc Ninh) television viewer.

FIG. 4.3. Quan họ by the river. A "typical" natural setting reconstructed for film.

The way that locality informs televisual representations of quan họ is evident in the work of director Nguyễn Trung, who works at the provincial Bắc Ninh Radio and Television Station.[6] This emerges in Nguyễn Trung's framing of the material means of production in Bắc Ninh and also in the implications of the dreamlike quality of his television film called *Seeking in a Song* (*Tìm Trong Bài Hát*). *Seeking in a Song* tells the story of a young woodcutter who finds a woman's shoe in the fields and begins to dream the story of who this young woman might be. He dreams her as a young quan họ singer in the nearby village. She lives with her evil stepmother and stepsister who treat her poorly and, among other things, prevent her from joining in the village festival and its quan họ singing. Her story, as the woodcutter imagines it, is loosely based on the *Tấm Cám* folk legend (which has many similarities with the Cinderella story). In this legend, two young girls, Tấm and Cám, share the same father but have different mothers. At the time the story unfolds, the father and Tấm's mother have both died and the good-hearted and somewhat naive Tấm lives at the mercy of the whims of her greedy and unkind sister and stepmother. Throughout the story, Tấm periodically receives help from a kindly deity and she is also miraculously reborn several times with the help of this deity after being killed by her stepmother and sister. Near the end of the story, she meets and weds the young prince (whose role the woodcutter dreams himself in) who had been looking for the owner of the lost shoe. After this marriage, however, she is still beset upon by the stepmother and stepsister, who want the prince for the stepsister.[7]

The film's story, though based on the legend, is not simply broken down into dream and reality (that is, the legendary story and the "real" story of the woodcutter) but contains many different layers of past-ness and dreaming. The most striking of these is the figure of the woodcutter himself, who is shoeless and dressed in a simple brown loincloth and turban that are immediately reminiscent of Vietnamese folk paintings and of an idyllic rural Vietnamese past. In fact, the film generates a certain temporal irony in that with the current strong and pervasive revival of quan họ festivals in Bắc Ninh, the image of the woodcutter begins to feel more "past" than the images of quan họ despite the fact that, in the film, the images of quan họ are linked with the legend, and the woodcutter with the film's present. Nowhere in the woodcutter's appearances in the film is there any evidence of modern life—he sleeps next to a small fire out in the fields and carries his bundle of sticks on his back. The woodcutter, even while he is dreaming a legend, is himself already a figuration of past-ness and nostalgia. That is, he is a figment of a modern imagination that seeks to define itself in terms of a rural past.

Nguyễn Trung uses the story of *Tấm Cám* not as a morality tale, as it would have been used in the past that is referenced in the film, but rather as a commentary on the dream-like quality of the quan họ imaginary in modern Bắc Ninh society. We dream in quan họ, he seems to be saying, but we can never quite achieve that which we seek. Indeed, in discussing the film with me, he remarked that "it is all a dream (*giấc mơ*) in the end, like quan họ." But, in waking from this dream at the end of the film, it is as if we find ourselves in yet another dream of the past (or, the woodcutter's past-present).

The theme of searching for something just out of sight runs through the film. The film's title, *Seeking in a Song*, expresses this as does the body language of the singers and characters in the film who continually crane their necks and shade their eyes to look off into the distance. This is a performance style for quan họ that was first introduced by the Bắc Ninh *Quan Họ* Folk Song Troupe and is now pervasive in performances of quan họ. The songs used in the film, which are all new compositions in the quan họ style, and not *quan họ cổ*, further articulate a search for something out of sight and out of time (or, in the past). Their titles include: "Sent back to *quan họ*" (*Gửi về quan họ*), "Returning to Kinh Bắc" (*Về Kinh Bắc*), and "Searching in an afternoon at the Lim Festival" (*Tìm Trong Chiều Hội Lim*).[8]

This last song is quite well known and was composed by Nguyễn Trung himself. The music and lyrics, which often directly reference the sound and lyrics of village quan họ, express nostalgia for an authentic quan họ experience. For example, "Whoever stands in the cool breeze will feel nostalgic longing" (*bâng khuâng ai đứng trong gió lạnh*), or "Where are you? Let me always look for you" (*Em ở đâu? Để anh mãi đi tìm*) and "I look for you in how many words. A heart-to-heart language that I seek in how many songs" (*Tìm trong bao lời nói. Một tiếng nói tâm tình tìm trong bao giọng hát*). Several phrases that appear in the song, such as *gió lạnh* (cool breeze) and *cây trúc xinh* (beautiful bamboo), are direct references to titles of *quan họ cổ* songs as is the use of helping words and phrases such as *ư hự ư là hội hư*, which have no meaning but are immediately recognizable as *quan họ cổ*. These lyrical references to *quan họ cổ* directly link this new, modern song with a sound and an image of an idealized, past quan họ situated in the village. However, the sound of nostalgia and longing in the song indicates that this, like the film, is a musical dream of the past, not an actual return. In addition, the use of *quan họ cổ* lyrics in these new songs indicate that Nguyễn Trung's songs are, in many ways, a direct product of the revolutionary project to build a new national culture based upon the folk past, discussed in chapter one. It is through this very process of direct reference to local lyrics in the national context, that the local director establishes his claim to local authenticity.

Despite the fact that they are constantly searching for something, the characters and singers in the film *Seeking in a Song* never fully discover what they seek: "it is all a dream in the end." The young woman in the dream must run off from the festival as soon as her stepsister shows up. In the process, she loses the shoe, which starts the woodcutter dreaming. In the last scene of the film, the woodcutter wakes up in front of his fire (holding her shoe) and the story of love and fulfillment by way of quan họ song vanishes and dissolves into the credits. The stories in the film are inter-cut with each other in a way that emphasizes temporal and narrative ambiguity. For instance, the woodcutter himself appears to be a part of his own dream when he awakens holding the quan họ singer's shoe, which itself should have been a part of the dream. The fact that the woodcutter is himself an imaginary figuration of the past highlights the impossibility of the television film to make the connection between real life and the idealized construction of a local history and culture. This televisual mediation recognizes that it, too, is just one more idealized construction of quan họ.

LEARNING QUAN HỌ ON LOCAL TELEVISION

As discussed above, in the eyes and ears of the older village singers, television does not provide the proper social context for quan họ. In village practice, quan họ is not quan họ unless certain rules of practice are followed during singing events. On the other hand, as one elderly village singer claimed, on television, singers "can sing whatever they like" and so they do not have to "follow the rules of the elders from the past." One cannot sing a response to a song on television and vice versa. Nonetheless, others can watch the Bắc Ninh television show to teach quan họ and learn to sing along with the television. Or, they can sing along with one of a number of commercially available karaoke quan họ compact discs. As unrelated as televised quan họ may be to village quan họ, for its singers, the modernized style is a new and meaningful cultural idiom through which they express their identity as performers of Bắc Ninh traditional culture. For these singers, television is a medium through which they enact pride in their local culture, an important skill in today's world in which local cultures everywhere are embracing, performing, and marketing their traditions in national and international contexts.

Students at the Bắc Ninh Secondary School of Culture and Arts, the best of whom feed into the professional provincial quan họ troupe, frequently appear in programs of quan họ folk song on Bắc Ninh television. These students recognize that they are singing a modern form, one that appeals to

modern life, yet still maintain that they are more traditional in their singing than those from outside the province because, first, they are from Bắc
Ninh and therefore understand quan họ deeply, and second, they are less
"theatricalized" (sân khấu hóa) than non–Bắc Ninh singers who sing quan
họ songs on television (see Fig. 4.1). The perception that real quan họ can
only be sung by the voices of people from Bắc Ninh is implicit in the Bắc
Ninh Television Station's program to teach quan họ to viewers. On this show,
a retired singer from the Bắc Ninh *Quan Họ* Folk Song Troupe who now
teaches at the Bắc Ninh Province Secondary School of Culture and Arts
teaches modernized quan họ to a group of students from the school. The
show is taped at the Bắc Ninh Television Station in a small room whose back
wall is hung with blue drapes upon which the show's logo is mounted. Also
in the room is a podium for the teacher, some chairs, a few tables lined up
against one wall (several of them with bouquets of fake flowers on them),
and several microphones. Next to the door is a large glass window leading
to the control and edit room. Each show lasts between thirty and forty-five
minutes, depending on the length of the song taught, and is broadcast four
times over two weeks. The program proceeds as follows: first, the teacher will
introduce the song and then demonstrate how it is sung. Next, the teacher
reads out the lyrics one line at a time. The lyrics are simultaneously written
in graphic form across the bottom of the television screen. Then, he teaches
the song, line by line, to the students in the studio who are seated, as if in a
classroom, at the tables at the back. The students are paid by the television
station to appear on the show.

Because the show is produced for and broadcast on the Bắc Ninh provincial station, its target audience is the local Bắc Ninh population. The station sees part of its mission to be the education of its viewers in their own
local culture. However, the show's set, arranged like a classroom, facilitates
a particular modern pedagogical method. First, the students write down the
lyrics before beginning the lesson. This is then transmitted to the viewers
by way of the screen itself, which is imprinted with the lyrics, line by line,
with the understanding that the viewer at home is also copying them down.
Learning line by line in this way is a new method for teaching locals how
to be local citizens in a nationalized context.[9] In her discussion of classes
to teach karnatic music on the radio in 1950s India, Amanda Weidman
demonstrates how "[t]he learning process changes from one of inadvertent
absorption to one of conscious drilling. The long years of casual, almost
unconscious listening are replaced by the punctilious timing and infinitude
of radio broadcasting" (2003:470). As a result, she argues, "[t]he student's
identity is oddly augmented, for now he or she hears not only the voice of

the teacher, but the voice of a student repeating the teacher; it is as if one can step back (or simply stay home) and listen to oneself learn" (ibid.). Likewise, the television viewer-learner of quan họ is able to imagine himself or herself in the place of the learners on the screen; from the comfort of home, viewers can see themselves learning to be representatives of Bắc Ninh culture.

What is broadcast on the show to teach quan họ is not just a different pedagogical method but also a new temporality of learning and singing. In contemporary society (and on television), one thinks in minutes. Now, one can learn a song in four thirty- to forty-minute blocks over two weeks. The essential difference here is that the elder village singers define learning quan họ as a socially embedded process. One learns new-style quan họ, however, as the result of a new pedagogical method based upon repetition in television-time. The televisual learning process trains viewers not just how to sing quan họ songs, but also how to contribute to their preservation. By writing down songs in Bắc Ninh, one becomes a collector of folk culture and, specifically, of one's own culture. Television, then, teaches the modern viewer at home how to learn quan họ and to sing along and, at the same time, the show teaches Bắc Ninh viewers how to be "Bắc Ninh" people by identifying themselves with quan họ. To be a modern citizen of Bắc Ninh, one must be aware of quan họ culture and contribute to its popularization and preservation.

STAGING LOCAL CLAIMS TO AUTHENTICITY

The views on authenticity of quan họ expressed by the students at the school and professional singers are at times markedly different from those expressed by village quan họ singers. Important, one common complaint that village singers have is that researchers and television crews spend such a short time in the village that they cannot possibly truly understand quan họ. For these singers, what distinguishes quan họ is a long-term engagement with the form and, particularly, the strong sentiment that is generated between singers in the act of singing itself. Therefore, a brief encounter with a camera is insufficient, in their view, to engender true understanding of quan họ. I observed a number of film shoots in Bắc Ninh by Bắc Ninh Television, Vietnam Television, and international film crews. At one shoot in Diềm Village of a documentary about Vietnamese culture for Vietnam Television, the filmmaker asked one of the singers if he could film her teaching some of the children present to dance. The request confused the singer so the filmmaker then demonstrated by twirling his hands and said, "like on stage."[10] One of the researchers from the Bắc Ninh Center for *Quan Họ* Studies then explained that they never have dancing in a *canh hát*, only singing, at which point the filmmaker dropped his request. Local Bắc Ninh Television producers use a similar argument about immersion in a culture to situate themselves in opposition to outside television crews who, they feel, cannot truly or deeply understand quan họ. Outside productions do not have the daily, easy access to the village singers and the professional singers of Bắc Ninh that local producers have and that they feel leads to correct and authorized knowledge about quan họ.

Assertions of authenticity are a crucial part of the struggle for representational control over quan họ on television. I would argue that the emphasis on the impossibility to access "authentic" quan họ by way of television is itself part of the argument with which Bắc Ninh Television asserts its authority to represent quan họ. When Nguyễn Trung walked me through the studio where his station films the program to teach quan họ songs to viewers, he pointed out how small and simple the studio and its equipment were. However, he claims that while the Bắc Ninh station is poor and does not have the means of production that the national stations have, the content of its quan họ programming is superior:

> If one compares us based on the quality, it is true we are substandard because we are very poor. How can we compare ourselves to our friends at the central television station? Our means are insufficient. But we have our own strengths, that is, we live on a bit of land strong with quan họ, we have a storehouse of village singers and professional performers to utilize. . . . Compared to our friends in the center, when it comes to technical aspects we appear to be inferior but when it comes to content, nobody can compete with us. (pers. comm., 6/15/04)

His emphasis on the station's lack of material means is one way of articulating the power imbalance between provincial television stations and the national station. But, he argues, means of production do not, ultimately, matter; knowledge and access matter.[11] Thus, Bắc Ninh insiders believe that they will produce more authentic shows about quan họ in spite of their material disadvantages.

In Bắc Ninh, television producers, directors, and cameramen live in direct proximity to what are perceived as the vanishing traditions of village quan họ; but they are also, as producers of electronic media, directly implicated in the changes to quan họ through the popularization of a new, non-village form. (Indeed, many of Nguyễn Trung's films use elements of dance, props, and styles that had no place in "traditional" quan họ.) These producers are a part of the quan họ story in present-day Bắc Ninh. By emphasizing the inferiority of the material means of television production in Bắc Ninh, Nguyễn Trung is directly appealing to a notion of the amateur to bind his films to the authenticity seen to reside in the non-professional village singers (even though the singers in his films are professionally trained). Among village singers, researchers and local intellectuals, authentic quan họ is seen to reside in the bodies and voices of the non-professional village singers. Their sound, rougher and less polished yet authentic or real, is heard in direct opposition to the sound of the professional singers. Because the station's poverty is immediately visible in production quality, it stands in direct opposition to the polished, expensive productions out of the center. In Bắc Ninh televisual discourse, the polished (national) production does not reveal but obscures the story of authentic (local) quan họ behind the medium (video) whereas the inferior quality productions in Bắc Ninh highlight a connection to the authentic and rougher but still romanticized village practices.

The Bắc Ninh televisual discourse implicates village quan họ and televised or modernized quan họ in a unified field of practice much more effectively than do national and provincial academic discourses, which mark village quan họ as "authentic" and new quan họ as "modernized." By an explicit emphasis on the material poverty of the station and its productions and by asserting a deep understanding of the content represented, Bắc Ninh Television programming articulates the intangibility of modern dreams of representational power.

CONCLUSION

A successful performance relies upon meeting the social expectations of and conforming to the conventions of a genre, community, or society. The "socially appropriate ways" of communicating with an audience (Bauman 1975:293), or with other singers, is dramatically different in the performance of quan họ on the stage and the social practice of quan họ in the villages. Whereas in village quan họ, embodied practices generated social relationships based on sentiment, on the stage or on screen social relationships must answer to an audience of viewers who are not directly linked to the performer through relationships of sentiment. Whereas in the village, singers sat, sang, and imagined things, now they, and everyone else, can see these things enacted literally on screen. Village singers created meaningful ties of sentiment that were in sync with the rhythms and values of village life and inter-village relationships. Singers of modernized quan họ create social meaning by enacting provincial culture in the role of Bắc Ninh cultural "insiders." The social expectations for performed quan họ result in its being "watched" by a formal audience whose members can imagine themselves as participant in and owners of traditional Bắc Ninh provincial culture.

5

Broadcasting to Ourselves at the Quan Họ Festivals

At about 10:30 p.m. on February 24, 2004 (February 5, by the lunar calendar), the night before the main day of the Diềm Village Festival, the performance of modernized quan họ that had unfolded on a stage set up at the end of the village green in front of the communal house (*đình*) concluded. As the dense crowd quickly dispersed and headed home, a friend reported hearing a man who, with a few companions, was making his way into the less crowded courtyard of the Vua Bà Temple (the temple to the quan họ ancestral deity) say, "let's encourage them a little and see how it is" (*động viên một tý xem thế nào*).[1] He was referring to the quan họ singers who had earlier that evening gathered together in a circle on a few mats spread in front of the temple to *hát hội* or "festival sing." This is a fairly informal style of quan họ singing that is closely integrated with the function of festivals in village life, which is "each year to pray together for happiness, luck, prosperity in an animated and lively way, together with the hope that the next year will bring better sustenance than the last" (Đặng Văn Lung, Hồng Thao, and Trần Linh Quý 1978:24). In Diềm, the singers first sing three songs in offering (*hát thờ*) to the quan họ ancestral deity, Vua Bà, then take turns singing in pairs. The three offered songs are, first, a song to greet the deity (*bài chúc thánh*), which is the same tune as *La Rằng* but with different words; second, a song to greet the villagers, which is to the tune of *Kim Lan* (Soul Mate); and, third, *Gió Mát* (Cool Breeze). The singers must sing these three tunes or "voices" (*giọng*). After these three songs, those who feel like it sing and in no special sequence.

In 2004, however, the singing was more formal because of the presence of a film crew from the Institute of Culture and Information of Hanoi that was there to document traditional quan họ activities at the festival. Several times, a pair of singers began singing, but had to stop again to allow the film crew to set up the camera and microphones. There was also some direction on who should sing next, which occasionally seemed to cause confusion among some of the older singers.[2] Thus, what those who came "to encourage and see" saw was the re-staging of an event to look and sound as it was perceived that such an event should look and sound on film. What the man above and others, such as the film crew, also saw and expected to see was the importance of the event as "heritage."

The seeming irony of the situation in which village singers were directed to make them appear to be more like themselves (authentic) echoed through the village during the whole several days of the festival. That first night before the main festival day, three points of sound had reverberated through the village simultaneously: the modernized staged quan họ on the village green, the traditional style quan họ in the temple yard, and the taped quan họ emanating from the village loudspeakers, which broadcast quan họ songs from morning to night. Always audible, the loudspeaker broadcasts attempted to set the stage and tone of the festival for the villagers themselves. Quan họ is "ours," the constantly echoing sounds of recorded quan họ seemed to say, so remember to "encourage it a little." Furthermore, the loudspeakers broadcast modernized quan họ, reinforcing the sense that these sounds echoing through the village are linked to a wider, nationalized form of quan họ and demonstrating how quan họ cycles back, in changed form, into its "origin" villages.

At village quan họ festivals, aural and visual representations of culture are mutually constructed and more fully experiential than a focus solely on visual representation alone would indicate (see Bendix 2000). Viewing and listening are cultural practices, and thus, "directed, learned activity" (Sterne 2003:19), which are employed in specific ways in order to construct the contemporary cultural landscape (see Hirschkind 2006). The question is, what are festival participants directed to hear and see? This chapter focuses on a particular form of staging of traditional culture, village festivals in Bắc Ninh Province, to explore how visual imagery and sound have been used to frame quan họ as Bắc Ninh provincial culture; this, in turn, is part of the broader project to popularize the genre as a form of cultural heritage. I examine how sound and image are used to construct an "authentic" picture of quan họ by investigating how festival attendees learn to "see" the picturesque when they "hear" quan họ. I will consider this form of broadcasting as a kind of amplification that echoes beyond the local and that is indicative of the rising importance of cultural heritage in a global setting.

THE RETURN OF THE VILLAGE FESTIVAL

Village festivals, particularly in the pre-revolutionary period, were occasions in which villagers gathered to worship local gods, to enjoy themselves in the slack time after the spring and fall harvests, to come together and understand each other better, and to learn more about and practice their rituals and customs, a rare opportunity for villagers busy with subsistence farming throughout the rest of the year (Toan Ánh 1974:10–15). Villagers, government officials, and academics in Vietnam today refer to village festivals as an important (and often timeless) example of the communal (*cộng đồng*) nature and rural origins of Vietnamese culture.

However, immediately following the 1945 Revolution, Vietnamese village folk festivals were reduced in scale and frequency and in some places disappeared altogether. In particular, the religious and ritual elements of festivals were greatly reduced if not banned outright by the government. In contrast to its focus on the collection of folk culture, "the state in this period did not regard festivals as a critical component in their [*sic*] broader cultural agenda to create a new socialist society and culture" (Malarney 2007:525). Instead, festivals were aggressively discouraged by the Party as sites that encouraged wasteful spending, social evils, superstition, and backward or reactionary customs (see Malarney 1996, 2002). The government and Party began to spell out their ambivalent attitude towards festivals more explicitly in the 1960s, emphasizing that festivals should be geared towards educating the people by presenting acceptable national or cultural heroes as models of behavior (Malarney 2007:525–526). The State viewed festivals as sites of potential social disorder and tried to ensure that their organization was "improved" to conform to Party ideology (ibid.). Throughout the 1970s and 1980s, village festivals were openly discouraged and restoration of festivals that had not been held for a while was banned (Endres 2002:306).

Since the *Đổi Mới* reforms were initiated in the mid-1980s, folk festivals and other ritual practices have seen a resurgence or, in Luong Van Hy's (1993) terms, an "intensification." Anthropologists have remarked on the return of ritual and festivals and linked it to the changing political and socioeconomic conditions of Vietnamese society since reform resulting from greater surpluses, a lessening of the State's concern with ideological control, and feelings of economic vulnerability arising in the new market system (Luong Van Hy 1993; Malarney 1996; Taylor 2004). However, the impact and impetus for this resurgence cannot be relegated to political or economic motivations alone. Endres (2002), for example, argues that social science and humanities scholarship in Vietnam played an important role in the shifting State discourse on village festivals following reform. Beginning in the mid-1980s, scholars began writing about how village festivals were closely linked to communal life, agricultural cycles, and religious belief (Đinh Già Khánh and Lê Hữu Tầng 1993; Nguyễn Chí Bến 2000). Endres explains that this emerging discourse de-emphasized the negative aspects of festivals under socialist ideology and reframed village festivals as an important part of social and communal life in rural Vietnam. This new emphasis in the social sciences treated "festivals as a 'communal cultural activity' (*sinh hoat van hoa cong dong*) which contributes to the construction of national identity" (Endres 2002:303).

The 1989 "Regulation on Opening Traditional National Festivals" (*Quy Chế Mở Hội Truyền Thống Dân Tộc*, No. 54/VHQC) was, according to Endres, "a milestone in the politics of festivals" (2002:311, note 34) and since its passage, official interest in "the history and mechanics of festivals" has intensified (Malarney 2007:527). The regulation has subsequently been rewritten twice, in 1994 and 2001. What is notable is that the regulation has become increasingly specific about details such as, what is permitted or prohibited at the festivals, the definition of what kinds of festivals fall under the regulation's jurisdiction, the legal procedures for seeking approval or registering festivals, and so on. It should also be noted, as Endres' article nicely demonstrates and as festivals in Bắc Ninh Province support, that legislation often tends to lag behind the realities of practice. As such, the 2001 "Regulation on Organizing Festivals" (*Quy Chế Tổ Chức Lễ Hội*, No. 39/2001/QĐ-BVVTT) is the first of these three regulations to use the term "communal" (*cộng đồng*) in regard to village festivals.

The renewed interest in festivals as traditional culture must also be seen in light of how Vietnam views its culture in the international context. In their report at the 1993 Conference on Festivals, Trương Thìn and Phó Vụ refer to the success and limitations of implementing the 1989 Regulation on Opening Festivals in terms of the Party and government's program to improve national culture and also as a "response to the decade of cultural development launched by UNESCO" (1993:11).[3] In this context, encouraging people to value and preserve their traditions is no longer done only for the sake of "fostering a sense of shared national identity" (Endres 2002) but is also calculated to negotiate a place for Vietnam on the stage of world cultures. National cultural development, that is, is enmeshed in international cultural politics. This is not to assert that international exchanges and awareness of Vietnam's place in an array of world cultures is new. Rather, this awareness and its translation into the representational practices of the State, both nationally and locally, is increasingly institutionalized both in legislation at the national level (in dialogue with academia and provincial officials) and in practice at the local level (Đỗ Thị Minh Thúy 2004b; Nguyễn Chí Bến 2003).

While the impetus for the revival of festivals may not have been initiated by the State, recent attempts to control representational practices and governmental focus on these festivals at the local level indicate that the State continues to play an active and significant role in the direction cultural activities will take and believes itself to have a stake in how such activities are represented. In this context, since the early 1990s, national and Bắc Ninh regional authorities have become increasingly involved in regulating and representing regional quan họ activities, in general, and village quan họ activities and village festivals, in particular. Some representative dates include: 1991, the establishing of the regional spring quan họ competition in Bắc Ninh City; 1994, the Vua Bà Temple in Diềm Village (temple to the quan họ ancestress) was accepted into the national registry of historical relics and Vua Bà was officially recognized as the founding ancestor of quan họ; 1998, the Bắc Ninh Province Secondary School of Culture and Arts was established and the best students from the quan họ faculty began to feed directly into the professional Bắc Ninh *Quan Họ* Folk Song Troupe. And, as one singer in Diềm Village told me, since 1991 national and provincial officials have been attending the Diềm Village Festival, whereas in the past, only locals and friends from partner villages attended.

The State's current concern with controlling the ways that festivals are conducted is indicative of Vietnam's growing socioeconomic presence in international trade and cultural exchanges. This orientation, however, is not purely or single-handedly driven by the State. Rather, it is a process of collaboration between national and local officials, scholars, professional and non-professional singers, and ordinary citizens in the places in which these events unfold. These changes are visible in the fact that the public face of quan họ at Bắc Ninh village festivals has grown in recent years. Quan họ is drawn out and "shared," not just between singers who share long-term bonds of affection forged through singing, but between singers and non-singers in the village, and between villagers and festival attendees from elsewhere. Furthermore, quan họ is no longer one event among many at the village festivals of those localities with a quan họ tradition, but has become an overarching cultural theme of these festivals. Quan họ is a form of shared cultural capital that becomes the conceptual glue binding villagers to their heritage.

HỘI LIM, THE "MOST TYPICAL" QUAN HỌ FESTIVAL

The Lim Festival is held in the beginning of spring—on the thirteenth day of the first lunar month, honored guests from every region in the country and from abroad gather together to attend, making this into a major festival; it bears the spirit of the nation (Trần Thị Ngọc Lan 2003:19)

> Two pagoda festivals in three years,
> No one would miss falling under its spell.
> Old, young, girls and boys,
> Race each other to put on their shoes and come see it.
> The Lim Festival, whoever sees it longs for it,
> Tổ tôm, bài điếm,[4] pork sausage, nothing is missing.
> It is rumored that there is a weaving contest,
> And a restaurant with a hundred items that omits nothing delicious.
> (A folk verse from the Lim region, quoted in Trần Đình Luyện
>   (2000b:133)

In the chilly damp of the northern Vietnamese spring of 2003, I found myself standing in the middle of a bone-crushing crowd on muddy Lim Hill. Echoing all around me was a cacophony of over-modulated (hence distorted) and competing sound systems, each one broadcasting a variety of quan họ songs performed by the different quan họ clubs and local troupes, which were, that day, housed in blue-tarp-covered tents pitched up and down the side of the hill leading up to the Hồng Ân pagoda (Fig. 5.1). To my surprise, when I squeezed my way through to the crowded ring of small stools that served one tent's audience, the spectators appeared to be engrossed in and absorbed by the music, swaying and singing along (Fig. 5.2). While I heard the feedback and painfully loud crackling of the speakers, these spectators heard quan họ. This was the famous Lim Festival, touted as the most famous and well-attended of the spring quan họ festivals in Bắc Ninh.

The aural chaos that I experienced upon arriving at the festival seemed to me to contradict the claims and stories I had heard and read about the most famous and "picturesque" or "alluring" (hữu tình) of the quan họ festivals. I had heard the festival spoken of by the news media and people I knew in terms steeped in nostalgia and romantic visions of traditional culture and beautiful scenery. Instead, through dense crowds, I heard the distorted

FIG. 5.1. Tents on Lim Hill, Lim Festival, 2004.

FIG. 5.2. Audience gathered at a tent, Lim Festival, 2004.

and very loud sounds of singing voices filtered through microphones and poor-quality speaker systems set up under the tents. These voices were accompanied by musicians (a modern addition) or recorded instrumental accompaniment, which fought the voices of the singers for airspace. Adding to the din were the sounds of the hawkers calling through loudspeakers in the modern game booths set up along the road between the highway and the hill. I wondered how a festival so famous for its song could be so painful to the ears. It was evident that I was "listening" to something quite different from the other festival participants.

The Lim Festival is held on the thirteenth day of the lunar month of January in what is today the township of Lim, Tiên Du District, Bắc Ninh Province. Many of the regional festivals associated with quan họ are closely connected with temples and pagodas (Đặng Văn Lung, Hồng Thao, and Trần Linh Quý 1978:27). Likewise, the Lim Festival is held at the Hồng Ân pagoda to honor the death day of Bà Mụ Ả, who is both the village protective deity and the deity to whom the pagoda is dedicated. In pre-revolutionary times, the communal house festivals of the four villages surrounding Lim Hill were combined into the Hồng Ân Pagoda Festival. According to Đặng Văn Lung, Hồng Thao, and Trần Linh Quý, it is unclear when the Lim pagoda was built. According to legend, a woman named Bà Mụ Ả from Duệ Đông came to the pagoda to take orders and while there reached enlightenment. After this, whenever there was a drought, the local people prayed to Bà Mụ Ả for rain and later, because of her ability to work miracles, named her as the village protective deity (Đặng Văn Lung, Hồng Thao, and Trần Linh Quý 1978:36; Trần Đình Luyện 2000b). Based on the epitaph of his royal tomb, it is believed that in the first half of the eighteenth century mandarin Đỗ Nguyên Thụy donated a large sum of money and fields to the whole district of Nội Duệ to develop customs, festivals, and pagodas, including the Hồng Ân pagoda (Trần Đình Luyện 2000b:126). Subsequently, at the end of the eighteenth century, a high-ranking mandarin named Nguyễn Đình Diễn from the area donated money and fields to repair the pagoda, expand its activities, and change the date of its festival to the 13th day of the first lunar month (from the 15th of the 8th month, a full moon day) in honor of Bà Mụ Ả (Trần Đình Luyện 2000b:126ff., 2005; Trần Thị Ngọc Lan 2003).

Hồng Ân pagoda sits at the top of Lim Hill (Hồng Vân Sơn), on which the Lim Festival's main activities take place. The Lim Festival was not always held on a large scale every year, as it is now. In the second half of the eighteenth century, it was held only once in three years. After the Revolution and during the War of Resistance against the French and the American War, the festival was not held at all except during a brief period in the late

1950s. It was not until the 1980s that the festival was again regularly held, and, newly, every year (Trần Đình Luyện 2000b:134).

There are a number of different activities and games at the Lim Festival that are common to most village and pagoda festivals in northern Vietnam. These include the ritual procession (*rước*), wrestling competitions, cock-fights, a traditional swing on which two people stand and swing together, a card game called *tổ tôm*, tug-of-war, and others. The Lim Festival is most famous today, however, as the most "typical" (*tiêu biểu*) quan họ festival in the Bắc Ninh region. The Lim Festival is often called "typical" but, in fact, is in some respects fairly distinctive: "singing on the hill," for instance, is a practice particular to the Lim Festival. "Typical," in this usage, means, rather, that the distinctive (and shared) activities of the festival have come to represent the general, shared quan họ culture of Bắc Ninh.

Descriptions of quan họ activities at the pre-1945 Lim Festival emphasize the importance of the exchange of quan họ songs between young men and women that took place at the festival. In the days following Tết Nguyên Đán (the Vietnamese Lunar New Year) and leading up to the festival, the quan họ groups (*bọn*) of the different hamlets in the village would formally invite groups from their partner villages to come sing with them (Đặng Văn Lung, Hồng Thao, and Trần Linh Quý 1978:37). On the main festival day, however, quan họ groups from all over the region came to sing freely (that is, no specific invitation was needed), a practice that was called "singing on the hill" (*hát ngoài đồi*):

> The singers stood and sang with each other anywhere they chose on the hillside and were always surrounded by dense crowds of people. . . . If they liked each other after a few songs are exchanged, they would continue singing, otherwise they would go seek other partners. (ibid.:40)

Today, one still encounters dense clusters of people gathered around the singers on the hill. However, at the 2004 and 2005 festivals, the groups of singers did not wander freely on the hill seeking partner groups. Rather, they were housed in tents that had to be applied for from the festival organizing committee. The tents were set up as small, outdoor theaters, enclosed on top and three sides by blue plastic tarps (see Fig. 5.1). Singers stood under the tent and sang, facing outward, to the crowds gathered to listen. Each tent had a banner announcing the pair of clubs it housed and had its own speaker and amplification system broadcasting out to the crowd. Occasionally, the singers in the tent would invite audience members to join them, which emphasized the shared and communal feelings and atmosphere of the festival's singing activities. Therefore, the tents simultaneously created a sense of performance or theatricality and a sense of communal, shared culture. The singing on the hill, despite these changes to the way it is practiced, still looms large in the visual imagination and representation of the Lim Festival today.

REVIVALS: BROADCASTING THE INSIDE OUT AT THE LIM FESTIVAL

In 2005, at the request of the Tiên Du Culture Center, the UNESCO-sponsored quan họ clubs organized singing in three venues at the festival: the Bắc Hợp Temple (Fig. 5.3), a tent on the hill, and a private house. These three venues were chosen to represent "correct tradition" (cho đúng truyền thống). The teacher and director of the Hanoi UNESCO club informed me that the function of the UNESCO clubs was to restore (khôi phục lại) the way quan họ was practiced in the past at festivals. The temple singing was meant to represent festival singing (hát hội) in the communal house, the singing in the tent on the hill was to represent "singing on the hill" (hát ngoài đồi), and singing in the house would represent both the practice of groups singing with each other in houses (canh hát) and of villagers greeting each other at home on festival days (Thanh Ngân, pers. comm.). All three of these venues were set up in such a way that their activities were on display and broadcast to those outside their immediate space. Both the temple and the house had a speaker placed outside their doors to lure people in and the tent, like the other tents on the hill, was set up as a stage.

The UNESCO "house" at the 2005 Lim Festival was set up at the home of the quan họ club leader for Lim Township. The house, which lies on Highway 1 to the north of Lim Hill, consists of an older room in front, facing the road, and a newer house in back in which the daily lives of the inhabitants now take place. This older anteroom was set up with mats, a few stools and chairs, and the makings of the phoenix-shaped betel and areca on a plate on the floor, which some people were busy carving out (Fig. 5.4), and tea.[5] And, of course, there was also the amplification system. A large speaker rested on the sidewalk outside the door to this room, its broadcast songs acting as a call to passersby to come in and participate. Visitors came in from the street to "festival sing" in a recollection of traditional festival activities. Visits to the houses of family and friends are still an important social activity during village festivals in Bắc Ninh. Many of the visitors to the quan họ house at the 2005 Lim Festival were friends or acquaintances of the host, but a number of other people also wandered in, drawn in by

FIG. 5.3. The UNESCO quan họ club at the Bắc Hợp Temple, Lim Festival, 2005.

the sounds of singing. Many came in and sang a song or two; some stopped outside and looked in. Everyone who entered was encouraged to sing, and books of lyrics were passed around for those who did not know the words.

In a certain sense, the three UNESCO venues took on the character of a living museum in that they were representations of themselves. Regardless of UNESCO sponsorship, friends, acquaintances, and relatives would have stopped in to visit, drink tea, snack, and perhaps sing a few songs at the quan họ "house" and temple. However, because the venues announced themselves as such, by broadcasting out on to the street, they became a call to widen the communal nature of traditional practices beyond one's own circle of acquaintances. Anyone who can listen to the songs emanating from the house, temple, or tent speakers and "hear" tradition (in the form of quan họ) can participate in, or perform, its representation.

The three UNESCO sites were not the only places that broadcast quan họ to festival attendees in 2005. Singers at the communal house were also set up with speakers, the singing in the boats on the town pond was amplified, and one also encountered private groups of people singing in their own houses or shops.[6] With all the speakers, one merely had to follow one's ears

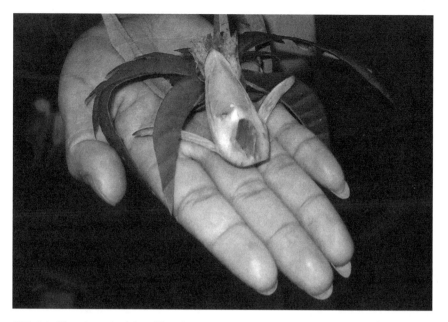

FIG. 5.4. The phoenix-shaped betel and areca.

to find out where the quan họ was. Walking around Lim Town at lunch-time, for example, my friend and I once again heard the sounds of amplified quan họ as we rounded a corner. In a small auto parts shop, a group of men were sitting down to eat and sing on some mats set up on the floor. We excused ourselves for interrupting and stopped to ask a few questions: I asked if they were *nghệ nhân* (village singers who trained over long years in the traditional oral manner) and they responded that, no, they were simply ordinary laborers who love quan họ. Today, they said, they were just "festival singing" and relaxing with some friends from another village because they enjoy singing quan họ. They explained that they had learned to sing and preserve old-style quan họ from village singers. I found that many people who practiced traditional-style quan họ, even in villages, do not refer to themselves as *nghệ nhân*. People reserve this term for those singers with a more officially recognized role in the preservation and dissemination of *quan họ cổ*. While it refers to singers who play an important role in transmitting *quan họ cổ* to the next generations and who have had long experience singing, it leaves those who do not fall under its designation, or who do not self-identify with the term, in an ambiguous place (particularly with regard to scholarship and legislation; see Meeker 2013). This group of men had gathered in an intimate setting to share a meal and some songs in a traditional (cổ) manner (and without musical accompaniment). They themselves asserted that they were just ordinary folk without a special or official connection to quan họ, yet they too cycled their song through the stereo system. They were sharing quan họ with one another in an intimate setting, a shared meal in a private (if open) space, and yet, their amplified song announced its presence to all nearby.

HEARING FOLK FESTIVALS, AMPLIFYING OURSELVES

Today, quan họ festivals in Bắc Ninh are heard by way of "amplification." That is, songs and activities are amplified internally, within the confines of the festival space, but with the larger intention of framing these festivals and quan họ as Bắc Ninh culture. I use the concept of amplification to refer, first, to the concrete practice of employing sound systems to augment and amplify singing and, second, to the transmission of sound that enables festival participants to hear themselves as participants in and representatives of a cultural form distinctive to their locality. In the first sense, the augmented and amplified sound has an aesthetic purpose. It contributes to the animated, noisy, and lively (rầm rộ, sôi nổi) atmosphere of the festival and is linked to relaxation and enjoyment. In the latter sense, I use amplification as a metaphor for the process that renders quan họ folk song audible beyond the confines of village practice and, ultimately, beyond the provincial borders. I would argue that amplification is that which connects the inside with the outside. Amplification links the inside of the Vietnamese home with the passerby on the street, links local culture to national culture, and ultimately by extension, links Vietnamese culture to world culture. It draws an audible, concrete version of Vietnamese culture out of the background of "the past" or "tradition" and, thus, makes it audible as cultural heritage.

Amplification is, metaphorically, and by way of an odd sort of circularity, that which allows Vietnamese to "hear" their traditions. The fear of disappearing traditions makes it necessary for tradition to double back to those places from which it is said to be disappearing, armed with the assertion that if we cannot hear ourselves as traditional, we are no longer in possession of our traditions. Once there, however, tradition "returned" must re-assert its claims to authenticity. Theories of media and recording technologies (sound and images) are often based on the premise that such technologies separate the body from its senses, rendering bodily productions (such as songs) external and hence, visible or audible (Crary 1998; Kittler 1990; McLuhan 2000 [1962]). That is, these technologies have "the power to split sources and copies" (Sterne 2003:20). This, in turn, leads to a distinction between "authentic" originals and copies. The voice, as a bodily function and the purveyor of tradition in quan họ singing, is drawn out from the body via electronic mediation and made material through recording technology. Older village quan họ singers often stressed that they sang "naturally" or "simply" (*hát mộc*) (literally, plain or unvarnished), that is, in an unembellished way and without the use of microphones; the voice alone carries the song. This style of singing is necessary to achieve the intimacy and social connectedness that is created among partnered singers in the village context. In contrast, the amplified voice is removed from the body of the singer and, thus, metaphorically removed from the "source tradition." No longer belonging only to the singer, it has become representation. Of course, folk songs as collective cultural creations and performances have always been shared and have never "belonged" to an individual singer. What sets the amplified song apart is that when it is channeled electronically through speakers, it is also physically removed from the social body.

Nevertheless, Sterne cautions that in focusing on "sources" and "copies," we focus only on the "product" not on the "process" with the result that "technology vanishes, leaving as its by-product a source and a sound that is separated from it" (2003:21). In this context, the amplified quan họ song at the village festival must be seen not as a poor copy of a village original but, rather, a process of authentication that occurs in a different social order from the social practice of quan họ. The work of the folk festival in the context of heritage culture, thus, is to appear to reconnect the voice and its electronically mediated representation such that the festival participants hear something that is authentic, is Vietnamese, and is "ours." Thus, the louder such amplification grows, the more self-consciously it is controlled. The new heritage culture of Vietnam increasingly seeks to minimize the appearance of amplification and mediation but all the while counts and depends on it as that which will announce Vietnam's arrival on the global stage of world culture.

SINGING THE PICTURESQUE

The amplified quan họ heard at the festivals is closely linked to the "picturesque." The picturesque is a form of contemporary representational practice that has been used to great effect in the popularization of quan họ with a national audience while at the same time emphasizing quan họ's connection to the land and customs of Bắc Ninh Province. This is reflected strongly in the practice of singing in boats on the village pond, a popular festival activity in which a group of singers paddle around the pond in a colorfully painted dragon-shaped boat (Fig. 5.5). Singers use remote microphones linked to a speaker system on the shore. Often, they will sing along with piped-in instrumental backup. The singing on the pond always draws large crowds of spectators who gather on the banks of the ponds. The singers on the boats are most often local villagers who sing in the modernized style. Some villages also invite the professional Bắc Ninh *Quan Họ* Folk Song Troupe to sing on the boats.

Singing in the boats on the pond is often referred to as a "tradition" of the quan họ festivals. However, I have found no mention of this practice in the pre-reform literature on the Lim Festival.[7] Nonetheless, several of my Vietnamese friends and colleagues with whom I attended these festivals (none of whom are quan họ singers) remarked to me that the singing on the boats seemed "more natural" to the music than some of the other quan họ events. One friend, for instance, commented that the scene of quan họ singing on the boats at the Lim Festival was more suitable to quan họ than the singing on the hill where the singers were set up in tents. It "fit better," she said, with the music and "made it more beautiful." In similar fashion, at the Diềm Festival in 2005, a film crew from the Institute of Culture and Information filmed a couple of young singers out by the Cầu River, which runs

FIG. 5.5. Singing on the pond, Diềm Village Festival, 2004.

past some of the village fields. A farmer who tended some of the mulberry fields came by, concerned that the crew were trampling her new seedlings. I asked her if she sang quan họ, to which she replied that she did not. She then added, gesturing to the singers, that "they sing next to the river to be correct." All my inquiries to village singers, however, indicated that they did not sing outside in this manner in Diềm. Therefore, even local non-singers linked quan họ with a picturesque and natural outdoors setting.

The strong association between the picturesque and quan họ revealed in the comments and the claims that quan họ sung out of doors is the most "correct" is closely linked to the modern quan họ performance style. To be sure, many quan họ lyrics express a romantic and lyrical sense of the rural landscape and singing on the hill was an important part of the Lim Festival in the past. However, the exchange of songs between groups of singers in village practice did not depend upon a visual picture of quan họ as picturesque. Rather, the socially oriented singing practices of *quan họ cổ* required an ear trained to hear the creation of long-standing relationships based on sentiment through the act of singing itself. Interestingly, with the scene of the singing on the boats, a link between nature and sound is constructed by way of visual imagery. Rather than hearing the quan họ inside temples and communal houses or on Lim Hill as that which is most "authentic," my friends *saw* the singing on the boats as most natural. Singing on the boats is a visual depiction of a scene that explicitly links nature, as timeless and organic, to a vision of "authentic" quan họ. Without the timelessness of the imagery, the sound of the singing would have less impact as "tradition" and would, rather, be heard as modernized song. Explicitly linking quan họ to nature allows it to be cast as timeless and unchanging regardless of whether it is in the old or the new style. But to frame quan họ in this way requires a removal of the voice from its culturally embedded place in the bodies of singers and the social relationships between groups of singers.

"Authentic" quan họ for these festival participants does not depend on its sound (as clean or as audible) but rather on its ability to reference what Sutton (1996) calls "the auditory imagination."[8] Quan họ's significance at the festival lies not in the mechanics of hearing, per se, but rather in the social practice of listening. The people gathered around the tents and ponds listened to quan họ as Bắc Ninh local tradition or, more widely, as Vietnamese tradition. What initially appeared to me as the chaos, aural and visual, of the festival was often described in positive terms by those attending and those writing about it in the media. The atmosphere was said to be lively or exciting and happy (*sôi nổi* and *vui vẻ*) but also an example of "our local culture."

COMMERCIALIZATION

At the Lim Festival in 2004, near the top of Lim Hill, my friend and I ran into some women we had met the previous Saturday at the annual Bắc Ninh quan họ competition at the Cultural Center in Bắc Ninh Town. They gave us some stools to sit on while we watched them assembling the betel and areca in the form of phoenixes (see Fig. 5.4). One of the competitors from the other day handed me one and said it was a "souvenir" (kỷ niệm). As we sat, some of the other women in the group were putting up the tarps and setting up speakers. We got up to go look around some more and the woman making the betel and areca phoenixes asked for a donation, so I put 2,000 Vietnamese Đồng (roughly .15 USD) on the plate. As we walked away, my friend looked quite surprised and said "so commercial!" "Traditionally," one would never have asked for money in return for offering betel and areca, the traditional way of inviting guests. Betel and areca are very important to the social exchange and politeness of quan họ practice in the villages and more generally in Vietnamese culture. Betel chewing in Vietnam, while still common among the older rural population is less common among urban dwellers and young people, both rural and urban. However, it still remains an important cultural and social symbol in many areas of Vietnamese life including weddings, temple and altar offerings, and village quan họ. It is always present at quan họ events in the villages and many of the older women will sit and prepare it throughout the event, either in the shape of the phoenix or in the more common wedges. Therefore, the direct exchange of money for betel in this context was seen by my friend as a breach of etiquette, and a violation of a fundamental rule of social exchange. Offering betel and areca is one of the first steps in establishing a social relationship; acceptance of the betel and areca indicates a willingness to enter into the relationship. At the singing on the hill in past practice, for instance, new relationships were initiated based upon the offering and acceptance of betel and areca between groups of singers. Acceptance meant acceptance of an exchange of songs and of the potential for a long-term singing relationship.

Later that day, at the village pond, where singers were paddling around in a dragon-shaped boat, the people lined up at the shore were also giving money, placing it in a large round quan họ hat held by one of the female singers. These latter donations were not seen as commercial to the same degree as the money that was given in exchange for betel phoenixes. Giving a donation to the singing groups on the boat was seen as a donation of "support." Donations given at the tents were similarly framed, yet because they were in actuality a direct monetary transaction, they were seen as "commercial" and inappropriate by my friend. Giving in certain contexts is seen as a duty. At staged performances by the local quan họ troupes at village festivals, people give donations during the performance. Periodically the "MC" will announce the names of the donors and the amounts given. Such support, following the logic of the gift (Mauss 1990) is framed as a gift, but is never absolutely voluntary.[9] The donations at the pond, therefore, were seen as more acceptable because they were framed in terms of a notion of collective responsibility important to village communities; giving is a demonstration of membership in the community.

In 2005, the setup for the singing on the boats at the Lim pond was the same as the previous two years, with the one large speaker on the side of the pond and people crowded around three sides of the pond to watch. That year, however, there was also a very large advertising board erected on the little island in the middle of the pond. The board was so big that it actually obstructed the view of the opposite side of the pond—and at times the singers in the boat—and dominated the whole scene. The sign was composed of lyrical pictures of quan họ singers interspersed with flashy car advertisements and was topped by a banner reading "The Traditional Lim Village Festival. . . . We will meet again" (Hội cổ truyền quan họ làng Lim. . . . Đến hẹn lại lên) (Fig. 5.6). The expression "we will meet again," is a phrase from a quan họ song and has become a catchphrase or slogan of quan họ and quan họ festivals in the region. It embodies the strong sentiments of friendship and longing for those times when one can again meet and sing with one's friends. Therefore, the incorporation of this phrase on an advertising board, visually announced quan họ as an advertisement for the Bắc Ninh region and directly linked quan họ to modern progress and development in contemporary Bắc Ninh. The point is even more striking in light of the growing calls, which intensified in 2004, to cut back the commercialized practices of the festival.[10]

At this "most typical" (and, therefore, the most attended) quan họ festival, the Lim Festival, the question of staging is emphasized precisely through the removal of the traces of the stage. Beginning in 2004, I began to hear, both from officials at the Bắc Ninh Department of Culture and Information and in the news media, a growing emphasis on the need to "restore" the festival (and others in the region) and its atmosphere to its "traditional" state. For example, in November of 2004, the newspaper Văn Hóa Chủ Nhật (Sunday Culture) reported on the conference "The Lim Festival—traditional and modern" organized by the Department of Culture and Information of Bắc Ninh and the Tiên Du District People's Committee in anticipation of

FIG. 5.6. Advertisement on the town pond with singers on the boat in the background, Lim Festival, 2005.

the next year's festival: "most of the opinions [expressed at the conference] were in agreement that the Lim Festival is a traditional cultural activity most typical of the Northern Kinh Bắc region, the place which cultivated and developed a special form of *quan họ* folk song" (NG. H. 2004:3). Participants of the conference expressed particular concern about how to preserve the traditional value of the festival today and, for instance, criticized the way in which the tents on Lim Hill are lined up one next to the other such that "the sound of singing of this tent drowns out the sound of singing of the next tent." This situation resulted in sound that was "chaotic, blaring, and causes the diminishment of the beauty of *quan họ* folk song" (ibid.).

The phrase, "the sound of singing of this tent drowns out the sound of singing of the next tent" (*Tiếng hát của lán này lấn át tiếng hát của lán kia*), ironically invokes the phrase "the sound of the singing drowns out the sound of the bombs" (*tiếng hát át tiếng bom*). This latter phrase is often cited to invoke the way that song mobilized and inspired people during the Revolution and the War of Resistance. By invoking bombs, this article simultaneously references the power of music as a mobilizing force for national culture and the potential threat to a sense of harmonious representation of community by the chaotic clash of sounds. Therefore, the attempt to reduce the echo to a more harmonious level seems to be a call to mobilize sound once again for a more socially unified purpose. This implies that the objection is not to the echoing broadcast of sound per se but rather to the internal clash of sounds, which would point to the uncontrolled proliferation of market competition on Lim Hill (indeed, these objections to sound are raised in the context of "commercialization").[11] At the festival, the representation of quan họ is held as a shared responsibility. The sounds transmitted through this form of public broadcasting, thus, should aurally transmit a "shared" culture and reinforce the "communal" nature of the festival as expressed in current discourse. In doing so, the sound of the hill becomes the sound of the festival itself and the place of the festival, Lim Hill and its environs, becomes a stage in and of itself.

In response to concerns over the clashing sound systems in the tents, in 2005, the organizing committee permitted fewer tents on the hill, only six, in order to improve the sound. Indeed, the tents were not just fewer in number, but were also spaced farther apart on the hill and no two tents were set up directly across from each other. It was still very loud on the hill, but the overall sound was less chaotic than in previous years. On a brief trip back to Vietnam in March of 2006, not long after that year's Lim Festival, a friend and colleague reported that the festival had been significantly changed that year. It had "returned" to the traditional way of "singing on the hill" by eliminating the tent setups and having groups of singers wander the hill freely "as they did in the past."[12] This "return" to the old way of singing on the hill is by no means a return to the old forms of social practice to which it belonged. It is, instead, a new engagement with the notion of staging such that the entirety of the festival becomes the stage. The festival does not merely stage cultural heritage events but is itself staged as cultural heritage. Indeed, the organizers of the folk festivals discussed here are ever more concerned with minimizing the "negative" impacts of modern life on traditional culture by hiding those traces behind a facade of "authenticity." The more they attempt to hide the traces of staging, however, the more the festival, and by extension the villages themselves, become stages.

Trần Đình Luyện, a scholar and former director of the Bắc Ninh Department of Culture and Information, expressed this in his call to expand the "space" (không gian) of the Lim Festival in the future to include a wider array of Bắc Ninh cultural attractions: with its "center at Lim hill, [the festival will] open up more widely to include all the villages/communes in Lim Township, [including] the commune of Nội Duệ and the commune of Liên Bão, and all the surrounding tourist areas: historical and cultural sites, quan họ villages, and trade villages" (Trần Đình Luyện 2005:19). The call to extend the cultural "space" of the festival to include other regional attractions embodies a recognition that in this context, the stage of culture is, in fact, Bắc Ninh itself.[13] Thus, Vietnamese performers, academics, governmental officials, and all other citizens, are all envisioned as purveyors and consumers of provincial heritage, including quan họ.

REVIVALS, AGAIN

At the Châm Khê Village Festival in 2005, a stage was set up at one end of the communal yard, along the pagoda's side wall. When we arrived in the morning, quan họ singers from several villages had already gathered on stage to sing. They sat on straw mats in a semicircle. A sound system was set up to the left of the stage and there were two large and very loud speakers on either end of the stage. The singers on stage sat with their co-villagers: Bồ Sơn on the right, Diềm at the back right, Xuân Ổ at the back left; the left side had a rotating group of people (Fig. 5.7). Local quan họ singers told

FIG. 5.7. Châm Khê Village Festival stage, 2004.

me that Châm Khê has only set up the festival stage for five or six years. Before that, they explained, *quan họ cổ* singing at the festival was only held in people's houses or at the pagoda. In the past five or six years, then, *quan họ cổ*, as a form of local tradition, has been "shared," displayed, and literally staged as culture in the Châm Khê Festival setting. The singers sitting on stage faced outward to a densely packed audience of locals and visitors from elsewhere in the region who crowded around the stage. In doing so, these singers announced, or sang, their presence as the embodiment not of the tradition of quan họ singing itself, but rather of its ability to be staged as cultural heritage. At one point, audience members, including one man from Hanoi, were invited on stage to sing, though not necessarily quan họ songs. This particular local stage demonstrates the extent to which the work of representing quan họ has become the work of all, from the village level to the provincial level and up to the national level.

CONCLUSION

Festivals have become an important visual and aural manifestation of folk tradition in the heritage culture of Vietnam. Their construction in academic discourse as "communal," how they have been affected by and are situated within the market economy, and the growing international interest (both economic and cultural) in Vietnam, have played an important role in how festivals have returned and continue to evolve in the post-reform period. The centrality of festivals in the current discourse on culture emphasizes the continuing, if changed, importance of local cultures to the national culture. All locals, now, must become the arbiters of and in possession of their own culture if Vietnamese culture as a whole is to maintain and assert its objective status as heritage on the world stage.

As discussed throughout this book, local culture has played an important role in the construction of a national culture since the Revolution. Since the *Đổi Mới* reforms initiated in the mid-1980s, practices such as those described in this chapter are increasingly taking place at a point of intersection between the renewed attention to and restoration of local cultural practices in Vietnam and the growing infiltration of a globally informed, internationally defined concept of culture as "heritage" into local spaces. Today, the idea of local culture derives force and value from its embedded place in the global discourse on cultural heritage, which itself emerged in an international context in which notions of cultural relativism and cultural rights are deployed by both nation-states and ethnic groups trying to negotiate space for themselves on the stage of world cultures. The particular way in which folk festivals in the quan họ region are heard today by participants reflects the shifting discourse on village festivals. Participants at these festivals are asked to step outside of themselves in order to "hear themselves" in such a way that everyone is included in the work of constructing an audible representation of quan họ folk song as Bắc Ninh culture. By tuning in, as it were, to themselves as participants in a local cultural form, they become attuned to the wider discourse on heritage that represents them as the owners and practitioners of something of value. Such representational practices work on several levels: to draw locals into a space of national culture conceived of as encompassing a diversity of local cultures and to draw nationals into the space of global culture.

Conclusion

Heritage and the Afterlife of Songs

One of the core concerns of this book is how discourses on quan họ folk song have been constructed and deployed over time by various national and local actors. Struggles to gain representational control over quan họ since the Revolution are firmly situated in the historical conditions of the time, the politics of local and national culture, and the dramatic transformations of society and social life since the Revolution. As argued in chapter one, these struggles were particularly intense after the Revolution as the Party and government in the North worked to consolidate their power and to build a new socialist culture for the nation. In this context, they marshaled local folk forms as the building blocks of a new national culture. After the *Đổi Mới* reforms initiated in 1986 that began the process of political and economic liberalization, these struggles have taken on new dimensions. The focus on and resurgence of numerous traditional cultural and religious practices since reform has given rise to new questions and concerns for academics and the government including fears about the loss of traditional culture as the elder generation of folksingers born prior to the Revolution passes away, the question of how to balance preservation of quan họ with its popularization, and how to promote the value of Vietnamese culture on the global stage. Quan họ singers share concerns about the loss of their tradition but also must grapple with the impact that increased attention to their activities has on their musical practice and daily lives.

Since the development of new-style quan họ in the late 1960s, representations of quan họ often split practice into two poles of "age-old/traditional/rural" and "new/modernized/urban" quan họ. This discursive division of practice into binary opposites tends to hide the ways that these two forms of practice are, in today's society, dependent upon each other. Yet, while this opposition may seem an oversimplification of the complex ways that old and new quan họ interconnect, it cannot be ignored; it reveals much about how Vietnamese culture more generally is constructed in contemporary society. In his research on the effects of urbanization on people living at the margins of Ho Chi Minh City, Erik Harms demonstrates how Vietnamese tend to conceptualize urban space in terms of the binary opposition between urban and rural. He argues that this reveals what he calls a " 'folk structuralism' that explains society through binary oppositions quite similar to those cast aside by poststructuralist theory" (2011:226). Whether or not such binaries are overly simplistic or an accurate representation of reality is somewhat beside the point; rather, they are "a fundamental element of the social landscape" that "do something" (ibid.).

Splitting quan họ practice into "old" and "new" forms does a number of things, as discussed throughout this book. In some cases, it is used to valorize certain practices as more authentic than others, as the focus on intangible heritage does for elderly village singers. In other contexts, it emphasizes the importance of development of culture, as the creation of the Bắc Ninh *Quan Họ* Folk Song Troupe did in the late 1960s. Or, as seen in the period following 1945, the "old" folk culture was used as a building block for the new culture and a new national music under socialism. Articulation of this binary is pervasive among Vietnamese scholars, government officials, and singers, although different groups deploy it for different purposes.

One concept that ties this binary together into a single discursive field is sentiment (*tình cảm*). Feelings of sentiment and the relationships of exchange that sentiment is based upon bind people to the music they sing, regardless of what style they perform. Yet, how sentiment is embodied and enacted in different time periods and contexts varies. Musicians in the post-1945 period used the concept of sentiment to indigenize international socialist ideology, even going so far as to articulate an "ideology of sentiment" that would enable music simultaneously to be properly socialist and truly Vietnamese. They sought traces of sentiment in folk music and then attempted to incorporate it into their compositions. For them, sentiment was a form of ideological musical practice rooted in an essential Vietnamese character. While, for these musicians, sentiment was rooted in folk culture, for village quan họ singers, it is rooted in the body and in social interaction. It is the act of exchanging songs and proper speech and gestures that cement enduring friendships between partnered singers. As such, sentiment is a form of social practice. In staged performances of quan họ, on the other hand, sentiment is enacted in ways that index changing social values of contemporary society. Here, sentiment is a representation of and reference to an idealized picture of social life rooted in village tradition.

Regardless of the different ways that sentiment is understood and deployed across time and venue, it is always *felt* to be Vietnamese and to be Vietnamese is to feel proper sentiment. Sentiment is an embodied concept that is embedded in the broader social order of the times. The Vietnamese concept of sentiment highlights how the emotional (felt and lived experience) is inseparable from social action: one is seen to have proper sentiment in quan họ or in Vietnamese social life more generally only when one acts in morally, socially, and at times politically appropriate ways. Thus, sentiment is a form of Vietnamese cultural performance that binds singers to their social order.

Another theme that runs throughout this book is the impact that the focus on intangible cultural heritage has had on quan họ in the past decade. Placing sentiment at the center of an analysis of quan họ practice and discourses problematizes the intangible cultural heritage model. Intangible cultural heritage forms, despite the rhetoric that culture is process (UNESCO 2010), rely upon an identifiable standard that can be registered (for example on the UNESCO lists) and against which all other forms can be measured. George Yúdice quotes the president of the World Bank, James D. Wolfensohn, as saying "Heritage gives value. Part of our joint challenge is to analyze the local and national returns on investments which restore and draw value from cultural heritage—whether it is built or living cultural expression, such as indigenous music, theater, crafts" (2005:9). Influential international institutions, Yúdice argues, such as the European Union, the World Bank, and the Inter-American Development Bank have been integral to the reshaping of culture as "resource" as part of broader neo-liberal and development agendas. Indeed, in order to be funded, culture must provide at least "an indirect form of return" that is in some way quantifiable (ibid.:13, 15). Yet, sentiment is not "quantifiable" and cannot be owned. Experiential, it is truly intangible, embodied, and becomes manifest only through social interaction. Sentiment, thus, cannot be articulated effectively as intangible cultural heritage, in which culture becomes a form of capital or a "resource for both socio-political and economic amelioration" (ibid.:9) in the global marketplace for culture. A full understanding of Vietnamese culture, thus, necessitates an ethnographic attention to the processes through which truly immaterial practices and feelings, such as sentiment, are formed.

An issue related to the development of cultural heritage is the concern with preservation and development of traditional culture. Quan họ researcher Lê Danh Khiêm told me that "if we want to develop *quan họ*, then we cannot simply preserve it in its original form because then it would only exist in the bodies of the *nghệ nhân* [village singers]" (pers. comm., 6/13/04). The particular emphasis on the need to preserve (*bảo tồn*) folk music sits uneasily with the pressure to develop (*phát triển*) it in part because of the early policy to build a new national music based on a foundation of folk music. According to musicologist Bùi Trọng Hiền, there is a need to define what, precisely, each of these terms means in relation to music in order to avoid the "paradoxical situation" in which preservation has come to mean "not developing" and development to mean "not preserving" (n.d.: 6). Ethnomusicologist Tô Ngọc Thanh similarly emphasizes the need to distinguish clearly between preservation and development, which, he says, should exist parallel to each other. He does not object to original compositions that are inspired by folk music. However, he argues that an "original" form must also be maintained for its own sake and not changed or "corrected" to make a new composition, otherwise Vietnam's musical history and heritage will be lost (pers. comm., 3/28/05).

Bùi Trọng Hiền also contends that a lack of understanding of what preservation entails leads to ideas that traditional music is "backward" (*lạc hậu*), that only a selection need be preserved (to be added to one's performance repertoire), and that it merely serves as the raw material for other musical composition. In recent decades, in the context of increasing emphasis on intangible cultural heritage, the Party and government has increasingly emphasized and funded the preservation and reconstruction of traditional culture. In fact, the selective nature of preservation that Bùi Trọng Hiền objects to is central to the process of institutionalizing the cultural heritage and why the paradigm of cultural heritage takes on such force in the world today. Cultural heritage relies upon individual countries to transform social practices into representations of culture in order to make it marketable as heritage on the world stage. This process selects the most visible and salient practices as representative of the whole. To do so, it must transform (and politicize) the original social function of those practices, even while the resulting representation depends upon referencing that social function. By casting this process as cultural rather than political in what Pemberton (1998) calls a "culturalist discourse," the heritage paradigm in some ways becomes a more influential and totalizing force than revolutionary ideology.

The emphasis on intangible cultural heritage introduces a new and different form of ambiguity into how the new/old binary is applied to quan họ by enforcing the adoption of an internationally defined concept of authenticity along with a preservation agenda that may not be entirely compatible with local (indigenous) concepts and agendas. I conclude here with two discussions that illustrate the impact of the heritage discourse on quan họ, each of which raises broader questions about the impact of the culture of heritage on local places. I describe, first, how one of the oldest quan họ songs has been resurrected in the heritage context and second, how the story of quan họ Bắc Ninh continues to unfold for local singers in the post-UNESCO inscription years.

HỪ LA: THE AFTERLIFE OF A SONG

Hừ la vui vẻ thế này
Vui bằng đám hội đốt cây nhang trầm
Yêu nhau điếu đổ lăn xe
Phải duyên thì lấy chớ nghe ai dèm.

Hừ la, as happy as this,
As happy as lighting a stick of incense at the festival
If you fall in love with someone and you think it is your destiny,
You must get married, do not listen to anyone's disparaging words.[1]

Hừ La is said to be one of the oldest, most traditional, and most difficult quan họ songs. *Hừ La* also has become emblematic of what academics and older village singers see as the fate of *quan họ cổ*: a genre in danger of disappearing because of the modernization and mass mediation of songs, the younger generation's lack of interest, and a new, faster pace of life.

During my time in the field, I heard *Hừ La* sung only twice. Once was at the final meeting for the joint UNESCO and Vietnamese Ministry of Culture and Information Pilot Project to select a list of quan họ "living treasures" held at the Museum of Ethnology in Hanoi in January 2004, and the other was in Châm Khê Village in Bắc Ninh.[2] The two elderly male singers who sang the song in the first of these instances are said to be the only remaining village singers who remember how to sing it. However, when one of them later sang it for me in Châm Khê Village, even he had to reference jotted down lyrics and frequently stopped to redo a phrase. As quan họ researcher Lê Danh Khiêm remarked, today the song can only be "groped for" (mò)[3] by a couple of older singers (pers. comm., 6/13/04). These two singers explained that many people had considered the song "uninteresting" (không hay). This resulted from the particular style of singing Hừ La in Châm Khê, in which the second and fourth lines of verse are switched with each other. As a result, the singers above explained, "while the poetry is very pleasing to the ear, when it is sung, it is backwards," which makes it "confused," "incoherent," and "nonsensical." As a result, people did not like to listen to it and stopped singing it. In addition, the song is structurally one of the most difficult to sing. The Châm Khê version of Hừ La, for instance, has only four lines of poetry but takes about ten minutes to sing. An elderly singer in Diêm Village also remembers the words to Hừ La as sung in her village and remembers being taught the song but cannot sing it anymore because it is "so difficult." She says she failed to learn it well in the first place because the woman who taught her many years ago was very old at the time and, therefore, was not "precise" when she sang it.[4]

For older village singers, Hừ La is a sign of that which has already disappeared because they no longer sing it in village practice and those outside the village or academia would not know what Hừ La was. It is something that was let go because no one wanted to sing it anymore and thus was a part of the organic evolution of an oral folk form. However, in the context of cultural heritage and as a result of the attention of Vietnamese and foreign researchers, Hừ La signifies the passing of the previous generation, those who taught the elderly singers of today. It also signifies the passing of a genre of music embedded in village life and centered on the generation of social bonds between singers. Hừ La has become the discursive sign of that which has been lost; even the last two singers of Châm Khê Village who can sing the song, stumble or grope their way through it. Thus, Hừ La is in a way doubly lost: lost to the singers themselves and lost to the electronic record of heritage culture that seeks to collect that which is disappearing. Indeed, when the singer in Châm Khê sang Hừ La for me to record, he made a point of saying that this was for reference and as a form of academic collection only. This was because he was singing alone, not as a pair, and because of the rough nature of his memory of the song. Yet, instead of being forgotten, Hừ La has been picked up as a sign of the importance of the work of cultural heritage. Despite its "disappearance," it remains as a discursive warning about the importance of preserving the cultural heritage and the dangers of inattention to those songs now on the verge of disappearance.

Elderly quan họ singers are seen to embody quan họ, but often in such a way that it becomes inaccessible to those outside the tradition as demonstrated by the example of the singer who was unable to learn *Hừ La* well because her teacher was too old. Her teacher held *Hừ La* in her memory and body, but because of age was no longer able to sing precisely enough to pass it on. In this sense, the bodies of the singers become an important context for the designation of tradition. This process enables intangible cultural heritage to become tangible, that is, to become policy and a form of cultural capital for the State. That which cannot be articulated, or that which exists only in the bodies and faded memories of elderly singers, *can* (the discourse goes) be represented by the State or by scholars. But what of these elderly singers? How precisely do they become living traditions and what does it mean for them?

PREPARING FOR UNESCO

In the summer of 2009, I interviewed village officials and residents of Diềm Village for a new research project on the planned tourism development of the quan họ region. In a group interview, representatives of the Diềm Village Elders' Association, Women's Union, and Youth Union all described their role as serving the needs of the village and of guests to the village, which might include greeting village guests, showing them around, making sure they get where they need to go, feeding them, etc. They saw this role as continuing with the development of quan họ tourism in their village.[5]

When we asked the secretary of the Youth Union what he hoped for with regard to tourism development in Diềm, he directly linked it to UNESCO, responding that "today, above all, the wish of the Ministry of Culture is to try to get *quan họ* accepted as world cultural heritage." Interestingly, he expressed this as the wish of the ministry (not himself, as the question had specified). When asked why this wish, he responded: "Because this wish belongs to all Diềm villagers, in particular, and all of Vietnam, in general. Once the 'world' [i.e., UNESCO] accepts it, quan họ will be famous all over the world, many guests will know about it and come here [Diềm] for a visit." However, this official view seemed to be in tension with feelings of distance between villagers and foreigners. As one interviewee said, "we don't understand foreigners very much." This is in large part because of the language barrier, which all the representatives felt to be a problem. There was also a secondary sense of distance in that foreign visitors were often guests of the village or provincial leadership. In this context, the members of the organizations might provide services (food, open up historic monuments, etc.) for these visitors, but have very little or no interaction with them. What struck me in particular was the comment of the representative of the Elders'

Association that "recently we hosted a group, probably from UNESCO, in preparation for this acceptance of cultural heritage [to the Representative List of the Intangible Cultural Heritage of Humanity]. In general, that group had a lot of foreigners, a few Japanese men, also Koreans. They all came here. There were a lot of them but we were only on the outside; their only direct [contact] was with the leaders of the district, or the cultural [cadres] of the commune. We were only the committee to provide service from the outside." Implicit in this statement is a sense that the cultural gatekeeper is always somewhere above: for the mass organizations, it is the village leadership; for the village leadership it is the province. These comments also complicate the claims that the cultural heritage inscription process through UNESCO includes the full participation of local populations.

QUAN HỌ AFTER UNESCO

In the summer of 2010, I returned to Bắc Ninh and Diềm Village to visit friends and see firsthand what changes the September 2009 inscription of quan họ to the UNESCO Representative List of the Intangible Cultural Heritage of Humanity had brought to the village and quan họ practice. In fact, very little had changed with regard to quan họ and the expected tourists had not yet arrived. The most dramatic changes to the village had more to do with redistricting: the village had recently been placed under the jurisdiction of the provincial capital, Bắc Ninh City, and thus was being enfolded into the municipal infrastructure (such as water and waste pipelines). Diềm Village was slowly merging with the city as new housing popped up along the roads between city and village.

In an interview with an official at the Bắc Ninh Department of Culture, Sport and Tourism that July, I asked what plans and accomplishments the UNESCO designation had brought about for the province. After carefully detailing the fourteen-point plan for preservation and development of quan họ and placing a strong emphasis on local-level management of preservation and teaching of quan họ, he explained that the UNESCO designation is for recognition only and does not provide any support. He then mentioned that one of the difficulties of the designation is that many people keep checking in on their progress in implementing their plans. With mild exasperation, he remarked that it had only been a few months since the designation and theirs were long-term plans. How could they have accomplished their goals this quickly?

While the provincial officials work through their plans for preservation and development, what of the elderly singers who have been designated "living treasures" (in Vietnamese, *nghệ nhân*)? On this same trip back to Bắc Ninh in 2010, I asked one of these "living treasures" to tell me about her experience with UNESCO (or, as she called it *công ty S-Cô*, "S-Co Company"). I include the transcript of her response here in its entirety as it embodies succinctly and neatly many of the themes discussed in this book and raises important questions about the value of the living treasure designation for those so named.

INTERVIEW TRANSCRIPT WITH ELDERLY SINGER, JULY 26, 2010

First, to prepare the list [of living treasures of quan họ], UNESCO invited me to Hanoi for a meeting. Then I was invited to a meeting of the Department in Bắc Ninh [Department of Culture and Information]. At the UNESCO meeting in Hanoi, I sang a few phrases, then we were taken to lunch. I had lunch with Mr. Trần Đình Luyện, the director of the Department, and [another singer]. A few months later, I was invited to a meeting of the Department in Bắc Ninh. They said UNESCO was going to recognize quan họ as [belonging to] the world's cultural heritage. They discussed the way to prepare the necessary paperwork for qualified artists. At first, I did not go for it since they said the artist had to have been actively performing by 1945 or earlier. But after reading the documents carefully, I realized that they accepted anyone who was in any quan họ singing group by 1945 or earlier. In 1945, I was learning quan họ at my grandmother's house, since she hosted a quan họ group. So I did the paperwork . . .

When I was about eleven or twelve, I was able to perform well, and thus was accepted as a junior singer in the group of the girls at my grandmother's house. They let me go to events in Bịu Village and sing a few times. As time passed by, the old women in the group passed away, and the group disbanded when I was sixteen. I then created a quan họ group by myself, with about eight or nine girls. Some of them were at my age, and some were older. I taught them quan họ, and we came to sing at village festivals, or any appropriate occasions. . . . We did not have many partnerships (*kết nghĩa*), but some male singers often came to visit us to sing together (*hát giao lưu*).

In 1990, there were eleven quan họ groups in my village, including my group. The village committee told us to stop acting as separate groups and form a single quan họ team. So we formed a team, and I was elected to be the team leader. I was the team leader from 1990 to 2002. Then, my husband fell ill and I stopped participating in the team and being the team leader. Since then I have been teaching quan họ. I teach quan họ classes in the village. Children, adults, even old people my age.

Among my quan họ students, there were four singing pairs who got the first prize at the quan họ singing competition of our province. There were also some pairs who got the second prize and the third prize. Some of my young students got A prizes at the competitions on June first (the International Children's Day). The Bắc Ninh School of Culture and Art sends me quan họ students every summer for one month, so that I can teach them. This has been going on for about eight or nine years.

So I wrote all those things in my profile to UNESCO. They said I deserved the first place in the list of forty quan họ artists in Bắc Ninh Province, since I had contributed a lot, achieved a lot, and received a lot of certificates for those contributions. After that, I was recognized by UNESCO as a quan họ artist, although they were only supposed to recognize people who were eighty and above and I was only seventy-nine at that time. After the recognition, the Bắc Ninh government had a party to congratulate us. The party was for one day and one night. Each artist received a certificate and five million VND [about 250 USD]. So there were forty artists in our province, Bắc Ninh Province. Seven of them are in Diềm Village . . .

Before the seven of us were recognized as quan họ artists, they only invited me and [one other singer] to the meeting in Hanoi. UNESCO did not go to Bắc Ninh. They only issued the certificates in Hanoi. Then our provincial government went to Hanoi to get the certificate and brought the certificate to Bắc Ninh. Our province had a very big celebration, which went on for several days. There were so many guests, and the province spent more than ten billion VND [about 520,000 USD]. They had an extremely big party. A representative of UNESCO came to the celebration. The artists did not sing at the celebration. We had other quan họ singing groups and other performing groups in the province perform at the celebration. There was a great variety of performances. All types of performing arts that we have in Bắc Ninh were shown there. But they did not tell us the artists to sing. We just needed to attend the celebration. We went there two times on two consecutive days. On the first day, we stayed from the afternoon until night, and on the second day, we stayed from the morning until night. On the evening of the second day, each artist received a certificate and a laurel wreath from the Bắc Ninh government.

In Bắc Ninh Province, now the four eldest artists receive a monthly salary from UNESCO. I don't receive the money since I'm not that old. They only offer it to people who are ninety years old. This salary is just an allowance for the eldest artists.

That's all from UNESCO. I have not heard from them since then. That's all I have to tell you.[6]

WHOSE HERITAGE?

In 2005, the Folklore Association of Vietnam established age criteria for *nghệ nhân*, which it translates as "masters of folklore" and is elsewhere referred to as living treasures, in which a person must be at least seventy years old (in 2005) to qualify (Tô Ngọc Thanh 2007:19). This calculation is based upon the age of the *nghệ nhân* at the time of the 1945 Revolution. The generation of quan họ singers now (in 2011) in their eighties and nineties were trained by the last generation to be fully trained before 1945 and, thus, they are already one generation removed from the "origins" of quan họ (Lê Danh Khiêm, pers. comm.). Some village quan họ singers also refer to themselves in this way, signaling that many of these villagers are themselves conversant in the academic discourse on heritage culture. One singer in Thị Cầu Village who was in his sixties in 2004, for instance, described himself as belonging to the "fourth generation" of singers. These singers also have had long experience with politically motivated changes to quan họ practices at the village and provincial level, as the singer's story about her "living treasure" designation, above, indicates.

In the reform era, the 1945 Revolution continues to loom large in the academic understanding of the practice and place of folk music in Vietnam. As discussed for the revolutionary period, Vietnamese ethnomusicologists often pinpointed this year as a turning point in the research and the practice of folk music. However, since reform, there has been a subtle shift in the way 1945 is referenced in relation to music. While it continues to serve as a dividing point between "old" and "new" music, 1945 now marks a new concern with what is believed to be a rapidly disappearing cultural heritage that necessitates a preservationist's attention. The reframing of culture as heritage in recent decades has served to institutionalize this temporal marker in new ways. Whereas after the Revolution 1945 was institutionalized in law and policy as a symbolic marker of the new socialist nation, after the rise of cultural heritage, 1945 is institutionalized as a sign or brand of Vietnamese cultural authenticity. The singer who applied to UNESCO was told that 1945 was an absolute marker of authenticity; she just fell in (barely) behind the line and thus was able to apply for recognition of her authentic status as quan họ artist. For villagers 1945 is an arbitrary marker in the continuum of quan họ practice; it does not affect what they know or do. Therefore, the fact that this singer was given recognition for her accomplishments and work teaching and organizing quan họ activities in the village seems quite reasonable, "despite" the fact that her age was under eighty at the time. For the Party and government and for all who read through the UNESCO inscription, however, 1945 indexes authenticity by drawing a line in the sand between the past and the present. In the name of culture, the UNESCO inscription has reinforced and made permanent what continues to be a politically expedient symbol of Vietnamese nationhood.

While I offer a critique of how the discourse on intangible cultural heritage focuses attention on origins and authenticity and thus risks obscuring other forms of quan họ practice that do not live up to the standard it establishes, I also stress that it is important to recognize that worries about culture loss are shared by quan họ singers, young and old. In recent Western scholarship, the concept of "authenticity" has been critiqued for naively attributing a sense of origins to something that is in fact a cultural construction originating in the Western tradition (see Handler 1986). The implication is that in the contemporary world, those who buy into the concept of authenticity are somehow duped into romantically or naively partaking of a false and commercialized shell of what was once real culture. However, when faced with research subjects who enthusiastically embrace the concept of authenticity, some anthropologists have contested this view by demonstrating how indigenous groups are in fact taking up the Western notion of authenticity with active agency in order, for instance, to survive in the tourist market (Bunten 2008) or to protect what they see as their "authentic" culture from outsiders (Muehlmann 2008). Thus, while I agree that the concept of authenticity should be considered as a form of discourse and that a search for "real" origins is a red herring, I too find this view leads to troublesome questions in the field. Many Vietnamese singers, scholars, officials, and ordinary people are concerned with authenticity and feel strongly that it can be found, restored, and preserved. At the same time, they are fully aware of the political context in which they practice their cultural forms. Like Harms' claim that the binary opposition between urban and rural "does" something, authenticity too does many things in contemporary Vietnam. Attention to what it does can reveal much about what is experienced as real and meaningful in contemporary Vietnamese society. Authenticity, like sentiment, is felt to be real and, thus, is an important component of social life.

NOTES

INTRODUCTION

1   In 1997, Hà Bắc Province was divided into what are today Bắc Ninh and Bắc Giang provinces.

2   The Hùng kings are said to be the first Vietnamese dynasty and said to be of legendary origins (see Taylor 1983). For the full legend of Vua Bà, see chapter three.

3   The villages identified in the 2009 application to UNESCO to inscribe quan họ on the Representative List of the Intangible Culture of Humanity are the same as those identified by Đặng Văn Lung Hồng Thao, and Trần Linh Quý (1978).

4   See Woodside (1988) for a detailed discussion of the imperial examination system.

5   For example, the second line of the song *Gió Mát Giăng Thanh* (Cool Breeze, Bright Moon) as taught by a Diềm Village elder is *"Bỗng đâu thấy khách bên tỉnh sang chơi"* which corresponds to the line *"bỗng đâu có khách bien đình sang chơi"* (when from the frontier a guest turned up) from the *Tale of Kiều."*

6   For more on the importance of the concept of "home place" (*quê*) in contemporary Vietnam, see (Jellema 2007).

7   The Convention Concerning the Protection of the World Cultural and Natural Heritage was adopted by UNESCO at its seventeenth session held in Paris on November 16, 1972 and the issue of intangible heritage was raised by some of its members. The 1980s and 1990s saw a proliferation of UNESCO activities related to furthering the goal of safeguarding intangible cultural heritage around the world. Chronologies, resolutions, and other histories of this process can be found on UNESCO's website: http://www.unesco.org/culture/ich/en/convention/.

8   In 2004, a colleague from the Vietnam Institute of Culture and Information explained to me that the Institute's director, Dr. Nguyễn Chí Bền had recently requested that researchers at the institute use the term "cultural heritage" (*di sản văn hóa*) instead of "traditional culture" (*văn hóa cổ truyền*).

9   Proclamation of the World Decade for Cultural Development, A/RES/41/187, 8 December 1986, 100th Plenary Meeting of the UN General Assembly. The

proclamation can be accessed online at: http://www.un.org/depts/dhl/resguide/r41.htm

10 The "Convention for the Safeguarding of the Intangible Cultural Heritage" convened by UNESCO in Paris in 2003 defines intangible cultural heritage as follows: "The 'intangible cultural heritage' means the practices, representations, expressions, knowledge, skills—as well as the instruments, objects, artefacts and cultural spaces associated therewith—that communities, groups and, in some cases, individuals recognize as part of their cultural heritage. This intangible cultural heritage, transmitted from generation to generation, is constantly recreated by communities and groups in response to their environment, their interaction with nature and their history, and provides them with a sense of identity and continuity, thus promoting respect for cultural diversity and human creativity"(UNESCO 2003).

11 A candidature file for the Worship of the Hùng Kings in Phú Thọ was submitted in 2011.

12 Malarney explains that: "The main idea behind this ethic is that the village constitutes a moral and affective unity in which villagers should be ready to assist each other in their times of need, not simply out of obligation, but out [sic] ties of affect, sympathy, and compassion. In mundane moments, the realization of this ethic entails common courtesies, mutual respect, a willingness to compromise, and assistance if requested" (2002:129).

CHAPTER 1. MUSIC AFTER THE REVOLUTION

1 Shaun Malarney explains that the term "feudal" "assumed tremendous significance from the 1940s onward. Feudal was a catchphrase used to describe any idea or practice that either reproduced relations of inequality or asserted the existence of non-empirically verifiable causality in human life. At a general level, party ideology defined all aspects of the culture and ideology of the pre-colonial social order as feudal as they validated the inequalities of pre-revolutionary social life, such as husbands over wives or mandarins over commoners" (2002:58–59).

2 The word *lành mạnh*, which I here gloss as "wholesome," is often used in opposition to that which characterizes "social evils" such as prostitution, pornography, gambling, etc.

3 He maintains that it is not so much a Marxist influence as a Russian and Stalinist influence in the first period of the Revolution that leads to these tasks. Patricia Pelley maintains that, in the 1950s and 1960s, Vietnamese post-colonial historians looked to Stalin's five-stage model of history "not because Vietnamese writers nurtured Stalinist proclivities, but because the Stalinist model recognized the importance of prehistory," which was important in re-claiming a Vietnamese past as Vietnamese (2002:48).

4   Gironcourt (1942) includes a short annotated bibliography on research on music and general ethnological works on Indochina that touch upon music from the colonial period. See also Waterman et al. (1949).

5   Today, some ethnologists, while still valuing Nguyễn Văn Huyên's contributions, are beginning to question the lack of historicization of Huyên's cultural analyses as was made evident in a series of lectures on Vietnamese culture by Nguyễn Chí Bền I attended at the Culture University in Hanoi in March and April of 2004. See also, the work of Hoàng Yến (1919).

6   This quote is from a translated reprint of Le Van Hao's article "Fifteen Years of Ethnological Research in North Viet Nam" ("15 nam nghien cuu dan toc hoc o mien bac") originally published in *Nghien cuu Lich su* (Historical Research), no. 133 (July–August 1970).

7   In the 1950s and 1960s, Vietnamese post-colonial historians were also working to create a new historical canon for Vietnam. The shape that this "new history" (*lịch sử mới*) took was determined both by the need to reconfigure the past in terms of Marxism-Leninism and to write against colonial histories of Vietnam that portrayed it both as merely derivative of China's history and culture and as the primitive recipient of a beneficent French civilizing force (Pelley 2002:7–8).

8   Interestingly, Phạm Văn Chùng uses the word *di sản*, which I have here translated as "inheritance." This is the word that is translated as "heritage" in the current Vietnamese discourse on culture and has gradually taken precedence over the use of "traditional culture" (*văn hóa truyền thống* or *văn hóa cổ truyền*). His use of the word here emphasizes an objective status of what is collected that enables it to be put to use in service of the new nation. I have chosen to use "inheritance" here to avoid confusion with the contemporary usage.

9   A focus on the voice in its connection to tradition is also found in post-colonial India. Weidman finds that the twentieth-century South Indian discourse on classical music relied on what she calls a "politics of the voice" in which "the voice came to be associated with Indianness and not Westernness, originality and not reproduction, humanity and not mechanization, tradition and not modernity." She argues that the particular way that the voice is valorized in karnatic music is itself modern "for it is precisely *within* modernity that the voice comes to occupy such a privileged position" (2006:6; emphasis in original).

10 Even today, many musicians and performers repeatedly refer to how folk song genres and individual songs within a particular genre are abundant (*phong phú*).

11 In *chèo*, a northern genre of Vietnamese folk theater, *vỉa* is an introductory verse that is sung freely and without rhythm. It is accompanied by music but not by drums, which are essential to other, rhythmic *chèo* songs.

12 These three principles, translated here by Marr as "patriotism," "mass consciousness," and "scientific objectivity" are *dân tộc hóa*, *đại chúng hóa*, and *khoa học hóa*. A literal rendering could be national-ization, mass-ization, and science-ization as the suffix *hóa* connotes a process of becoming. Kim Ngoc

Bao Ninh, with whom I agree, prefers "nationalization" to Marr's "patriotism" because of the complicated nuances of the word *dân tộc*: "there is a sense of great urgency and an edge of desperation in Trường Chinh's version of *dân tộc hóa*. The phrase thus means more than 'people' or 'nation' or even 'patriotism.' It demands an active return to what is uniquely Vietnamese, or, simply put, it asks for Vietnamization" (2005:29).

13 This was Trường Chinh's report to the Second National Culture Conference in July 1948. This argument is also found, more succinctly, in the short document "Some Major Principles of Today's New Culture Movement" (*Mấy nguyên tác lớn của cuộc vận động văn hóa Việt-Nam lúc này*) (1985 [1945]).

14 The article defines "the new person" (*con người mới*) at length as follows: "The new people, new heroes are ordinary simple people, every day self-sacrificing and resolutely struggling laborers. They are factory workers, miners, construction workers, farmers, who industriously produce to restore and develop the economy. They are people who experienced land reform and are excited to go down the road of cooperative production. They are soldiers who day and night protect our borders, who make every effort to train the body and study politics, military affairs and culture in order to protect the motherland, protect the peaceful work of labor for the people. They are the intellectuals who ardently contribute to the task of building the economy and culture of our country. They are active people, loveable characters of our society who our brothers and sisters in our country's arts need to make every effort to praise and glorify" (1957:8). For more on the concept of the "new person," especially in relation to Hồ Chí Minh's role in fostering a new moral code for the new society, see Malarney (2002:chap. 2).

15 Patricia Pelley details how, in the war period, the concept of "national essence" (*quốc túy*) came to be emphasized over the idea of national unity. The Vietnamese understanding of national essence was built upon Japanese influence, their readings of German and French romantic nationalists, and from what she calls a deliberate misreading of Stalin's *Marxism and the National Question* (2002:140–142). Writings on music that I have reviewed more commonly use the term "national character" (*dân tộc tính*) or "national spirit" (*tinh thần dân tộc*) to express similar ideas (see Viện Nghệ Thuật 1972).

16 The *Music Review* (*Tập San Âm Nhạc*) was published by the Musicians Union until 1957, when it changed its name to *Âm Nhạc* (*Music*). The *Music Review* contained essays contributed by many of the prominent musicians and composers whose opinions were reflective of the times.

17 For detailed accounts of the period and its main proponents see Boudarel (1990) and Kim Ngoc Bao Ninh (2005).

18 In 1960, the authorities announced that several of the participants had been tried for treason and given harsh prison sentences (Boudarel 1990:172–173).

19 This was the second National Arts Congress organized in the DRV. The first was held in 1948.

20 One might translate *luồng sáng tác* literally as "schools of composition." "School" here is comparable to its use in "school of thought."

21 For more on Vietnamese revolutionary policies on superstition see Malarney (1996).

22 There is no inclusion of the original lyrics with the song or any contextualization as to its original content or the type of song it was beyond the title. The song was "collected and given new lyrics" by Nhật Lại and "harmony and instrumentation" by Tạ Phước.

23 According to Tô Ngọc Thanh, only songs with improved lyrics have been integrated into the school curricula (pers. comm., 4/15/04). See Norton (2002) for discussion of how *chầu văn*, the music used in spirit mediumship ceremonies, was altered to conform to political and ideological imperatives.

24 There are many different terms used for this type of music (see Arana 1999 and Le Tuan Hung 1997). I have followed Arana's use of *nhạc dân tộc hiện đại*, which she translates as "modern national folk music."

25 Tô Ngọc Thanh comments that this interim section very often mimics "birdsong."

26 Although "texture" is potentially very interesting, he gives no further explanation of how he uses this term, nor does he provide the Vietnamese term.

27 In attendance at performances of this music, I was continuously struck by the musicians' demonstrations of virtuoso in the form of Western-style solos that attempted to dazzle audiences with their ability to appear to exceed their instrument's capacity. Such virtuosity usually took the form of ever-increasing speed and melodic complexity.

28 Such ornamentation is at times "improvisational" in the Western sense of spontaneous and creative rendering of a base tune. However it can also be fixed phrasing, as in village quan họ singing in which ornamental additions to a base poem and melody are always sung in the same way by pairs of singers. This is necessary as the two singers are meant to sound "as one" so a high degree of coordination is required. Pairs of singers from different localities, however, will sing different variations. For a good discussion of how a musical base melody is expanded in Vietnamese instrumental performances, see Norton (2009).

29 Borrowing is often evident, for instance, in certain quan họ songs. Village singers are aware of this crossover and will sometimes indicate, for instance, that "this is *quan họ chèo*" (that is, a *chèo* song adopted by quan họ). For examples of borrowing of other genres within quan họ see Hồng Thao's comprehensive collection *300 bài dân ca Quan họ Bắc Ninh* (300 Quan Họ Bắc Ninh Folk Songs) (2002).

30 For more on the concept of "mode" in Vietnamese music see Trần Văn Khê (1992).

31 *Hơi* or *hơi thở* means "breath." The breath is central to the particular performance style of Khuốc village, where this singer is from. However, Trần Văn Khế translates *hơi* as "modal nuances" and *điệu* as "mode" by which he means

a system composed of a number of pentatonic scales and refers specifically to the "tuning on an instrument according to the different modal scales (such as *Bắc* (Northern) or *Nam* (Southern))" (1992:552). There are a variety of terms, depending on the region of use, for "mode," which include *giọng* (voice) and *cung* (refers to the notes in the traditional pentatonic and the seven-note scales) (see also Tran Van Khe 1980). I have chosen to translate *hơi* here as "breath" in this instance as this singer was emphasizing the lack of musicological method in the past and because of the particular emphasis on breath in this village.

32 This can be seen as a mapping of Western musical reality onto the Vietnamese along the lines of Thongchai's conceptual framework in *Siam Mapped: A History of the Geo-Body of a Nation* (1994). He argues that a Thai sense of identity and nationhood developed by the overlapping with and eventual displacement of an indigenous sense of space, boundaries, and margins by Western ones that were determined by the introduction of the map as a mediator between human perception and spatial reality and by notions of sovereignty.

33 This issue, of course, has changed with the widespread availability of electronic recording technology. For example, the province of Bắc Ninh has made it a policy to archive and collect quan họ on tape. However, this new technology comes with new issues such as limited access to the collections and the deterioration of collections under poor storage conditions and poor tape quality. Poor quality of materials continues to be a problem today even with the introduction of CDs and DVDs now widespread in Vietnam.

34 It was only through learning by direct oral transmission, for instance, that I was able to distinguish the subtleties of the vastly different vocal techniques of quan họ folk song and *chèo* theater.

35 The songbooks were published in 1960 and 1961. They were based on a collection compiled by the Committee for Musical Research–Department of Arts, under the Ministry of Culture, in the 1950s and published by the Music Publishing House (*Nhà Xuất Bản Âm Nhạc*).

36 This designation only appears on the front of one of the songbooks, *Dân Ca Tày* (Tày Folk Song), though other books are listed in this category on the back cover of the book.

37 The "you" of the passage is a translation of the Vietnamese word *bạn* or literally "friend." This is an informal, egalitarian, and inclusive form of direct address that is still used today.

38 Some of the regional variations that Văn Cao identifies have different names such as Lý Con Sáo (southern and southcentral versions), Con Sáo Sang (Phú Thọ version), and Lý Giang Nam (Quảng Trị version) (Văn Cao 1972:161).

CHAPTER 2. EMBODIED PRACTICES AND RELATIONSHIPS OF SENTIMENT

1 Quan họ lyrics of a song from the *La Rằng* song type as recited by Nguyễn Thị Bàn, Diềm Village. *Người* literally translates as "person" or "people." In this case,

the "people" are quan họ singers from another group with whom the singer has a friendship or partner relationship.

2   More generally, the word *chơi* is used to mean "to do something for fun" as in "*đi chơi*" or "go play" and can also be used to mean "play music" (*chơi nhạc*).

3   Lê Danh Khiêm contends that "until the end of the 19th century, beginning of the 20th century, the word '*bọn*' was used to indicate a homogeneous (social, economic) collective and did not carry the negative meaning of today" (2001:189). The word *bọn* today is often used with a negative connotation to mean "a group of people" with the understanding that they are up to no good. It can, however, be used informally with an affectionate meaning of "my group of friends" (e.g., *bọn tôi*).

4   Elderly singers in Diềm Village claim that there were eleven *bọn* in their village.

5   An exception to this is Thị Cầu Village, which only had men's *bọn*.

6   According to Lê Danh Khiêm, there are two theories as to why each *bọn* must have at least five *liên anh* or *lien chị*. One relates the number to the five elements of yin and yang (*âm dương ngũ hành*) and the other is that it is based on the five-tone scale (*ngũ âm* or *ngũ cung*) (2001:191).

7   *Giọng* can also mean "accent," as in northern accent (*giọng miền Bắc*).

8   In chapter four, I will discuss how the interpretations of the lyrics change when quan họ is put on the modern stage.

9   See, for instance, Hồng Thao's annotations in his "300 Bài Dân Ca Quan họ Bắc Ninh" (300 Quan họ Bắc Ninh Folk Songs) (2002).

10 The words of the base poem are highlighted as bold text. These are the first two lines of a response song (*bài đối*) in the *La Rằng* melody (*giọng*). This version is taught by Ngô Thị Nhi in Diềm Village.

11 In fact, the evenness of the tempo or rhythm prompts some non-singers to complain that village quan họ is monotonous in comparison with modernized quan họ.

12 This aspect of *quan họ cổ* singing is crucial and caused me some confusion at first as I had read in a number of English-language articles on quan họ that it is "improvisational," which did not seem compatible with this very coordinated and synchronized pairs singing. In the past, I have been told, a local troupe would have had one literate person who composed lyrics for them, occasionally composing a response song (same melody with different lyrics) on the spot to counter the other troupe's song. Also, there are variations on the same songs that occur from village to village in Bắc Ninh. However, I did not encounter anything resembling "improvisation" in singing, as it is understood in English.

13 The Linguistics Institute's Vietnamese Dictionary defines *bụng* as: "Stomach of the human being, regarded as the symbol of thinking and deep sentiments in relation to person and actions" (*Từ Diển Tiếng Việt*, 2001). *Bụng* is also associated with kindness, as in the phrase "*người tốt bụng*" (a kind or kindhearted person).

14 "*Chơi vừa nghèo về kinh tế nhưng lại giầu về tình cảm.*"

15 Some singers did refer directly to the feelings of respect and deep emotional attachments singers had for each other. All singers I spoke with were in agreement about this latter aspect.

16 *"Hai bên hiểu nhau lắm, hiểu nhau bằng những câu nói, câu hát. Chứ không phải là nói với nhau người ta quý nhau. Người ta hiểu nhau ở trong cái câu hát."*

17 Bùi Trọng Hiền explained that the angle at which a pair of *quan họ cổ* singers face each other is that at which the ideal resonance between the two voices occurs (pers. comm.).

18 Eye contact in Vietnam today, particularly between men and women, can be a sign of intimacy. I learned this the hard way on one of my first visits with local officials in Diềm Village when one of them joked awkwardly about how "deeply" I gazed into his eyes after I had made eye contact when speaking with him.

19 As related to me by a female singer in Diềm Village.

20 Village singers at times refer to the other group of singers as quan họ.

CHAPTER 3. "HOW MUCH FOR A SONG?"

1 In this chapter, I use the word "center" as a direct translation of the word most frequently used in this context by the village singers I worked with.

2 *Lề lối* literally means the "way of doing" and is used to refer to the oldest group of songs that must be sung at a gathering of village singers, called a *canh hát*.

3 The authors use the phrase "to correct (*chỉnh lý*) the lyrics," by which they mean to rewrite lyrics to bring them in line with socialist ideology and goals.

4 The conferences were held in 1965, 1967, 1969, 1971, 1974, and 1981 (Lê Hồng Dương 1982:697).

5 In this case, the singers were speaking with me, an American researcher. They may very well have tailored their responses, out of politeness, and answered differently with Vietnamese researchers. It is, however, important to point out that the American War is not an essentialized marker for these singers but rather exists in the broader continuum of the revolutionary period.

6 For more on the history of Vietnamese conservatories, see Le Tuan Hung (1997). For more on the Bắc Ninh Province Secondary School of Culture and Art, see the 2003 booklet issued by the school for its fifth anniversary, "5 Năm Trường Trung Học Văn Hóa Nghệ Thuật Bắc Ninh" (5 Years of the Bắc Ninh Secondary School of Culture and Arts).

7 In the summer of 2004 I sat in on these classes with the fifth quan họ class, which was then in its first year of study and I sat in on the summer 2008 classes. Certain other villages in Bắc Ninh also stake their own claims to the birthplace of quan họ.

8 The designation also excludes. Those who are not recognized as *nghệ nhân*, regardless of what they actually *do*, tend to fall outside the authenticity net cast

by culture workers. As there is no equivalent term for *nghệ nhân* in English, I use the Vietnamese term in this book when appropriate (Meeker 2013).

9 This teaching model is also used at the National Conservatory in folk music classes (though the teacher might hand out a photocopied sheet of lyrics).

10 At the 2004 competition, for example, the first prize was a gift of 1,000,000 VNĐ, or approximately 70 USD.

11 By March of 2006, ten months after I left the field, a portion of the final stretch of dirt road into Diềm Village had been paved. In the subsequent three years, many new houses have been constructed along this road, rendering the village ever "closer" to the center. In 2008, Diềm, which was formerly in Yên Phong District, was administratively placed under the jurisdiction of Bắc Ninh City.

12 This is a game in which a ball must be wrested away from other contestants and placed into a square hole dug into the earth. The game represents harmony between the earth and sky or the heavens. The ball's round shape and red color represent the heavens and the hole in the earth is square, representing the earth. When the winner places the ball in the hole, harmony is achieved. The game is also played as part of a ceremony to pray for rain in times of drought.

13 This story was related to me by an elderly singer in Diềm Village. There are slight variations in the details of the legend according to the teller (for instance, some leave out the second contest, saying that Vua Bà had no choice but to accept the results of the first contest of *cướp cầu*, and others tell that Vua Bà "descended" to earth after the storm to found Diềm Village). The legend is retold by researchers and is also recounted in a small pamphlet put out by the Đền Vua Bà, the temple to Vua Bà. The princess in the legend is worshipped here as the ancestor of quan họ (*Thủy tổ Quan họ*). See, for example, Trần Đình Luyện (2000a:58).

14 The word that the storyteller used initially for "king" is *vua*. She moved from "king" to "mandarin" (*quan*) by saying, "All the *quan* stopped," that is, all the attendants to the king stopped. For other versions of this legend see Đặng Văn Lung, Hồng Thao, and Trần Linh Quý (1978) and Lưu Khâm, Nguyễn Viêm, and Nguyễn Đình Tấn (1956).

15 Thanks to Ben Junge for this insight.

16 Diềm is the folk name (*nôm na*) for Viêm Xá, which is the official character-based name of the village. I have chosen to use Diềm Village, as it is the name most commonly used by villagers themselves. See also Trần Chính (2000:30–31).

17 George Yúdice argues that in today's globalized world, culture has become a "resource for both socio-political and economic amelioration." His argument resonates well with the ways that folk culture is increasingly framed as heritage in Vietnam (2005:9).

18 This team, also sometimes called the Đội Quan Họ, is the official organization for quan họ practice in the village today.

19 Từ Điển Tiếng Việt 2001. In the past, a night watchman would strike a tocsin at the start of each of these time periods.

CHAPTER 4. STAGING QUAN HỌ, TELEVISING NEW SOCIAL RELATIONSHIPS

1 *Chèo* theater has a long-established dance tradition that was familiar to northern Vietnamese at the time that the modernized quan họ form was developed.

2 In the past five years, however, with the proliferation of national and cable channels and increased selection of available programs, television viewers are less likely to encounter programs about quan họ.

3 *Lưu không* (literally, "keeping or holding space") is a musical interlude that marks the division of one lyrical phrase from the next. In *chèo* theater, for instance, this is an interlude that allows the singer to catch his or her breath. This was the only time I heard the term used in reference to quan họ singing, which indicated a familiarity with music terminology that would explain his direct equation of these helping words with "music."

4 These authors also reported in 1962 that some of these customs had changed in certain villages. For example, Diềm and Bịu villages now may marry, despite their *kết nghiã* relationship and singers from Bồ Sơn and Y Na still may not marry each other but if singers from Bồ Sơn partner with a group from Khả Lễ, they are permitted to marry (Nguyễn Văn Phú et al. 1962:23, note 1).

5 Rivers figure centrally in quan họ songs as the quan họ region is cut through by a number of rivers. For more on traditional Vietnamese architecture see Nguyen Khac Tung (1993).

6 During my research in Bắc Ninh, I worked extensively with Nguyễn Trung. I base much of the substance of the following discussion on his work and views.

7 For an extended discussion of this legend and a collection of a number of different versions see Đinh Gia Khánh (1999).

8 The Lim Festival is the most well-known and widely attended quan họ festival in Bắc Ninh. In the past, quan họ groups (*bọn*) would gather on Lim Hill and seek out other groups with whom to sing and form partnerships. For more, see Đặng Văn Lung, Hồng Thao, and Trần Linh Quý (1978).

9 In contrast, as discussed in chapter three, elderly singers in the quan họ villages speak of spending all their time, as youths, "following older singers around" in order to learn to sing. Because they were always surrounded by the music in this way, they claimed, when they actively began to learn songs taught by older singers, they picked them up quickly and easily without writing anything down.

10 The twirling hand motions he made were in imitation of the *chèo* theater dance style.

11 This is not to say that there are not producers at the national station who claim to speak about "authentic" quan họ. I interviewed one producer of traditional music programs from Vietnam Television, for instance, who is very careful in her choice of singers and of the accuracy of her information on traditional

music. She emphasizes the importance of giving her viewers a true understanding of folk music and is very concerned with issues of authenticity. As a result, she always consults and often incorporates the commentary of scholars of traditional music in her shows. She is, perhaps, exceptional in that she is married to a scholar of traditional music.

CHAPTER 5. BROADCASTING TO OURSELVES AT THE QUAN HỌ FESTIVALS

1 Thanks to Đỗ Thị Thanh Thủy for sharing this with me.

2 Some of this direction came from one of the local singers who was acting as a sort of director of ceremonies as well as a liaison between the singers and film crew.

3 They are referring to the World Decade for Cultural Development, 1988–1997 (Proclamation of the World Decade for Cultural Development, A/RES/41/187, 8 December 1986, 100th Plenary Meeting of the UN General Assembly).

4 A traditional card game played at festivals.

5 Betel and areca constructed into a phoenix is particularly associated with quan họ in Bắc Ninh. The body of the phoenix is made from the areca nut and the wings and head from the betel leaf.

6 Vietnamese houses and shops generally are directly open to the street. Doorways are often wide double doors (for houses) or, for stores, the entire width of the store is open to the street (these would have a roll-down gate). In other words, they are open and visible to passersby.

7 Singing on the boats is also dependent upon electricity and remote microphone technology. At the 2005 Diềm Village Festival, for example, the singing on the boats ended early because the village lost electricity. I was also told that singing on boats is traditionally a part of the Thổ Ha Village Festival but Thổ Ha is not one of the "original" quan họ villages, indicating that it is also a new practice there. At this festival, singers invite each other to sing on boats on the river. Scenes depicting singing on the river are frequently incorporated in Bắc Ninh Television productions such as those of Nguyễn Trung, discussed in chapter four.

8 Sutton describes the overlapping sounds at special public events in Java in terms of *ramé* or the positive connotations given to busyness, noisiness, and the sense of not being alone as a possible explanation for Javanese seeming unconcern with poor sound quality. He proposes that a cassette tape of poor quality may be a "trigger for the auditory imagination" to Javanese rather than an inconvenience, as many Westerners would consider it (1996:261).

9 The obligatory nature of the donation was made clear to me at a staged performance of new quan họ by the village troupe at the Diềm Village Festival. I was sitting with some village singers in the audience when a friend came over and informed me that she was beginning to hear some comments about how I had not yet donated to the group on stage. I immediately had a friend carry

up a donation. After it was announced, a woman behind me slapped my arm playfully and complained, "why did you give so much!" The donation, in my case, was augmented by a "request" that I also get up on stage and sing a quan họ song. In this case, the money was expected (as it was from everyone else) but singing the song was an act that would cement the feelings of sentiment between me and the village.

10 Such calls to reduce the commercial aspect of the festivals are not entirely new. They are present in legislation following reform and were also discussed as early as 1993 at the Conference on Festivals (Trương Thìn and Phó Vụ 1993).

11 The objection to competition, however, is limited. The competition that occurs in "traditionally" and officially sanctioned ways is supported.

12 Thanks to Nguyễn Thị Kim Chi for sharing this with me.

13 Trần Đình Luyện's use of the word "space" resonates with many of the entries on the UNESCO Representative List of the Intangible Cultural Heritage of Humanity, many of which have "Cultural Space" in their titles. This includes Vietnam's inscription "the Space of Gong Culture."

CHAPTER 6. CONCLUSION

1 *Hừ La* as taught by Nguyễn Công Trúc and Nguyễn Công Rứa from Châm Khê Village, Bắc Ninh. I owe thanks to Nguyễn Kim Chi for help with this translation.

2 At the time I heard the song sung at the Museum of Ethnology meeting, I was unaware what I was hearing until I was later told *Hừ La* was sung.

3 The word "*mò*" means to grope or feel around in the dark for something. The physicality of this term is in itself interesting, indicating that there is some concrete, real form of *Hừ La* extant and waiting to be caught hold of behind the faded memories and vocal attempts of these singers.

4 This singer's version of *Hừ La* is slightly different from the two men from Châm Khê Village. Additional transcribed versions from other villages can be found in Hồng Thao's collection of quan họ songs (2002).

5 Mass organizations, such as the Youth Union are the "core" of society, according to the Diềm Village leader. They are active in the organization and implementation of the cultural activities of the village, such as festivals, quan họ activities, sports events, and so on. Diềm has six organizations: the Cooperative, the Farmer's Union, the Women's Union, the Elders' Association, the Youth Union, and the Veterans' Association.

6 Thanks to Phuong Minh Cao for help with this translation.

GLOSSARY

anh hai, anh ba, anh tư, etc.—"second older brother," "third older brother," "fourth older brother," etc. The term of address for male quan họ singers.

bài đối—response song in a singing event (*canh hát*).

bài ra—opening song in a singing event (*canh hát*).

bọn—"group." In quan họ this refers to a group of at least five singers from the same village. All singers in the group are of the same gender.

canh hát—a singing event in which two groups of quan họ singers from different villages (one male and one female) gather at a host's house to exchange songs. Songs must be sung in a particular order (depending upon the locality), and strict rules of politeness followed. In the past, this event sometimes lasted several days and nights.

câu—literally, "phrase." In quan họ, the lyrical variant of a melody (*giọng*).

chị hai, chị ba, chị tư, etc.—"second older sister," "third older sister," "fourth older sister," etc. The term of address for female quan họ singers.

chơi quan họ—to "play" or "practice" quan họ (used by village singers).

cổ—ancient, old-style.

cổ truyền—traditional, with the implication that something is inherited whole cloth from the past.

di sản văn hóa—cultural heritage.

đội quan họ—A village-level quan họ troupe consisting of both male and female members of all ages (to be distinguished from the *bọn quan họ*). These groups only emerged after the Revolution.

giọng—voice; a complex term in quan họ that refers both to tune categories and melody variants.

giọng giã bạn—"goodbye" voice; the third of three groups of songs that must be sung at a *canh hát*.

giọng lề lối—the "way of doing" or "method" voice; the first of three groups of songs that must be sung at a *canh hát*.

giọng vặt—"miscellaneous" voice; the second of three groups of songs that must be sung at a *canh hát*.

hát đều—when paired singers sing evenly and symmetrically such that the two voices become as one.

hát đôi—to sing in pairs. In quan họ, the voices of the two singers must be well matched and sound "as one voice."

hát đối đáp—To exchange matching songs with another quan họ group.

hát hội—festival singing. An informal style of gathering and singing at village festivals that does not follow the same strict song order of the *canh hát*.

kết bạn—an official partnership between two quan họ groups (*bọn*).

liền anh—a male member of a *bọn quan họ*.

liền chị—a female member of a *bọn quan họ*.

lối chơi quan họ—the "way of practicing" quan họ, including the rules of behavior and song exchange in village practice.

nghệ nhân—village performers or craftspeople who are officially recognized as highly skilled in a folk art or craft and who play an important role in teaching that skill to subsequent generations. Sometimes translated as "artists," "amateurs," "living treasures," or "masters of folklore," the word has no precise English translation.

quan họ cổ—old-style or village quan họ.

tình cảm—sentiment.

truyền thống—traditional, with the implication that something is in-the-style-of traditional practices.

Vua Bà—the quan họ ancestral deity, said to be the daughter of one of the Hùng kings and to have taught villagers in the region how to raise silkworms and to sing quan họ.

BIBLIOGRAPHY

Adorno, Theodor W. 1990. The Form of the Phonograph Record. *October* 55:56–61.

Anderson, Benedict. 1991. *Imagined Communities: Reflections on the Origin and Spread of Nationalism*. New York: Verso.

Arana, Miranda. 1999. *Neotraditional Music in Vietnam*. Kent, OH: Nhạc Việt, The Journal for Vietnamese Music.

Attali, Jacques. 1985. *Noise: The Political Economy of Music*. Translated by B. Massumi. Minneapolis: University of Minneapolis Press.

Ban Chấp hành Trung ương Đảng Lao Động Việt-nam (Vietnamese Workers' Party Central Executive Committee). 1957. Phấn Đấu Thắng Lợi cho Một Nền Văn Nghệ Dân Tộc Phong Phú [trích thư của Bản chấp hành Trung ương Đảng Lao động Việt-Nam gửi Đại hội Văn nghệ Toàn quốc lần thứ 2] (Fighting for the Success of a National and Abundant System of Arts [letter from the Vietnamese Workers' Party Central Executive Committee to the Second National Arts Congress]). *Tập San Âm Nhạc (Music Review)* 7:5–11.

Barthes, Roland. 1977. *Image, Music, Text*. Translated by S. Heath. New York: Hill and Wang.

Bauman, Richard. 1975. Verbal Art as Performance. *American Anthropologist* 77 (2): 290–311.

Bendix, Regina. 2000. The Pleasures of the Ear: Toward an Ethnography of Listening. *Cultural Analysis* 1:33–50.

Benjamin, Walter. 1977. *The Origin of German Tragic Drama*. Translated by J. Osborn. London: NLB.

Bergeron, Katherine. 1996. Prologue: Disciplining Music. In *Disciplining Music: Musicology and Its Canons*, edited by K. Bergeron and P. V. Bohlman. Chicago: University of Chicago Press.

———. 1998. *Decadent Enchantments: The Revival of Gregorian Chant at Solesmes*. Berkeley: University of California Press.

Bhabba, Homi. 1994. *The Location of Culture*. London: Routledge.

Boudarel, Georges. 1990. Intellectual Dissidence in the 1950s: The Nhân-Dân Giai-Phẩm Affair. *The Vietnam Forum* 13:154–174.

Bradley, Mark. 2001. Contests of Memory: Remembering and Forgetting War in the Contemporary Vietnamese Cinema. In *The Country of Memory: Remaking the Past in Late Socialist Vietnam*, edited by Hue-Tam Ho Tai. Berkeley: University of California Press.

Bùi Trọng Hiền. N.d. Đường đi của Âm Nhạc Truyền Thống—Những Điều Trông Thấy (The Path of Traditional Music—Things Seen). Unpublished manuscript. Viện Văn Hóa-Thông Tin.

Bunten, Alexis Celeste. 2008. Sharing Culture or Selling Out? Developing the Commodified Persona in the Heritage Industry. *American Ethnologist* 35 (3): 380–395.

Chan Ngoc Le. 2002. *Quan họ* Singing in North Vietnam: A Yearning for Resolution. Ph.D. diss., Department of Music, University of California, Berkeley.

Comaroff, John L., and Jean Comaroff. 2009. *Ethnicity, Inc.* Chicago: University of Chicago Press.

Con Sáo Sang Sông (The Magpie Crosses the River). 1956. *Tập San Âm Nhạc* (*Music Review*) 1:33–34.

Crary, Jonathan. 1998. *Techniques of the Observer: On Vision and Modernity in the Nineteenth Century*. Cambridge, MA: MIT Press.

Csordas, Thomas J. 1990. Embodiment as a Paradigm for Anthropology. *Ethos* 18 (1): 5–47.

———. 1994. *Embodiment and Experience: The Existential Ground of Culture and Self*. Cambridge: Cambridge University Press.

Cừ Huy Cận. 1972. Về Tính Đan Tộc Trong Âm Nhạc (On National Character in Music). In *Về Tính Dân Tộc Trong Âm Nhạc Việt Nam* (*On National Character in Vietnamese Music*). Hanoi: Nhà Xuất Bản Văn Hóa.

Đặng Đình Hưng. 1956. Hát Dân Ca (Singing Folk Song). *Tập San Âm Nhạc* (*Music Review*) 2:30–35.

Dang Nhat Minh and Pham Thu Thuy. 2003. Representations of *Doi Moi* Society in Contemporary Vietnamese Cinema. In *Consuming Urban Culture in Contemporary Vietnam*, edited by L. B. W. Drummond and M. Thomas. London: RoutledgeCurzon.

Đặng Văn Lưng. 1982. Quan Họ. In *Địa Lý Hà Bắc* (*Hà Bắc Geography*), edited by Lê Hồng Dương. Hà Bắc: Hà Bắc Department of Culture and Information.

Đặng Văn Lung, Hồng Thao, and Trần Linh Quý. 1978. *Quan Họ Nguồn Gốc và Quá Trình Phát Triển* (*Quan Họ: Origins and the Development Process*). Hanoi: Nhà Xuất Bản Khoa Học Xã Hội.

Đào Trọng Từ. 1984a. The "Quan ho" Peasant Song and Village Culture. In *Essays on Vietnamese Music*, edited by Đào Trọng Từ, Huy Trân, and Tứ Ngọc. Hanoi: Foreign Languages Publishing House.

———. 1984b. Renaissance of Vietnamese Music. In *Essays on Vietnamese Music*, edited by Đào Trọng Từ, Huy Trân, and Tứ Ngọc. Hanoi: Foreign Language Publishing House.

———. 1984c. Vietnamese Traditional Music. In *Essays on Vietnamese Music*, edited by Đào Trọng Từ, Huy Trân, and Tứ Ngọc. Hanoi: Foreign Languages Publishing House.

Darbellay, Etienne. 1986. Tradition and Notation in Baroque Music. In *The Oral and the Literate in Music*, edited by T. Yosihiko and Y. Osamu. Tokyo: Academia Music Ltd.

Đinh Gia Khánh. 1999. *Sơ Bộ Tìm Hiểu Những Vấn Đề Của Truyện Cổ Tích Qua Truyện Tấm Cám* (*Preliminary Understanding of Issues Concerning Legends by Way of the Tam Cam Story*). Hanoi: Nhà Xuất Bản Hội Nhà Văn.

Đinh Gia Khánh and Lê Hữu Tầng, eds. 1993. *Lễ Hội Truyền Thống Đời Sống Xã Hội Hiện Đại* (*Traditional Festivals in Modern Social Life*). Hanoi: Nhà Xuất Bản Khoa Học Xã Hội.

Đỗ Thị Minh Thúy. 2004a. Báo Cáo Đề Dẫn Hội Thảo "Xây Dựng và Phát Triển Nền Văn Hóa Việt Nam Tiên Tiến Đậm Đà Bản Sắc Dân Tộc" (Introductory Report for the Conference "Building and Developing a Progressive Vietnamese Culture Rich in National Identity"). In *Xây Dựng và Phát Triển Nền Văn Hóa Việt Nam Tiên Tiến Đậm Đà Bản Sắc Dân Tộc: Thành Tựu và Kinh Nghiệm* (*Quán triệt tinh thần Nghị quyết Trung ương 5 khóa VIII*) (*Building and Developing a Progressive Vietnamese Culture Rich in National Identity: Achievements and Experiences [grasping thoroughly the meaning of Central Resolution 5 of the Eighth Congress]*), edited by Đỗ Thị Minh Thúy. Hanoi: Nhà Xuất Bản Văn Hóa Thông Tin.

———, ed. 2004b. *Xây Dựng và Phát Triển Nền Văn Hóa Việt Nam Tiên Tiến Đậm Đà Bản Sắc Dân Tộc: Thành Tựu và Kinh Nghiệm* (*Quán triệt tinh thần Nghị quyết Trung ương 5 khóa VIII*) (*Building and Developing a Progressive Vietnamese Culture Rich in National Identity: Achievements and Experiences [grasping thoroughly the meaning of Central Resolution 5 of the Eighth Congress]*). Hanoi: Nhà Xuất Bản Văn Hóa Thông Tin.

Đoàn Chuẩn. 1956. Trở Về Với Âm Nhạc Dân Tộc (Returning to National Music). *Tập San Âm Nhạc* (*Music Review*) 4:4.

Drummond, Lisa B. W., and Mandy Thomas. 2003. Introduction. In *Consuming Urban Culture in Contemporary Vietnam*, edited by L. B. W. Drummond and M. Thomas. New York: RoutledgeCurzon.

Đức Siêu. 1998. Những Bước Đi Ban Đầu Của Đoàn Dân Ca Quan Họ (First Steps of the Quan Họ Folk Song Troupe). In *Sum Họp Trúc Mai*. Bắc Ninh: Đoàn Dân Ca Quan Họ Bắc Ninh.

Dumoutier, Gustave. 1890. *Les Chants et les Traditions Populaires des Annamites*. Paris: Ernest Leroux.

Endres, Kirsten W. 2002. Beautiful Customs, Worthy Traditions: Changing State Discourse on the Role of Vietnamese Culture. *Internationales Asienforum* 33 (3–4): 303–322.

Evans, Grant. 1985. Vietnamese Communist Anthropology. *Canberra Anthropology* 8 (1–2): 116–147.

Foucault, Michel. 1994. *The Order of Things: An Archaeology of the Human Sciences*. New York: Vintage Books.

Gammeltoft, Tine. 2002. The Irony of Sexual Agency: Premarital Sex in Urban Northern Việt Nam. In *Gender, Household, State: Đổi Mới in Việt Nam*, edited by J. Werner and D. Bélanger. Ithaca, NY: Southeast Asia Publications, Southeast Asia Program, Cornell University.

General Statistics Office of Vietnam. 2010. *2009 Vietnam Population and Housing Census, Part II, Major Findings* [cited June 16, 2011]. Available from http://www.gso.gov.vn/default_en.aspx?tabid=617&idmid=&ItemID=9811.

Gibbs, Jason. 1997. Reform and Tradition in Early Vietnamese Popular Song. *Nhac Viet* 6:5–33.

Giebel, Christoph. 2001. Museum-Shrine: Revolution and Its Tutelary Spirit in the Village of My Hoa Hung. In *The Country of Memory: Remaking the Past in Late Socialist Vietnam*, edited by Hue Tam Ho Tai. Berkeley: University of California Press.

Gironcourt, Georges de. 1942. *Recherches de Géographie Musicale en Indochine*. Saigon: S.I.L.J. Original edition, *Bulletin des Etudes Indochinoises* 17 (4): 3–174.

Handler, Richard. 1986. Authenticity. *Anthropology Today* 2 (1): 2–4.

Harms, Erik. 2011. *Saigon's Edge: On the Margins of Ho Chi Minh City*. Minneapolis: University of Minnesota Press.

Haug, Wolfgang Fritz. 1986. *Critique of Commodity Aesthetics: Appearance, Sexuality and Advertising in Capitalist Society*. Translated by R. Bock. Minneapolis: University of Minnesota Press.

Hershatter, Gail. 1993. The Subaltern Talks Back: Reflections on Subaltern Theory and Chinese History. *Positions* 1 (1): 103–130.

Hickey, Gerald C. 1967. *Village in Vietnam*. New Haven: Yale University Press.

Hirschkind, Charles. 2006. *The Ethical Soundscape: Cassette Sermons and Islamic Counterpublics*. New York: Columbia University Press.

Hoàng Kiều. 1956. Dân Tộc Tính trong Âm Nhạc (National Character in Music). *Tập San Âm Nhạc (Music Review)* 2:7–9.

Hoàng Kỳ. 1982. Giáo Dục. In *Địa Lý Hà Bắc (Hà Bắc Geography)*, edited by Lê Hồng Dương. Hà Bắc: Hà Bắc Department of Culture and Information.

Hoàng Yến. 1919. La Musique a Húe: Đờn Nguyệt et Đờn Tranh (The Music of Hue: Dan Nguyet and Dan Tranh). *Bulletin des Amis du Vieux Hué* 6 (3): 233–387.

Hồng Thao. 2002. *300 Bài Dân Ca Quan họ Bắc Ninh (300 Quan họ Bắc Ninh Folk Songs)*. Hanoi: Viện Âm Nhạc (Vietnamese Institute of Musicology).

Hue-Tam Ho Tai. 1992. *Radicalism and the Origins of the Vietnamese Revolution*. Cambridge, MA: Harvard University Press.

———, ed. 2001. *The Country of Memory: Remaking the Past in Late Socialist Vietnam*. Berkeley: University of California Press.

Hughes-Freeland, Felicia. 2008. *Embodied Communities: Dance Traditions and Change in Java*. New York: Berghahn Books.

Huu Ngoc. 2001. Kinh Bac: Cradle of Vietnamese Civilization. *Vietnamese Studies* 3 (141): 10–15.

Huynh Sang Thong, ed. 1996. *An Anthology of Vietnamese Poems: From the Eleventh through the Twentieth Centuries*. New Haven: Yale University Press.

Jankowiak, William. 1995. Romantic Passion in the People's Republic of China. In *Romantic Passion: A Universal Experience?*, edited by W. Jankowiak. New York: Columbia University Press.

Jellema, Kate. 2007. Returning Home: Ancestor Veneration and the Nationalism of Đổi Mới Vietnam. In *Modernity and Re-enchantment: Religion in Post-revolutionary Vietnam*, edited by P. Taylor. Singapore: ISEAS.

Khóa Son. 1956. Dân Tộc Tính (National Character). *Tập San Âm Nhạc (Music Review)* 4:32.

Kim Ngoc Bao Ninh. 2005. *A World Transformed: The Politics of Culture in Revolutionary Vietnam, 1945–1965*. Ann Arbor: University of Michigan Press.

Kittler, Friedrich. 1990. *Discourse Networks, 1800/1900*. Translated by M. Metteer. Stanford, CA: Stanford University Press.

Kleinen, John. 1997. The Village as Pretext: Ethnographic Praxis and the Colonial State in Vietnam. In *The Village in Asia Revisited*, edited by J. Breman, P. Kloos, and A. Saith. Delhi: Oxford University Press.

———. 1999. Is There a "Village Vietnam"? In *Vietnamese Villages in Transition: Background and Consequences of Reform Policies in Rural Vietnam*, edited by B. Dahm and V. J. Houben. Passau: Department of Southeast Asian Studies, Passau University.

Knosp, Gaston. 1922. Histoire de la Musique dans l'Indochine (History of Music in Indochina). In *Encyclopédie de la Musique et Dictionnaire du Conservatoire (Encyclopedia of Music and Dictionary of the Conservatory)*, edited by A. Lavignac. Paris: Librairie Delagrave.

Le Bris, E. 1922. Musique Annamite: Airs Traditionelles (Annamite Music: Traditional Songs). *Bulletin des Amis du Vieux Hué* 9:255–309.

Lê Danh Khiêm. 2000. Những Tiêu Chí Xác Định Làng Quan Họ và Danh Sách Những Làng Quan Họ Gốc (Criteria for Determining Quan Họ Villages and a List of Quan Họ Origin Villages). In *Một Số Vấn Đề về Văn Hóa Quan Họ (Some Issues Concerning Quan Họ Culture)*, edited by Nguyễn Thị Minh Đoàn. Bắc Ninh: Trung Tâm Văn Hóa Quan Họ Bắc Ninh.

———. 2001. *Dân Ca Quan họ: Lời Ca và Bình Giải (Quan họ Folk Song: Lyrics and Commentary)*. Bắc Ninh: Trung Tâm Văn Hóa Quan Họ Bắc Ninh.

Lê Hồng Dương. 1972. Về Tình Hình Của Phong Trào Ca Hát Quan Họ Trong Những Năm Qua Và Phương Hướng Nhiệm Vụ Sắp Tới (Concerning the State of the Quan Họ Singing Movement in Recent Years and Directions and Responsibilities To Come). In *Một Số Vấn Đề Về Dân Ca Quan Họ (Some Issues Concerning Quan Họ Folk Song)*. Hà Bắc: Ty Văn Hóa Hà Bắc.

———, ed. 1982. *Địa Lý Hà Bắc (Hà Bắc Geography)*. Hà Bắc: Hà Bắc Department of Culture and Information.

Le Tuan Hung. 1997. Traditional and Modern National Music in North Vietnam Between 1954 and 1975. *Nhac Viet* 6:35–70.

Le Van Hao. 1972. Ethnological Studies and Researches in North Viet Nam. *Vietnamese Studies* 32:9–48.

Luật Di Sản Văn Hóa (Law on Cultural Heritage). 2001. Hanoi: Nhà Xuất Bản Chính Trị Quốc Gia.

Luong Van Hy. 1992. *Revolution in the Village: Tradition and Transformation in North Vietnam, 1925–1988*. Honolulu: University of Hawai'i Press.

———. 1993. Economic Reform and the Intensification of Rituals in Two North Vietnamese Villages, 1980–90. In *The Challenge of Reform in Indochina*, edited by B. Ljunggren. Cambridge, MA: Harvard Institute for International Development.

Lưu Khâm, Nguyễn Viêm, and Nguyễn Đình Tấn. 1956. Tìm Hiểu Nguồn Gốc và Sinh Hoạt Của Quan Họ Bắc Ninh (Seeking to Understand Quan Họ Bắc Ninh). *Tập San Âm Nhạc (Music Review)* 1:17–21.

Lyon, Margot L. 1995. Missing Emotions: The Limitations of Cultural Constructionism in the Study of Emotion. *Cultural Anthropology* 10 (2): 244–263.

Mac Duong. 1977. Principal Stages in the Development of Ethnographic Knowledge in Vietnam. *Soviet Anthropology and Archaeology* 15 (4): 74–89.

MacDougall, David. 2006. *The Corporeal Image: Film, Ethnography, and the Senses*. Princeton: Princeton University Press.

Malarney, Shaun K. 1996. The Limits of "State Functionalism" and the Reconstruction of Funerary Rituals in Contemporary Vietnam. *American Ethnologist* 23 (3): 540–560.

———. 2001. "The Fatherland Remembers Your Sacrifice": Commemorating War Dead in North Vietnam. In *The Country of Memory: Remaking the Past in Late Socialist Vietnam*, edited by Hue-Tam Ho Tai. Berkeley: University of California Press.

———. 2002. *Culture, Ritual and Revolution in Vietnam*. London: RoutledgeCurzon.

———. 2007. Festivals and the Dynamics of the Exceptional Dead in Northern Vietnam. *Journal of Southeast Asian Studies* 38 (3): 515–540.

Marr, David. 1971. *Vietnamese Anticolonialism, 1885–1925*. Berkeley: University of California Press.

———. 1981. *Vietnamese Tradition on Trial, 1920–1945*. Berkeley: University of California Press.

———. 1995. *Vietnam 1945: The Quest for Power*. Berkeley: University of California Press.

Mauss, Marcel. 1979. Body Techniques. In *Sociology and Psychology: Essays*. Boston: Routledge and Degan Paul.

———. 1990. *The Gift: The Form and Reason for Exchange in Archaic Societies*. New York: W. W. Norton.

McLuhan, Marshall. 2000 [1962]. *The Gutenberg Galaxy: The Making of Typographic Man*. Toronto: University of Toronto Press.

Meeker, Lauren. 2013. Cultural Expert, Nghệ Nhân. In *Figures of Southeast Asian Modernity*, edited by J. Barker, E. Harms, and J. Lindquist. Honolulu: University of Hawai'i Press.

Muehlmann, Shaylih. 2008. "Spread Your Ass Cheeks": And Other Things That Should Not Be Said in Indigenous Languages. *American Ethnologist* 35 (1): 34–48.

NG. H. 2004. Cần Khôi Phục và Phát Huy Giá Trị Văn Hóa Hội Lim (We Must Restore and Develop the Value of the Lim Festival). *Văn Hóa Chủ Nhật (Sunday Culture)* 1041:3.

Ngành Nhạc Chuẩn Bị Đại Hội (The Discipline of Music Prepares for the Congress). 1956. *Tập San Âm Nhạc (Music Review)* 1:3–4.

Ngô Đức Thịnh. 2006. Vùng Văn Hóa Kinh Bắc (The Kinh Bắc Cultural Region). In *Vùng Văn Hóa Quan Họ Bắc Ninh (The Quan Họ Cultural Region)*, edited by Nguyễn Chí Bền, Trần Văn Túy, Nguyễn Tri Nguyên, Trần Đình Luyện, and Võ Hoàng Lan. Hanoi: Viện Văn Hóa Thông-Tin and Sở Văn Hóa Thông Tin Bắc Ninh. Original edition, Văn Hóa Vùng và Phân Vùng Văn Hóa ở Việt Nam (Regional Culture and Elements of Regional Culture in Vietnam), Nhà Xuất Bản Trẻ, 2004.

Nguyen, Phong T. 1991. Ethno-historical Perspectives on the Traditional Genres of Vietnamese Music. In *New Perspectives on Vietnamese Music*, edited by P. T. Nguyen. New Haven: Council on Southeast Asian Studies, Yale Center for International and Area Studies.

———. 1998. Vietnam. In *The Garland Encyclopedia of Music*, edited by T. E. Miller and S. Williams. New York: Garland Publishing.

Nguyen, Phong T., and Hong Thao. 1993. Social context and aesthetic concepts of the Quan ho. *Nhac Viet* 2(1) (1):15–26.

Nguyễn Chí Bền. 2000. Tổng Quan về Kho Tàng Lễ Hội Cổ Truyền Việt Nam (Overview of the Treasure of Vietnamese Traditional Festivals). In *Kho Tàng Lễ Hội Cổ Truyền Việt Nam (The Treasure of Vietnamese Traditional Festivals)*. Hanoi: Nhà Xuất Bản Văn Hóa Dân Tộc, Tạp Chí Văn Hóa Nghệ Thuật.

———. 2003. Di Sản Văn Hóa Phi Vật Thể, Từ Sưu Tầm, Nghiên Cứu Đến Bảo Tồn và Phát Huy (Intangible Cultural Heritage, From Collection and Research to Preservation and Development). In *Văn Hóa Dân Gian Việt Nam: Những Phác Thảo (Vietnamese Folklore: Sketches)*. Hanoi: Nhà Xuất Bản Văn Hóa Thông Tin.

———. 2004. Nhận Diện Chủ/Khách Thể Của Văn Hóa Việt Nam từ Năm 1986 Đến Nay (Recognizing the Subject and Object of Culture from 1986 until Today). *Văn Hóa Nghệ Thuật* 1 (235): 4–12.

Nguyễn Chí Bền, Trần Văn Túy, Nguyễn Tri Nguyên, Trần Đình Luyện, and Võ Hoàng Lan, eds. 2006. *Vùng Văn Hóa Quan Họ Bắc Ninh (The Cultural Region of Quan Họ Bắc Ninh)*. Hanoi: Institute of Culture and Information and Bac Ninh Department of Culture and Information.

Nguyễn Đình Phúc. 2006. Các Giọng Quan Họ (Quan Họ Voices). In *Vùng Văn Hóa Quan Họ Bắc Ninh (The Quan Họ Cultural Region)*, edited by Nguyễn Chí Bền, Trần Văn Túy, Nguyễn Tri Nguyên, Trần Đình Luyện, and Võ Hoàng Lan. Hanoi: Viện Văn Hóa Thông-Tin and Sở Văn Hóa Thông Tin Bắc Ninh. Original edition, Văn Nghệ, No. 114, 1956.

Nguyen Khac Tung. 1993. The Village: Settlement of Peasants in Northern Vietnam. In *The Traditional Village in Vietnam*. Hanoi: The Gioi Publishers.

Nguyễn Phúc. 1972. Tình Dân Tộc Trong Âm Nhạc Việt Nam. In *Về Tính Dân Tộc Trong Âm Nhạc Việt Nam (On National Character in Vietnamese Music)*. Hanoi: Nhà Xuất Bản Văn Hóa.

Nguyễn Thị Minh Đoàn, ed. 2000. *Một Số Vấn Đề về Văn Hóa Quan Họ (Some Issues Concerning Quan Họ Culture)*. Bắc Ninh: Trung Tâm Văn Hóa Quan Họ Bắc Ninh.

Nguyen Van Huyen. 1934. *Les Chants Alternés Des Garçons et Des Filles En Annam*. Paris: Librairie Orientaliste Paul Geuthner.

Nguyễn Văn Phú, Lưu Hữu Phước, Nguyễn Viêm, and Tú Ngọc. 1962. *Dân Ca Quan Họ Bắc Ninh (Bac Ninh Quan Họ Folk Song)*. Hanoi: Nhà Xuất Bản Văn Hóa.

Nguyễn Văn Tý. 1956. Nắm Thực Tế Như Thế Nào? (How to Catch Hold of Reality?). *Tập San Âm Nhạc (Music Review)* 2:4–7.

Nguyễn Xuân Khoát. 1956. Lá Thư Gửi Các Bạn Nhạc Sĩ Miền Nam (Letter Sent to Our Musician Friends of the South). *Tập San Âm Nhạc (Music Review)* 1:10–12.

———. 1972. Càm Xúc, Tâm Hồn, Chân Thành, Sâu Sắc Là Diều Kiện Trước Tiên Của Một Tác Phẩm Có Tính Đan Tộc Đậm Đà (Emotion, Soul, Sincerity, Depth: The Foremost Conditions for a Composition with True National Character). In *Về Tính Dân Tộc Trong Âm Nhạc Việt Nam (On National Character in Vietnamese Music)*. Hanoi: Nhà Xuất Bản Văn Hóa.

Nhật Lai and Ta Phước. 1956. Đợi Chờ (Waiting). *Tập San Âm Nhạc (Music Review)* 3:29–31.

Những nét lớn của Phong Trào Văn Nghệ Việt-Nam từ sao cách mạng tháng tám (Some Important Features of the Arts Movement in Vietnam since the August Revolution). 1957. *Tập San Âm Nhạc (Music Review)* 7:1–4.

Norton, Barley. 2002. "The Moon Remembers Uncle Ho": The Politics of Music and Mediumship in Northern Vietnam. *British Journal of Ethnomusicology* 11 (1): 71–100.

———. 2009. *Songs for the Spirits: Music and Mediums in Modern Vietnam*. Chicago: University of Illinois Press.

Pelley, Patricia. 1995. The History of Resistance and the Resistance to History in Post-colonial Constructions of the Past. In *Essays into Vietnamese Pasts*, edited by K. W. Taylor and J. K. Whitmore. Ithaca, NY: Southeast Asia Program, Cornell University.

———. 2002. *Postcolonial Vietnam: New Histories of the National Past*. Durham, NC: Duke University Press.

Pelzer, Kristin. 1993. Socio-cultural Dimensions of Renovation in Vietnam: *Doi Moi* as Dialogue and Transformation in Gender Relations. In *Reinventing Vietnamese Socialism: Doi Moi in Comparative Perspective*, edited by W. S. Turley and M. Selden. Boulder: Westview Press.

Pemberton, John. 1998. Disorienting Culturalist Assumptions: A View from "Java." In *In Near Ruins: Cultural Theory at the End of the Century*, edited by N. B. Dirks. Minneapolis: University of Minnesota Press.

Perris, Arnold. 1983. Music as Propaganda: Art at the Command of Doctrine in the People's Republic of China. *Ethnomusicology* 27 (1): 1–28.

Phạm Duy, and Dale R. Whiteside. 1975. *Musics of Vietnam*. Carbondale: Southern Illinois University Press.

Phạm Văn Chùng. 1956. Nghiên Cứu, Sưu Tầm và Phổ Biến Dân Ca (Researching, Collecting and Popularizing Folk Song). *Tập San Âm Nhạc* (*Music Review*) 4:1–3.

Phấn Đấu Thắng Lợi: Cho Một Nền Văn Nghệ Dân Tộc Phong Phú (trích thư của Bản chấp hành Trung ương Đảng Lao động Việt-Nam gửi Đại hội Văn nghệ Toàn quốc lần thứ 2) (The Struggle for Victory: Towards a Diverse System of National Arts [letter from the Vietnamese Workers' Party Central Executive Committee to the Second National Arts Congress]). 1957. *Tập San Âm Nhạc* (*Music Review*) 7:5–11.

Phan Huu Dat. 1999 [1978]. Les premiers acquis de l'ethnologie Vietnamienne. In *Mot So Van De Ve Dan Toc Hoc Viet Nam*, edited by Phan Huu Dat. Ha Noi: Nha Xuat Ban Dai Hoc Quoc Gia.

Phan Huy Lê. 2006. Research on the Vietnamese Village: Assessment and Perspectives. In *Việt Nam: Borderless Histories*, edited by Nhung Tuyet Tran and A. Reid. Madison: University of Wisconsin Press.

Phinney, Harriet. 2008. Objects of Affection: Vietnamese Discourses on Love and Emancipation. *Positions: East Asia Cultures Critique* 16 (2): 329–358.

Randel, Don Michael. 1996. The Canons in the Musicological Toolbox. In *Disciplining Music: Musicology and its Canons*, edited by K. Bergeron and P. V. Bohlman. Chicago: University of Chicago Press.

Rydstrøm, Helle. 2003. *Embodying Morality: Growing Up in Rural Vietnam*. Honolulu: University of Hawai'i Press.

Salemink, Oscar 2003. *The Ethnography of Vietnam's Central Highlanders: A Historical Contextualization, 1850–1990*. Honolulu: University of Hawai'i Press.

Schechner, Richard. 1985. *Between Theater and Anthropology*. Philadelphia: University of Pennsylvania Press.

Schieffelin, Edward L. 1985. Performance and the Cultural Construction of Reality. *American Ethnologist* 12 (4):707–724.

Schlecker, Markus. 2005. Going Back a Long Way: "Home Place," Thrift and Temporal Orientations in Northern Vietnam. *Journal of the Royal Anthropological Institute* 11:509–526.

Simmel, Georg. 1959 [1911]. The Ruin. In *Georg Simmel 1858–1918*, edited by K. H. Wolff. Columbus: Ohio State University Press.

Spivak, Gayatri Chakravorty. 1988. Can the Subaltern Speak? In *Marxism and the Interpretation of Culture*, edited by C. Nelson and L. Grossberg. Chicago: University of Illinois Press.

Sterne, Jonathan. 2003. *The Audible Past: Cultural Origins of Sound Reproduction*. Durham, NC: Duke University Press.

Stoller, Paul. 1989. *The Taste of Ethnographic Things: The Senses in Anthropology*. Philadelphia: University of Pennsylvania Press.

Sutton, R. Anderson. 1996. Interpreting Electronic Sound Technology in the Contemporary Javanese Soundscape. *Ethnomusicology* 40 (2): 249–268.

Taylor, Keith W. 1983. *The Birth of Vietnam*. Berkeley: University of California Press.

Taylor, Nora. 1999. "Pho" Phai and faux Phais: The Market for Fakes and the Appropriation of a Vietnamese National Symbol. *Ethnos* 64 (2): 232–248.

———. 2001. Framing the National Spirit: Viewing and Reviewing Painting under the Revolution. In *The Country of Memory: Remaking the Past in Late Socialist Vietnam*, edited by Hue Tam Ho Tai. Berkeley: University of California Press.

Taylor, Philip. 2004. *Goddess on the Rise: Pilgrimage and Popular Religion in Vietnam*. Honolulu: University of Hawai'i Press.

Thongchai Winichakul. 1994. *Siam Mapped: A History of the Geo-Body of a Nation*. Honolulu: University of Hawai'i Press.

Thụy Loan. 1993. The Impact of French Music on Vietnamese Music. *Vietnamese Studies* New Series 37 (107): 57–60.

Tiến tới Đại hội: Văn nghệ Toàn Quốc (Approaching the Congress: Arts of the Whole Country). 1956. *Tập San Âm Nhạc (Music Review)* 1:1–2.

Tô Ngọc Thanh. 1997. Liaison Officer: Vietnam. *Bulletin of the International Council for Traditional Music* XCI:40–41.

———. 2001. Sưu Tầm, Nghiên Cứu, Phổ Biến Âm Nhạc Dân Gian Việt Nam trong Thế Kỷ XX (The Collection, Research and Popularization of Vietnamese Folk Music in the 20th Century). *Văn Hóa Dân Gian* 2 (74): 29–31.

———. 2007. Nghệ Nhân Dân Gian: Tài Sản Vô Giá Của Nền Văn Hóa Việt Nam (Master of Folklore—An Invaluable Property of Vietnam Traditional Culture). In *Hội Văn Nghệ Dân Gian Việt Nam: Nghệ Nhân Dân Gian (Folklore Association of Vietnam: Masters of Folklore)*, edited by H. V. N. D. G. V. Nam. Hanoi: Nhà Xuất Bản Khoa Học Xã Hội.

Tô Ngọc Thanh and Hồng Thao. 1986. *Tìm Hiểu Âm Nhạc Dân Tộc Cổ Truyền (Seeking to Understand National Traditional Music)*. Vol. 1. Hanoi: Nhà Xuất Bản Văn Hóa.

Tô Vũ. 1972. Một Số Đặc Điểm Về Tính Dân Tộc trong Âm Nhạc (Some Characteristics of National Character in Music). In *Về Tính Dân Tộc Trong Âm Nhạc Việt Nam (On National Character in Vietnamese Music)*. Hanoi: Nhà Xuất Bản Văn Hóa.

Toan Ánh. 1974. *Nếp Cũ Hội Hè Đình Đám, Quyển Hạ (Old Ways: Village Festivals)*. Vol. 1. Thủ Đức: Sao Mai.

Trần Chính. 2000. *Nghệ Nhân Quan họ Làng Viêm Xá (Quan họ Artisans of Viêm Xá Village)*. Hanoi: Khoa Học Xã Hội.

Trần Đình Luyện. 2000a. Đền Vua Bà: Di Tích Về Thủy Tổ Quan Họ Bắc Ninh (The Temple of Vua Bà, Ancestor of Quan Họ). In *Một Số Vấn Đề về Văn Hóa Quan Họ (Some Issues Concerning Quan Họ Culture)*, edited by Nguyễn Thị Minh Đoàn. Hanoi: Trung Tâm Văn Hóa Quan Họ Bắc Ninh.

———. 2000b. Mùa Xuân Đi Trẩy Hội Lim (Traveling to the Lim Festival in Spring). In *Một Số Vấn Đề về Văn Hóa Quan Họ (Some Issues Concerning Quan Họ*

Culture), edited by Nguyễn Thị Minh Đoàn. Hanoi: Trung Tâm Văn Hóa Quan Họ Bắc Ninh.

———. 2005. Phát Triển, Đổi Mới Hội Lim (Developing and Renovating the Lim Festival). *Văn Hóa Nghệ Thuật* 1 (247): 16–19.

Trần Đình Luyện, ed. 1997. *Văn Hiến Kinh Bắc* (*The Civilization of Kinh Bắc*). Vol. I. Bắc Ninh: Sở Văn Hóa—Thông Tin Bắc Ninh.

Trần Linh Quý. 2006 [1974]. Làng Gốc Quan Họ và Bảo Tồn Bảo Tang Đối Với Quan Họ (Original Quan Họ Villages and Preserving Museums Regarding Quan Họ). In *Vùng Văn Hóa Quan Họ Bắc Ninh* (*Cultural Region of Quan Họ Bắc Nin*), edited by Nguyễn Chí Bền, Trần Văn Túy, Nguyễn Tri Nguyên, Trần Đình Luyện, and Võ Hoàng Lan. Hanoi: Viện Văn Hóa Thông Tin—Sở Văn Hóa Thông Tin Bắc Ninh.

Trần Linh Qúy and Hồng Thao. 1997. *Tìm Hiểu Dân Ca Quan Họ* (*Seeking to Understand Quan Họ*). Hanoi: Nhà Xuất Bản Văn Hóa Dân Tộc; Sở Văn Hóa Thông Tin Hà Bắc.

Trần Quốc Vượng. 2001. Notes on the Culture of Kinh Bắc. *Vietnamese Studies* 3 (141): 5–9.

Trần Thị Ngọc Lan. 2003. Hội Lim, Đến Hẹn Lại Lên (The Lim Festival, We Will Meet Again). In *Tiên Du, Di Tích Và Lễ Hội* (*Tiên Du, Vestiges and Festivals*), edited by Ủy Ban Nhân Dân Huyện Tiên Du (The People's Committee of Tiên Du District). Ủy Ban Nhân Dân Huyện Tiên Du.

Tran Van Khe. 1980. "Vietnam," in *New Grove Dictionary of Music and Musicians*, edited by S. Sadie. London: MacMillan.

Trần Văn Khê. 1992. The Concept of *Dieu* in Vietnamese Musical Tradition. In *Von Der Vielfalt Musikalischer Kultur: Fetschrift für Josef Kuckertz*, edited by R. Schumacher. Anif/Salzburg: Verlag Ursula Müller-Speiser.

Trường Chinh. 1985 [1945]. Mấy Nguyên Tác Lớn của Cuộc Vận Động Văn Hóa Việt-Nam lúc Này (Some Major Principles of Today's New Culture Movement). In *Về Văn Hóa và Nghệ Thuật* (*On Arts and Culture*). Hanoi: Nhà Xuất Bản Văn Học.

———. 1985 [1948]. Chủ Nghĩa Mác và Văn Hóa Việt-Nam (Marxism and Vietnamese Culture). In *Về Văn Hóa và Nghệ Thuật*. Hanoi: Nhà Xuất Bản Văn Học.

Trương Thìn and Phó Vụ. 1993. Báo Cáo Sơ Kết Ba Năm Thực Hiện Qui Chế Mở Hội Truyền Thống (Summary Report on Three Years of Implementing the Regulation to Open Traditional Festivals). In *Hội Nghị-Hội Thảo về Lễ Hội* (*Conference-Seminar on Festivals*). Vụ Văn Hóa Quần Chúng và Thư Viện.

Từ Diễn Tiếng Việt (*Vietnamese Dictionary*). 2001. Hanoi: Trung Tâm Từ Điển Học.

Turner, Victor. 1988. *The Anthropology of Performance*. New York: PAJ Publications.

UNESCO. 2003. *Convention for the Safeguarding of the Intangible Cultural Heritage* (cited 6/29/2011). Available from http://www.unesco.org/culture/ich/en/convention/.

———. 2010. *Quan Họ Bắc Ninh Folk Songs* (cited August 2011). Available from http://www.unesco.org/culture/ich/en/RL/00183.

Văn Cao. 1972. "Con Sáo Sang Sông" Theo Phong Cách Quan Họ Bắc Ninh ("The Magpie Crosses the River" in the Quan Họ Bắc Ninh Style). In *Một Số Vấn Đề Về Dân Ca Quan Họ* (*Some Issues Concerning Quan Họ Folk Song*). Hà Bắc: Ty Văn Hóa Hà Bắc.

Vân Đông. 1957. Dân Tộc Tính và Địa Phương Tính (National Character and Local Character). *Tập San Âm Nhạc* (*Music Review*) 8:3–4.

Viện Nghệ Thuật, ed. 1972. *Về Tính Dân Tộc Trong Âm Nhạc Việt Nam* (*Concerning National Character in Vietnamese Music*). Hanoi: Nhà Xuất Bản Văn Hóa.

Waterman, Richard A., William Lichtenwanger, Virginia Hitchcock Herrmann, Horace I. Poleman, and Cecil Hobbs. 1949. Bibliography of Asiatic Musics, Ninth Installment. *Notes, Second Series* 7 (1): 84–98.

Weidman, Amanda. 2003. Guru and Gramophone: Fantasies of Fidelity and Modern Technologies of the Real. *Public Culture* 15 (3): 453–476.

———. 2006. *Singing the Classical, Voicing the Modern: The Postcolonial Politics of Music in South India*. Durham, NC: Duke University Press.

Werner, Jayne, and Danièle Bélanger, eds. 2002. *Gender, Household, State: Đổi Mới in Vietnam*. Ithaca, NY: Southeast Asia Program Publications, Cornell University.

Wilson, William A. 2006. Herder, Folklore, and Romantic Nationalism. In *The Marrow of Human Experience: Essays on Folklore*, edited by J. T. Rudy and D. Call. Logan: Utah State University Press.

Woodside, Alexander B. 1988. *Vietnam and the Chinese Model: A Comparative Study of Vietnamese and Chinese Government in the First Half of the Nineteenth Century*. Cambridge, MA: Harvard University Press.

Xuân Mùi. 1998. Vinh Quang và Gian Khổ: Nhớ Lại Đoàn Quan Họ Những Ngày Đầu Thành Lập (Glory and Hardships: Remembering the Early Days of the Quan Họ Troupe). In *Sum Họp Trúc Mai*. Bắc Ninh: Đoàn Dân Ca Quan Họ Bắc Ninh.

Yang Mu. 1994. Academic Ignorance or Political Taboo? Some Issues in China's Study of its Folk Song Culture. *Ethnomusicology* 38 (2): 303–320.

Yúdice, George. 2005. *The Expediency of Culture: Uses of Culture in the Global Era*. Durham, NC: Duke University Press.

INDEX

Page numbers in italics refer to illustrations.

ABOUT THE AUTHOR

Lauren Meeker received her PhD in anthropology from Columbia University in 2007. She is currently an assistant professor of anthropology at the State University of New York at New Paltz and a research fellow affiliated with the Center for the Study of Vietnamese Philosophy, Culture, and Society at Temple University. Her research interests include cultural politics, performance, folk music and theater, and visual anthropology. She was co-director, with a Vietnamese colleague at the Vietnam Institute of Culture and Arts Studies, Hanoi, of the Visual Anthropology Initiative, a two-year collaborative project (2008–2010) funded by the Ford Foundation to train Vietnamese ethnographers in visual anthropology. She is currently editing her own ethnographic film *Singing Sentiment*, which focuses on a Vietnamese folksinger.

OTHER VOLUMES IN THE SERIES

HARD BARGAINING IN SUMATRA:
Western Travelers and Toba Bataks in the Marketplace of Souvenirs
Andrew Causey

PRINT AND POWER:
Confucianism, Communism, and Buddhism in the Making of Modern Vietnam
Shawn Frederick McHale

INVESTING IN MIRACLES:
El Shaddai and the Transformation of Popular Catholicism in the Philippines
Katherine L. Wiegele

TOMS AND *DEES*:
Transgender Identity and Female Same-Sex Relationships in Thailand
Megan J. Sinnott

IN THE NAME OF CIVIL SOCIETY:
From Free Election Movements to People Power in the Philippines
Eva-Lotta E. Hedman

THE TÂY SƠN UPRISING:
Society and Rebellion in Eighteenth-Century Vietnam
George Dutton

SPREADING THE DHAMMA:
Writing, Orality, and Textual Transmission in Buddhist Northern Thailand
Daniel M. Veidlinger

ART AS POLITICS:
Re-Crafting Identities, Tourism, and Power in Tana Toraja, Indonesia
Kathleen M. Adams

CAMBODGE:
The Cultivation of a Nation, 1860–1945
Penny Edwards

HOW TO BEHAVE:
Buddhism and Modernity in Colonial Cambodia, 1860–1931
Anne Ruth Hansen

CULT, CULTURE, AND AUTHORITY:
Princess Liễu Hạnh in Vietnamese History
Olga Dror

KHMER WOMEN ON THE MOVE:
Exploring Work and Life in Urban Cambodia
Annuska Derks

THE ANXIETIES OF MOBILITY:
Migration and Tourism in the Indonesian Borderlands
Johan A. Lindquist

THE BINDING TIE
CHINESE INTERGENERATIONAL RELATIONS IN MODERN SINGAPORE
Kristina Göransson

IN BUDDHA'S COMPANY:
Thai Soldiers in the Vietnam War
Richard A. Ruth

LỤC XÌ
PROSTITUTION AND VENEREAL DISEASE IN COLONIAL HANOI
Vũ Trọng Phụng
Translated by Shaun Kingsley Malarney

REFIGURING WOMEN, COLONIALISM, AND MODERNITY IN BURMA
Chie Ikeya

NATURAL POTENCY AND POLITICAL POWER:
Forests and State Authority in Contemporary Laos
Sarinda Singh

THE PERFECT BUSINESS?
ANTI-TRAFFICKING AND THE SEX TRADE ALONG THE MEKONG
Sverre Molland

SEEING BEAUTY, SENSING RACE IN TRANSNATIONAL INDONESIA
L. Ayu Saraswati

POTENT LANDSCAPES
PLACE AND MOBILITY IN EASTERN INDONESIA
Catherine Allerton